Finding Shapes

Rectangles

Diyan Leake

www.raintreepublishers.co.uk
Visit our website to find out more information about **Raintree** books.

To order:
 Phone 44 (0) 1865 888112
Send a fax to 44 (0) 1865 314091
Visit the Raintree Bookshop at **www.raintreepublishers.co.uk** to browse our catalogue and order online.

First published in Great Britain by Raintree, Halley Court, Jordan Hill, Oxford OX2 8EJ, part of Harcourt Education.
Raintree is a registered trademark of Harcourt Education Ltd.

Editorial: Diyan Leake
Design: Jo Hinton-Malivoire
Picture research: Maria Joannou
Production: Chloe Bloom
Originated by Dot Gradations Ltd, UK
Printed and bound in China by South China Printing Company

ISBN 1 844 21332 3
10 09 08 07 06
10 9 8 7 6 5 4 3 2 1

British Library Cataloguing in Publication Data
Leake, Diyan
516.1'5
Finding Shapes: Rectangles
A full catalogue record for this book is available from the British Library.

Acknowledgements
The publishers would like to thank the following for permission to reproduce photographs: Alamy pp. **13** (Rick Yamada-Lapides), **15** (Nic Cleave Photography), **17** (britishcolumbiaphotos.com); Corbis pp. **12** (McIntyre Photography), **14** (Abbie Enock); Getty Images pp. **5** (Stone/Erik Von Weber), **16**, **23** (crops, Photodisc; sides, Stone/Erik Von Weber); Harcourt Education Ltd pp. **6** (Tudor Photography), **8** (Malcolm Harris), **9** (Malcolm Harris), **10** (Malcolm Harris), **11** (Malcolm Harris), **18** (Malcolm Harris), **19** (Malcolm Harris), **20** (Malcolm Harris), **21** (Malcolm Harris), **22** (Malcolm Harris), **23** (cuboid, Tudor Photography; hollow, Malcolm Harris; straight, Malcolm Harris); back cover (card, Tudor Photography; drawer, Malcolm Harris)

Cover photograph reproduced with permission of Alamy

Every effort has been made to contact copyright holders of any material reproduced in this book. Any omissions will be rectified in subsequent printings if notice is given to the publishers.

The author and publisher would like to thank Patti Barber, specialist in Early Years Education, University of London Institute of Education, for her advice and assistance in the preparation of this book.

The paper used to print this book comes from sustainable resources.

Contents

Some words are shown in bold, **like this**. They are explained in the glossary on page 23.

What is a rectangle?

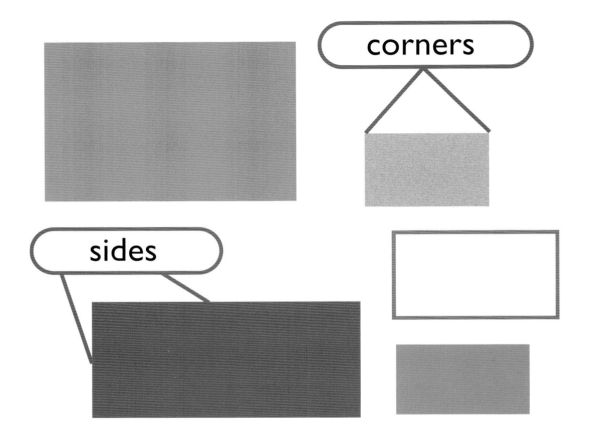

A rectangle is a **flat** shape with four **corners**.

You can see flat shapes but you cannot pick them up.

Rectangles have four **straight sides**.

The opposite sides of a rectangle are always the same length.

Can I see rectangles at home?

There are lots of rectangles at home.

Some of them are in the living room.

Cards can be rectangles.

What other rectangles are there at home?

There are rectangles in
the bedroom.

The front of each drawer is
a rectangle.

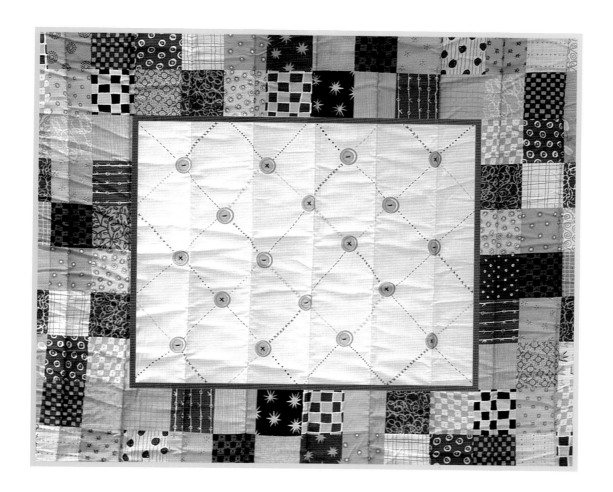

This quilt has a white rectangle
on it.

Can I see rectangles at school?

There are lots of rectangles at school.

Blackboards and whiteboards are rectangles.

This wall of bricks has rectangles on it.

Some rectangles are long and some are short.

Are there rectangles outside?

Some buildings have rectangles on the outside.

This brick school building has lots of rectangles.

You can see rectangles on a climbing frame.

This climbing frame is purple and yellow.

Are there rectangles in town?

We can see all sorts of rectangles in town.

The windows on these buildings are rectangles.

There are rectangles in car parks.

Each rectangle is the space for one car.

Are there rectangles in the countryside?

Fields in the countryside can be rectangles.

Farmers grow **crops** in the fields.

These hay bales are in a field.

Each **flat face** of the bales is a rectangle.

Can I see rectangles on other shapes?

faces

Rectangles can be part of a shape called a **cuboid**.

Each face on a cuboid is a rectangle.

You can stack cuboids on top of each other.

Have you ever seen a **hollow** cuboid?

A box is a **hollow cuboid**.

If something is hollow, you can put things in it.

People give presents in boxes.

This teddy will be a nice present.

What can I make with rectangles?

Make a pattern with rectangles of different colours!

Glossary

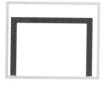

corners
parts of a shape where the sides come together

crops
plants that farmers grow in fields for food

cuboid
solid shape with six flat faces

flat
has no thickness to it

hollow
has space inside

sides
the outside lines of a flat shape

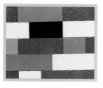

straight
not bent or curved

Index

Note to parents and teachers

Reading non-fiction texts for information is an important part of a child's literacy development. Readers can be encouraged to ask simple questions and then use the text to find the answers. Each chapter in this book begins with a question. Read the questions together. Look at the pictures. Talk about what the answer might be. Then read the text to find out if your predictions were correct. To develop readers' enquiry skills, encourage them to think of other questions they might ask about the topic. Discuss where you could find the answers. Assist children in using the contents page, picture glossary, and index to practise research skills and new vocabulary.

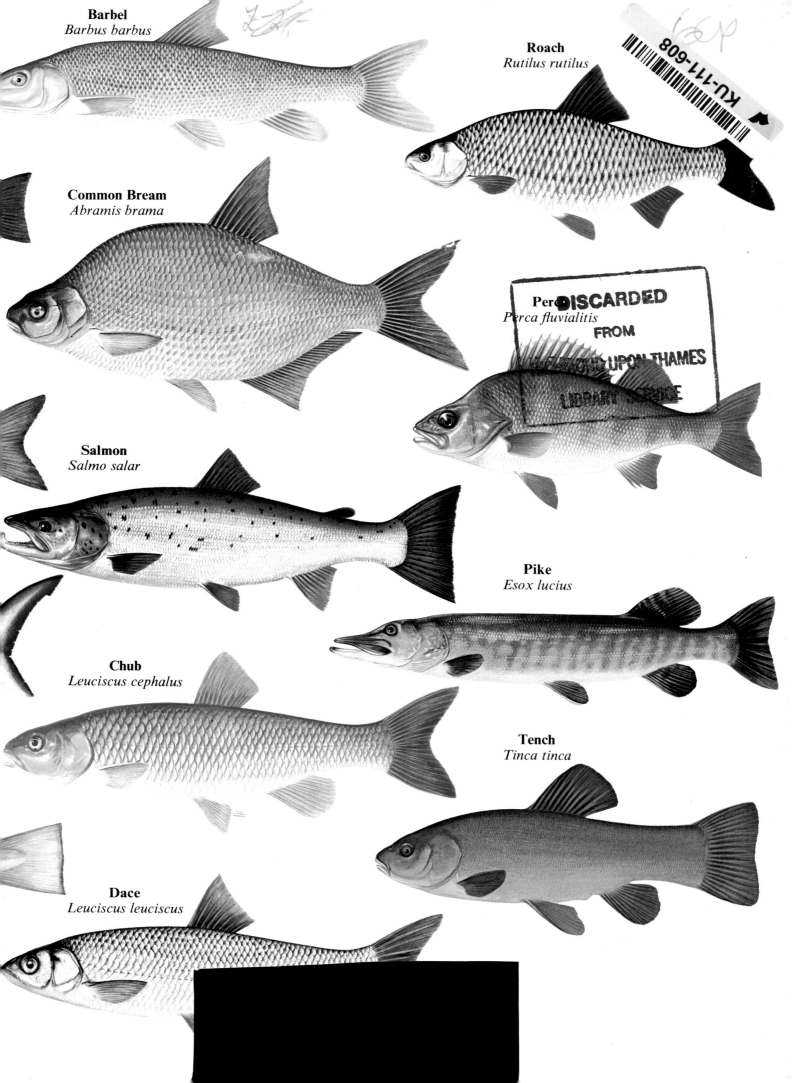

Barbel
Barbus barbus

Roach
Rutilus rutilus

Common Bream
Abramis brama

Salmon
Salmo salar

Pike
Esox lucius

Chub
Leuciscus cephalus

Tench
Tinca tinca

Dace
Leuciscus leuciscus

THE
BASIC GUIDE TO
ANGLING

An introduction to coarse fishing, sea angling and game fishing

TIGER BOOKS INTERNATIONAL
LONDON

Editor: Frances Jones
Consultant Editor: Len Cacutt
Art Editor: Caroline Dewing

This edition published in 1991 by
Tiger Books International PLC, London

Concept, design and production by
Marshall Cavendish Books Limited
119 Wardour Street, London W1V 3TD

© Marshall Cavendish Limited 1984
Reprinted 1986, 1991

Most of this material was first published
by Marshall Cavendish in the partwork
NEW FISHERMAN'S HANDBOOK

ISBN 1 85501 158 1

Printed and bound in Portugal

Picture Credits:
John Bailey: 42. Theo Bergstrom: 14(1), 27(r), 30, 32(t), 36, 39, 41(b), 43(tr), 50(t), 76(t), 78(bl&br), 79, 98(t), 101(r&br), 102(c&b). Don Bridgewood: 45(l). Len Cacutt: 95(tr). Kevin Clifford: 48. John Darling: 67(b), 74(t). A. J. Deane/Bruce Coleman Ltd 31(r). Pete Evans: 18. Ray Forsberg: 27(tl), 46. Trevor Housby: 37, 76(bl&br), 95(tl), 99(bl). Bill Howes: 25, 31(l), 40(b), 41(t), 45(r), 47(l&r), 49(t), 55(tr), 57, 63(t), 67(t), 70(bl, tr&br), 71(b), 72(tr), 73(t), 80(tl), 82(t&cr), 83(c), 87(c), 87(tl), 98(l), 103(l), 104(l&r). Ethel Hurwicz: 40(t). Irish Tourist Board: 74(c), 97(b). Hilary John: 96(b). Derrick Jones: 55(l). D. B. Lewis/Natural Science Photos: 47(c). Frederick Mancini: 35. Graham Marsden: 14(r), 16. Mike Millman: 44(r), 62(t), 62(t&b), 63(b), 64(c&b), 65(tl&cr), 66, 68(tl&cl), 69(bl&br), 73(c), 78(t&cr), 82(cl&b), 83(t&b), 84, 88(b), 91. Arthur Oglesby: 28, 94(tl&br), 97(tl&tr). Dave Plummer: 8, 49(b). Barry Potterton: 94(tr). Kim Sayer: 44(l). Peter Summerland: 58. Jim Tyree: 10, 15. P. H. Ward: 26, 55(br), P. H. Ward/Natural Science Photos 38, 43(tl, bl&br), 50(b). S. L. Ward/Natural Science Photos: 54(tr&br). John Watson: 20, 77(l). Ken Whitehead: 85(tl), 86(b). John Wilson: 4, 12, 22, 23, 24, 52, 54(l), 56. Zefa: 92.

Artwork Credits:
Lynn Cawley: 46, 48, 50, 72(tl), 74(r), 80(tr&bl), 85(tr), 101(l). Colin Newman: 29, 31, 33(t), 57, 103(r). Ralph Stobart: 66(bl), 73(cr). Rod Sutterby: 10, 11, 23, 27, 28, 30, 33(b), 34, 36, 38, 42, 44, 45, 48(t), 49, 51, 53, 55, 56, 58, 62, 63, 64, 65, 66, 68, 69, 70, 71, 72(bl&br), 74(b), 75, 77(tr), 81, 82, 84, 86(t&c), 87, 88, 88/9, 89, 90, 94(bl), 95, 96, 98, 100, 101(t), 102(t), 104(b).

Contributors:
Coarse fishing: John Bailey, Kevin Clifford, Tony Fordham, Frank Guttfield, Bill Howes, Charles Landells, Mike Prichard, Barrie Rickards, Gerry Savage, Peter Stone, Fred Taylor, Harvey Torbett, Jonathan Webb, Ken Whitehead, John Wilson.
Sea fishing: Des Brennan, Ron Edwards, Ray Forsberg, John Goddard, John Holden, Trevor Housby, Mike Millman, Mike Prichard, Mike Shepley, Hugh Stoker, Reg Quest.
Game fishing: Geoffrey Bucknall, Bob Church, Arthur Oglesby, Alan Pearson, Barry Potterton, Mike Shepley, John Veniard, Richard Walker, Barrie Welham.

INTRODUCTION

Will a worm on a pin catch a fish? It has been done. Those two simple elements are the lowest rung on the bottom of a ladder that stretches to the sky. This book sets the beginner to fishing firmly on the first rung and points the way to an absorbing outdoor sport. Whether it takes place in salt or freshwater, sportfishing is done with rod and line. So, armed with basic information on many of the fishes, the rods and reels, simple tackle accessories, together with elementary fishing skills, the reader will begin to see a structure in what seems at first a bewildering maze.

Each chapter in this book includes all the basic information that will enable the newcomer to the sport to join an army of sportfishers and find, as they have found, an invigorating, fresh-air pastime crammed with suspense, excitement, exasperation, jubilation, and an awakened awareness of the beauty of the countryside.

Fishing is a sport closed to no one, a sport with no fans, only participants. Its rewards are a respect for nature, and surroundings which are a pleasure in themselves even if the fish are not biting. For many anglers fish in the bag are a bonus, capping an enjoyable and relaxing day by the water.

NOTE: For freshwater fishing it is illegal to sell or use lead weights which are greater than 0.06 grams and less than or equal to 28.35 grams. All references to shots or shotting patterns for coarse or game freshwater fishing in this book should be taken to refer to the use of commercial lead weight substitutes and not to lead shot.

CONTENTS

ABOUT FISHING

There are three main branches of fishing: sea angling, coarse fishing and game fishing. Both coarse and game fishing are practised in freshwater, differing in the fishes. All freshwater fish, other than salmon, trout and sea trout, are coarse fishes. The chapters that follow reflect these natural divisions, which are themselves further subdivided into the fishes, the baits, tackle and tackle accessories, and fishing skills.

The fish species sought by the angler run into hundreds, and there are as many techniques for fishing for them. There are complete books on the various baits and the choice of fishable waters extends from the deep sea through huge man-made reservoirs, mountain streams, rivers, ponds, featureless Fenland drains—such a range would occupy volumes. Here we concentrate on essentials.

The ratio between numbers of coarse, sea and game fishermen is reflected in the space allocated to them, but none has any major element omitted.

Fishing the sea is free, the fishes themselves creating seasons when they are absent, either seeking warm water in our winter, moving to more prolific feeding grounds, or heading for long-established breeding places inaccessible to the rod and line angler. Therefore there is no sea angling licence, although many authorities make charges for fishing from piers, so check beforehand.

The general close season for coarse fishing is March 15 to June 15 inclusive, but some water authorities, such as the South West, have no statutory close season and in some areas anglers can fish for the coarse species all year.

The seasons for game fish vary according to authority areas, but in general salmon can be sought on rod and line from between 30 September and early November to late January-early April. Trout seasons are as varied, beginning in October and ending March or April in the North and in April-March to September-October in the South and West. In all cases, anglers should check with the local water authority controlling the fishery before setting out.

It must be remembered that while a licence allows the possessor to fish, it does not automatically allow him access to the water. In the case of water authority reservoirs, the licence includes permission, but where a riverbank is owned privately, the angler needs the appropriate licence and a ticket to fish, bought for the day, week or season.

One way the newcomer to fishing can help himself is by joining a local angling club. Most clubs have access to waters either through leasing their own or by coming to agreements with riparian owners. All the club angler needs then is the correct water authority licence. Most tackle retailers will have good information on local fishing and in many cases can sell licences and day tickets.

The management of fishing interests in Britain is overseen by the National Anglers' Council. This body is the angler's link between himself and those responsible for fishing legislation. The NAC has all the major bodies within its committees, including the Federations and Associations to which most clubs are affiliated. The NAC also runs what is probably the most criticised body in angling—the British Record (rod-caught) Fish Committee. Under a series of carefully drawn up rules this body accepts or rejects claims for record fish to be published in the official listings.

The beginner must remember when handling fish that these creatures have a complex nervous system. We do not know for sure whether they can feel pain as we understand the word, and we must not therefore infer that because

Above *Admire them, photograph them — then return your prize catch to the water.*
Right *There is nothing more exhilarating than casting from the beach into a fierce incoming tide.*

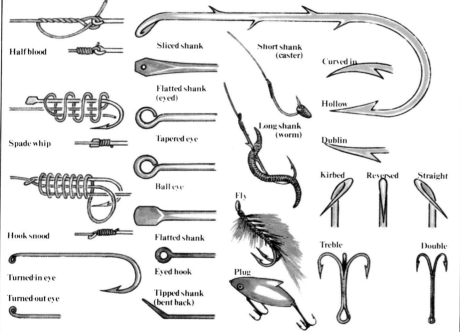

Half blood	Sliced shank	Short shank (caster)
		Curved in
	Flatted shank (eyed)	Hollow
		Long shank (worm)
Spade whip	Tapered eye	Dublin
	Ball eye	Kirbed · Reversed · Straight
Hook snood	Fly	
	Flatted shank	Treble · Double
Turned-in eye	Eyed hook · Plug	
Turned-out eye	Tipped shank (bent back)	

they do not shout 'Ouch!' when a hook is being clumsily removed no pain is felt. Never treat a fish in such a way that pain may be caused, either in the process of unhooking, handling or even in being confined in a keepnet that is too small. One of the fish's protections against disease and parasitism is its mucous covering and its scales. When these are torn off, or fins are frayed by thrashing about in a small keepnet, the mucus is removed, leaving the fish exposed to disease.

When fishing a venue for the first time, make yourself aware of the regulations controlling fishing. On trout reservoirs note the Fly Only rule, non-observance of which will have you thrown off the water immediately. There will be size limits to observe on both game and coarse fisheries; certain

baits may be banned, or spinning only possible at certain times. The number of rods allowed in use at the same time will usually be one—or two for those to whom ledgering is the preferred method.

All anglers need to know a few important knots, for one of the properties of nylon monofilament is that unless knots are tied in a special way they will not hold. A few important knots are shown above.

One important rule is TAKE YOUR RUBBISH HOME WITH YOU. It may not be put that way, but many a beautiful riverbank has been so spoiled by anglers' discarded tins, paperbags, sandwich wrappings, bits of tackle, old groundbait, that the owner has banned all fishing. The many suffered from the actions of the few. Certainly the gravest mistake an angler can make is to leave

coils of unwanted nylon on the bank-side or hanging from trees or bushes. There are some very sad photographs (we publish one on page 31) showing dead birds hanging from branches, their claws or bodies trapped by a few strands of nylon. Take it home and burn it.

Lastly, never hesitate to ask for advice from those more experienced than yourself. Do not, however, choose to walk up to an angler with a question at the moment when his concentration is focused on the tiny float, quivering and bobbing a split second before it dips to record that bite he has been waiting hours for. Your footsteps may well put down a fish about to take the bait. He will lose the fish and you will lose a friend.

USEFUL ADDRESSES

National Anglers' Council and British Record (rod-caught) Committee
11 Cowgate
Peterborough PE1 1LZ

National Federation of Anglers
Halliday House
2 Wilson Street
Derby DE1 1TG

National Federation of Sea Anglers
26 Downsview Road
Uckfield
Sussex TN22 1UB

Salmon and Trout Association
Fishmongers' Hall
London Bridge
London EC4R 9EL

Nine water authorities issue licences for angling in Britain. Anglers should ask at their local town hall or post office for the address and telephone number of the authority controlling their area.

COARSE FISHING

One day, someone will come up with an answer to the question: 'What is "coarse" about coarse fishing?' So far there has been no satisfactory explanation, for every freshwater fisherman will tell you that 'coarse' is the last word one could use to describe today's float rods, lines, hooks, to say nothing of the finesse and delicacy needed to lure an ultra-timid carp from the haven of a weedbed to take a morsel of floating crust.

So 'coarse' is the word we use to provide some means of telling the fly fisherman apart from the seeker of any species not belonging to the salmon and trout family. One facetious comment cannot be avoided though. Anyone who has tried eating a roach or bream will agree with the writer who said that coarse fish tasted like cotton wool stuffed with needles.

The beginner to fishing will, then, go to his local tackle dealer and buy the essentials of the angler's craft: a rod, reel, line, hooks, leads and floats.

A word of advice—buy carefully and do not necessarily buy the cheapest of the available range. Go for good quality at a reasonable price, and listen to the advice of the tackle dealer. He lives in a world of fishing tackle and knows, like all sensible retailers, that a satisfied customer comes back. He will willingly help the beginner to select a sound, basic range of tackle to start out on a life of infinite pleasure in the open air.

One of the most colourful displays will be the serried ranks of floats large and small, dull and brilliantly coloured. Attractive though they may be, half-a-dozen, again recommended by the dealer, will suffice.

A hundred yards of 5lb breaking strain (b.s.) nylon will do for line, while some hooks sized from 16 to 12 provide a range that will take maggots, bread and worms, the baits best used at first by the newcomer to the sport. Not absolutely necessary, but useful, will be a couple of plastic bait boxes and a disgorger.

There are many other gadgets and accessories but they can wait until some proficiency has been attained, together with an understanding of what kind of fish will be sought, where the fishing will take place and which techniques appeal most.

The important fish species are described in the following pages, together with the basic angling equipment needed to catch them. Unfortunately, space prohibits the inclusion of the crucian carp, an ornamental introduction from the East a few hundred years ago.

Anglers wishing to catch eels should seek any farm pond or backwater, for this still incompletely known fish wriggles over the land to find its eventual home-water. The muddy waters of the Fens and Broads are places where a ledgered worm is almost guaranteed to be taken by a wriggling, slimy bootlace impossible to hold and unhook. The secret is to lay it on a sheet of newspaper, where it will lie still while the hook is removed. Larger eels are another matter, and it is likely that any beginner who reels a thrashing double-figure eel to the bank will quickly seek help to subdue the slithering monster.

A branch of fishing not covered here is matchfishing. Simply, matchfishing is competitive angling where anglers vie with one another to catch more fish, or a greater weight of fish, in a given time.

The number of coarse fishermen has increased hugely in the past decade. This means that the available bank space is diminishing. Newcomers to the sport would be strongly advised to join a local angling club and gain the benefit from waters that become available by virtue of this membership. Clubs often affiliate to the large federations, and so the range of waters is increased. In clubs, too, beginners will find that all their questions—and there will be plenty—will be discussed and solutions offered. It is a known fact that each time an angler describes a recent catch the weight of the fish increases; not so well publicized is the fact that the beginner who joins a club and goes on fishing expeditions with the members will increase both the weight of his catch and the knowledge of his chosen sport.

Fishing is controlled in British waters by River Authorities who have the right to issue licences to anglers wishing to fish their waters. Licences range from day tickets to those covering a complete season. Most tackle shops sell these licences both for local waters and for other River Authorities. As well as the licences, the angler must also have permission from the owner of the waters, for all water other than the sea is owned by someone. This is where club membership is so important, for the member is able to fish his club's waters and only needs the River Authority licence.

Good quality tackle is not cheap. After every fishing trip check your reel and rod. Wipe off all bankside dirt, especially gritty mud. The reel mechanism needs to be absolutely free of abrasive matter, so wipe it over then apply a fine coating of oil. The rod ferrules should be given the same treatment.

Lastly, the beginner must remember that there is a close season for coarse fishing. From 15 March to 15 June fishing for freshwater fish other than trout and salmon is prohibited. The period was originally conceived to allow a three-month respite for the fish during their spawning season. But it seems that nobody told the fish, for tench have been known to spawn in July, as have other species well outside the statutory close season. Record sizes have been claimed for fish whose bellies were swollen with eggs, and while there seems no legal argument against such claims it is surely against the spirit of sporting angling.

CHAPTER 1
THE FISH

PIKE

Streamlined, powerful but graceful, the pike is the supreme predator in our rivers and streams because of the enormous size it can reach. It leads a solitary life, lying in ambush to dart out and feed on smaller shoal fish—species such as roach, rudd and bream. The pike is built for speed, but only over short distances. It prefers to wait until an unwary fish comes within striking distance, then, in a burst of energy, launches its body forward to grasp its prey. The pike is widely distributed throughout the British Isles. It is found in both flowing and stillwaters. Lakes, especially those containing vast shoals of small fish, will hold the larger pike. Loch Lomond and similar large expanses of water have an enormous food potential. Pike there feed on salmon smolts, trout and coarse fish in large numbers. River pike, on the other hand, have to keep up a never ending battle against running water in order to breathe and maintain control over their territory before they even attempt to make a kill.

Pike rods

First, the rod. A model like the Mark IV carp rod is too soft, not for playing pike, but for casting the baits so commonly used in piking. However, a strengthened carp rod is ideal. Several versions of these rods are available in hollow glass-fibre, but the best type are those with all-through action as opposed to the rods whose action is at the top.

For gravel pit pike, which can reach 30lb in the waters with prime food fish, a sturdy purpose-built or carp rod, 10-15lb b.s. line, and a wire trace carrying two or three treble hooks, is standard kit. Good baits are dead roach, small bream, herring and mackerel, which can be ledgered without lead on the bottom or, in breezy weather, cast out beneath a sliding float to work across water with the wind. A deadbait, cast far out and retrieved jerkily to simulate the erratic progress of a sick or injured fish, makes an effective bait when searching large areas of varying depth. Pike, like carp, regularly patrol channels and shallow bars through deep water. Such spots are always worth special attention.

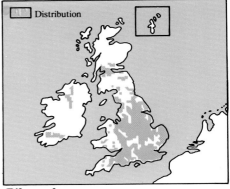
Distribution

Pike reels

When considering reels a ruthless approach cuts out thoughts of multipliers and centrepins, and homes in on the versatility of a good quality fixed-spool reel.

Pike can be caught by a variety of methods. Because of the fish's voracious appetite, it will attack both live and deadbaits. Fish, for example, can be presented either live, swimming in mid-water, or as deadbait, lying on the bottom. Practically any species can be used as a livebait—even small pike are an attractive lure for the larger ones.

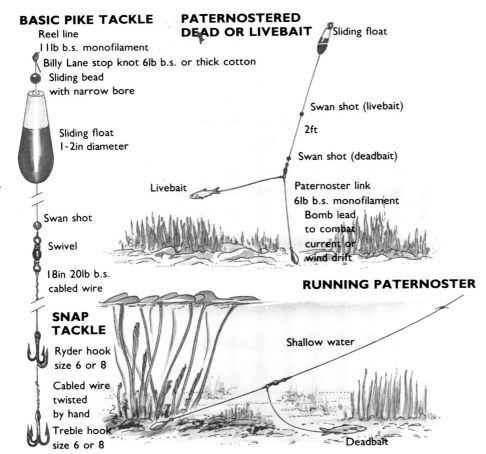

BASIC PIKE TACKLE
- Reel line
- 11lb b.s. monofilament
- Billy Lane stop knot 6lb b.s. or thick cotton
- Sliding bead with narrow bore
- Sliding float 1-2in diameter
- Swan shot
- Swivel
- 18in 20lb b.s. cabled wire

SNAP TACKLE
- Ryder hook size 6 or 8
- Cabled wire twisted by hand
- Treble hook size 6 or 8

PATERNOSTERED DEAD OR LIVEBAIT
- Sliding float
- Swan shot (livebait)
- 2ft
- Swan shot (deadbait)
- Livebait
- Paternoster link 6lb b.s. monofilament
- Bomb lead to combat current or wind drift

RUNNING PATERNOSTER
- Shallow water
- Deadbait

Above *This 16½lb Norfolk pike was taken in winter by Dave Plummer.* **Left** *Three basic tackle set-ups for pike fishing.*

FISHING FOR PIKE

Methods	Rod	Reel	Reel Line	Terminal Tackle	Hooks	Leads/ Weights	Bait	Groundbait/ Attractor	Habitat	Time of Season	Distribution
Float-ledgered deadbait	10ft stepped-up carp rod with 2¼lb test curve	Fixed-spool	11-12lb mono- filament	Snap tackle	8-6	1 swan shot	Roach, herring	Minced/ sliced fish	On all waters	Throughout the Open Season	Throughout the British Isles though average sizes run bigger in Fenland drains and in Scottish or Irish lakes
Ledgered deadbait/ livebait	As above	Fixed-spool	As above	Single treble or snap tackle	8-6	½oz-2½oz	Roach, herring or lip-hooked livebait	Minced/ sliced fish	On all waters	Throughout the Open Season	
Suspended deadbait/ livebait	As above	Fixed-spool	As above	Snap tackle	8-6	1 swan—½oz	Roach	Minced/ sliced fish	On all waters	Throughout the Open Season	
Paternostered livebait/ deadbait	As above	Fixed-spool	As above	Snap tackle	8-6	1½-2oz	Roach	Minced/ sliced fish	On all waters	Throughout the Open Season	
Plug fishing	9-11ft stepped-up carp rod with 2lb test curve	Fixed-spool or multiplier	11-14lb	Trace, link swivel	—	Anti-kink	Plug	Minced/ sliced fish	On all waters	Throughout the Open Season	
Spinning (1)	As above	Fixed-spool	11-12lb	Trace, link swivel	—	Anti-kink	Spoon, spinner	Minced/ sliced fish	On all waters	Throughout the Open Season	
Spinning (2)	7-8ft 1¼-1½lb test	Fixed-spool	6-9lb	Trace, link swivel	—	Anti-kink	Spoon, spinner	Minced/ sliced fish	On all waters	Throughout the Open Season	
Fly fishing	9ft Hardy jet	Intrepid Rimfly	Lead-cored	6in wire trace	—	—	5in fly	Minced/ sliced fish	On all waters	Throughout the Open Season	

The most important thing is to use a lively bait that will work well, swimming strongly in order to arouse the attention of a hungry pike. However, many anglers consider the use of one live fish to catch another as cruel.

Artificial lures play an important part in pike fishing. Spinning is both a pleasurable and successful method. Almost any material can be employed in the manufacture of lures but metal is most often used.

Other tackle
As well as the basics, you will also need a wide range of miscellaneous items such as a large landing net with a soft, knotless mesh; 8in straight artery forceps; long-handled wire cutters; ring whipping thread for stop knots; grease to make line float, and diluted washing-up liquid to make it sink and a fine file for sharpening hooks.

Record pike
The present record pike weighed 40lb when taken from Horsey Mere, Norfolk, by Peter Hancock in February 1967, but numerous specimens of over 40lb, and one of 53lb have been taken from Irish and Scottish waters. A 43lb pike was caught in this country in 1974 but, following a spurious claim, the fish was never credited to its true captor whose name did not enter the record fish lists. There is some evidence for the existence of pike of up to 70lb in British waters. Certainly, if you wish to join the record-breakers, it is advisable to fish in the early part of the season when many of the female fish are heavy with spawn.

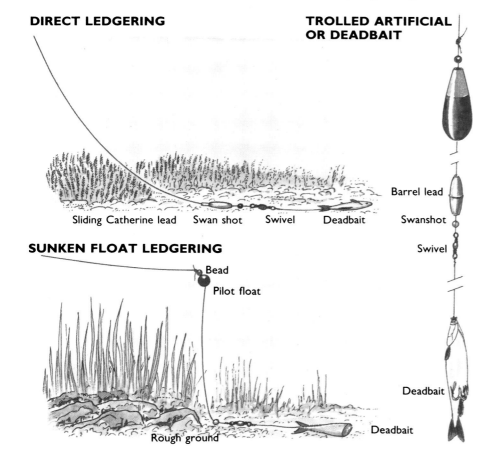

DIRECT LEDGERING

Sliding Catherine lead   Swan shot   Swivel   Deadbait

SUNKEN FLOAT LEDGERING

Bead
Pilot float
Rough ground
Deadbait

TROLLED ARTIFICIAL OR DEADBAIT

Barrel lead
Swanshot
Swivel
Deadbait
Deadbait

Left *Three methods of pike fishing using whole or half fish as deadbaits.*

ROACH

Roach are not much to look at, but their variety does begin with colour and shape. There are two extreme forms of coloration in mature fish. Most anglers are familiar with the bronze-flanked roach found in the Kennet or Hampshire Avon, as well as with the more common silver-flanked fish found in most areas. Both varieties are nevertheless found side by side in many waters.

Mature roach

The body shape of mature fish varies in that most roach are slim and streamlined, reminiscent of the dace, while, also found but less common, is the full-bodied, deep-bellied fish that is to be seen among the angler's specimens.

The haunts of roach are as variable as their shape and colour. However, they prefer gravel, rock or hard bottoms and will settle over hard clay or mixed sand rather than silt or soft mud. Often they have little choice as the waters in which they are found vary from the swiftest chalk streams to the most sluggish and coloured lowland streams and small ponds. To survive, shoals must locate good feeding. For this they turn to the weed beds, not only for their plant food but for insects and other creatures. Roach, therefore, often shoal within easy reach of such natural larders, which also offer them protection from predators.

In roach fishing the colour of the water is important. In bright conditions and with clear water, even the finest tackle is quite visible. You must then be ultra-cautious, be as quiet as possible, and use bankside shrubbery to camouflage your silhouette. As it is a shoaling fish, the roach is highly sensitive to alien vibrations, surface shadows, or anything suspicious. One frightened fish can easily lead the shoal out of the swim or make them disinclined to feed. Therefore the best roaching, particularly for larger, wiser specimens, is done in coloured water, at dusk and dawn.

A roach weighing a pound is a good fish in any water. Over this it is excellent. Two pounders are not common, and specimens above this size are, for most anglers, the fish of a lifetime.

Tackle for roach fishing

Despite the wide variety of conditions and waters in which roach are found, two rods suffice: a 12-13ft match rod

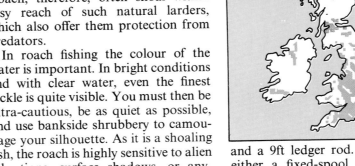

and a 9ft ledger rod. The reel can be either a fixed-spool with a sensitive clutch for light lines, or a free-running centrepin. The former is probably better because long and accurate casting is sometimes called for. Two spools are needed, one with 2lb b.s. line for float fishing, the other with 3-4lb line for ledgering.

Do not collect hundreds of beautiful different patterned floats, because you will not know whether your float is wrong or your method of fishing, although it will nearly always be the latter. A sensible range would be a set of four stick floats, carrying shot from 1BB to 5BB, for trotting in slow to medium-fast swims; a set of Avons, also for trotting, but taking shots ranging from 4BB to three swan and used to combat much faster, even turbulent water; a set of zoomers or antenna floats, with shotting ranging from 2BB to 4AA for sensitive presentation in stillwaters; and a few tiny floats for ultra-sensitive work.

As far as hooks are concerned, round-bends take a lot of beating. For large baits, such as worms and breadflake, use eyed hooks from No 10 to No 6, and tie them directly on to the line. For small baits, where neatness of presentation is essential, spade end hooks are better.

A good selection of split shot is also

Left *Two beautiful Norfolk roach captured by tackle dealer and specimen hunter John Wilson. Many anglers will go fishing for years before seeing a roach of this calibre.* **Below** *Fishing for roach like this 'goer' occupies the time of huge numbers of anglers throughout the coarse fishing season.*

FISHING FOR ROACH

Methods	Rod	Reel	Reel Line	Terminal tackle	Hooks	Leads/ Weights	Bait	Groundbait/ Attractor	Habitat	Time of Season	Distri- bution
Stick float	13ft hollow glass match	Fixed spool or centrepin	2lb	1½lb hook length	16-20	Small shot evenly spaced	Maggots, casters, hemp	Loose feed hookbait	River, stream	Summer/ Winter	Widespread in England, Wales, lower Scotland Local in Northern Ireland and the Republic of Ireland
Balsa stick	13ft hollow glass match	Fixed-spool or centrepin	2½lb	1½lb hook length	14-18	Balanced shotting	Maggots, casters	Loose feed hookbait	River	Winter	
Avon trotter	12-13ft hollow glass/progres- sive action	Centrepin	2½lb	2lb hook length	10-16	Grouped shots	Maggots, bread crust	Small balls of cereal	River	Winter	
Zoomer	13-14ft hollow glass	Fixed-spool	2½lb	1½lb hook length	14-18	Balanced shotting	Casters, maggots	Hookbait in cereal groundbait	Slow river, pond, pit	Summer	
Long antenna	13-14ft hollow glass	Fixed-spool	3lb	1½lb hook length	14-18	Balanced shotting	Casters, maggots	Hookbait in cereal groundbait	Reservoir, gravel pit	Summer/ Winter	
Dart or porcupine quill	12-13ft hollow glass	Fixed-spool or centrepin	2lb	1lb hook length	16-22	Balanced shotting	Casters	Loose feed hookbait	Canal, pond	Summer	
Peacock quill (float ledger)	12-13ft hollow glass	Fixed-spool or centrepin	2½lb	Mini link- ledger	10-16 tied direct	AA stop shot	Maggots, bread flake, worms	Loose feed with bait droper	Fast water	Winter	
Ledger – paternoster	9-11ft ledger	Fixed-spool	2½lb	Fixed lead on link	10-16 tied direct	Bomb or swan shots	Maggots, bread flake	Cereal balls	Lake, slow river	Summer/ Autumn	
Paternoster blockend	9-11ft ledger with quivertip	Fixed-spool	3lb	Fixed feeder on link	10-16 tied direct	None	Maggots	Maggots in feeder	River	Winter	
Sliding link	9-11ft ledger with swingtip	Fixed-spool	2½lb	Swan shot on sliding link	10-16 tied direct	None	Maggots, bread flake	Cereal balls	Lake, slow river	Summer	
Running bomb	9-11ft ledger Avon-action	Fixed-spool	3lb	Running bomb	8-12 tied direct	AA stop shot	Bread crust, flake, worms	Loose feed lumps of hookbait	Fast river	Summer	
Open-end swimfeeder	9-11ft ledger with swingtip	Fixed-spool	3lb	Running feeder	8-16 tied direct	AA stop shot	Maggots, bread flake	Hookbait and cereal in feeder	Lake, slow river	Summer/ Winter	
Freeline	9-11ft ledger, Avon-action	Fixed-spool	2½lb	Hook only	6-12 tied direct	None	Bread flake, lobworm	Loose feed hookbait	Stream, river	Summer/ Autumn	
Fly	9ft hollow glass	Fly reel	2lb	6X cast	14-16	None	Dry fly	None	Stream, river, lake	Summer	

required, plus an assortment of small swivels, Arlesey bombs, and open-ended swimfeeders for fishing far out or in fast water. The easiest spots to catch roach are stillwater lakes, pits or farm ponds. On such waters, many different techniques can be tried until you have success.

The basic technique
On a small, well-coloured water in summer, for example, start off float fishing with a 2BB quill float, with ⅛in of the tip showing and a size 14 hook holding two maggots. Begin by fixing both shots 6in from the hook and set the float overdepth to lay the bait on the bottom. Then scatter a few maggots around the float every so often and you will soon have the roach feeding.

Ledgering is also useful on slow or stillwaters, particularly for larger fish which prefer the bottom. Baits can be large, such as a bunch of maggots or breadflake, and tackle should be kept to a minimum. Use just enough lead to reach the swim or to hold bottom, set the rod low to the water in two rests, pointing at the bait, and use a ledger bobbin clipped on the line between the butt and second rod ring to indicate bites. By using a luminous bobbin, you can fish that last hour of daylight and even later into darkness, when the biggest roach show up. A more exciting way of taking a specimen roach does not exist.

Stillwater roach differ from their river counterparts in one very important way—they are nomadic. During the summer months especially, roach in really large stillwaters may cover huge distances in the course of 24 hours. But, luckily, they do have certain habits, visiting preferred feeding areas at around the same time each day, particularly early morning and late evening. This is when the roach characteristic of rolling on the surface gives their presence away to the dedicated fish spotter.

However, some waters, particularly gravel pits, possess certain character-istics which help the stillwater specimen roach hunter. For example, pits which contain large concentrations of perch as well as roach are potentially very big roach waters. This is due to a process of elimination, for the perch decimate the young roach shoals, and the comparatively small numbers of roach which reach, say, ½lb, put on weight rapidly with less fish to share the food. In such perch-populated pits and reservoirs, you usually catch only very small or very big roach.

Every roach water has at some time or other produced fish of at least 1½lb. But a water holding only the occasional specimen does not offer much of an opportunity for consistent success. To reap the best rewards you need to hunt out those waters containing good num-bers of this most popular of the coarse-fishing species.

Fishing is like stamp collecting, it is best to specialize to gain most satis-faction from the sport.

CHUB

The chub belongs to the carp family, though it does not resemble the carp in appearance. The mature fish is solidly built, with a blunt head, large mouth and thick, pale lips. The back is greenish brown, the flanks silvery, and the belly a yellowy white. The fins, which are well defined and powerful, can range from colourless to a rich red. It is easy to identify by its large scales.

Predominantly a river fish, the chub is found where currents flow fast over gravel or stony beds. It is a fish of clean, unpolluted waters where both oxygen and food exist in plenty. The species provides fishing of quality for the angler prepared to stalk this cautious and stealthy prey with great care and skill. A specimen chub, 4 or 5lb, is shy in habit—a solitary, thick-bodied ghost that fades into the depths at sight or sound of man or beast. Yet the chub is renowned for the dogged resistance it displays to the efforts of angler and rod.

Distribution

While the chub is found throughout most of England, it is absent from west Wales and from Scotland above the Forth-Clyde valley. It is one of Britain's bigger coarse fish, rarely exceeding 6lb, though weight tends to vary in different parts of the country. A large Hampshire Avon chub, for example, may weigh some 7lb, while one of 3lb would be considered good in Norfolk. The present British rod-caught record fish weighed 7lb 6oz and fell to Bill Warren fishing the Avon in 1957.

Chub holes

All rivers have known chub holes, which

Right *Angling author John Marsden fished the River Severn for this catch of handsome chub. They were the result of dedicated fishing and careful attention to tackle and bait. Once the chub become aware of your presence, go home or move to another swim.* **Below** *Artificial crayfish and frog chub lures.*

the seasoned angler can point out to the newcomer, but it is unlikely that more than one or two chub can be caught from the swim. Younger chub do shoal and form mixed shoals with dace and roach in areas that can provide the necessary abundance of food.

Unlike the tench and carp, which can be regarded as fish of the warmer months, the chub remains a year-round angling species.

Baits

Chub are famed for their wide-ranging appetites and can be taken on a variety of baits. Float-fishing with cheese, ripe fruits, especially berries, worms, silkweed, dried blood, slugs or maggots, are well-tried methods. Natural and artificial flies can also be used, as can other insects and grubs. The smaller members of a shoal will feed on aquatic insects and bottom-dwelling invertebrates, while the older fish will add a substantial amount of vegetable matter to their diet and will chase and eat the fry of many species, including their own.

There is no mistaking a chub bite. The fish will take the bait with a great splash, then rush back to its home among the tangle of tree roots, submerged branches, or weeds. If this happens you will lose it, so as soon as you strike keep firm control, trying to pull

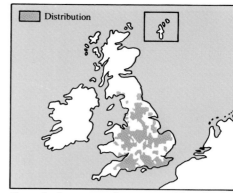

the chub away from trouble. Light tackle will be broken almost immediately, so use line of about 6lb b.s. and a powerful rod.

Though thought of as a pure river fish, the chub has been successfully introduced to stillwaters where it thrives and can grow larger than its river counterpart.

One very useful method of chub fishing is freelining. This is a technique to employ when having only limited success with the usual baits.

Quite simply, a piece of fresh bread flake is pinched on to the hook followed by a fair-sized piece of crust. The crust is only lightly pinched, however, so that a flick of the rod tip makes it break free. The baited hook is then allowed to travel with the current until it reaches the best point, when the crust is twitched

FISHING FOR CHUB

Methods	Rod	Reel	Reel Line	Terminal tackle	Hooks	Leads/Weights	Bait	Groundbait/Attractor	Time of Season	Habitat	Distribution
Float: Avon	12ft hollow-glass, soft tip	Centrepin or fixed-spool	3-4lb	2-3lb hook length	18-12	2 BB to 3 AAA	All baits	Groundbait, hookbait	All season	Fast-flowing rivers, weir-pools	Throughout England, southern Scotland, east Wales
Float: slider	13ft hollow-glass or carbon	Fixed-spool	3lb	2-3lb hook length	18-12	2-3 swan bulk shot	All baits	Stiff groundbait, hookbait	All season	Deep slow water	
Float: waggler (straw, peacock)	13ft hollow-glass or carbon	Fixed-spool	2-3lb	1-2lb hook length	20-16	Light terminal shot	Maggots or casters	Loose-fed casters or maggots	Mainly summer	Far bank of rivers and canals	
Float-stick	12ft hollow-glass or carbon	Centrepin or fixed-spool	2lb	1-2lb hook length	20-16	Strung out shot	Maggots or casters	Loose hemp, casters and maggots	All season	Rivers with steady flow	
Ledger: paternoster	10ft 6in hollow-glass, 1½lb test	Fixed-spool	3-5lb	2-4lb	18-6	Arlesey bomb or swan shot	All baits	Groundbait and hookbait	Mainly winter	Deep holes under river banks	
Ledger: bullet, roller	10ft 6in hollow-glass or split cane, 1½lb test	Fixed-spool	3-5lb	2-4lb hook length	10-4	Bullet lead	Crust, cheese, worm	Loose particles	All season	Fast-flowing rivers, weir-pools	
Blockend or open-end feeder	10ft hollow-glass, quivertip	Fixed-spool	4-8lb	3-6lb hook length	16-12	Swimfeeder	Maggots, casters, red worm	Samples in feeder	All season	Larger rivers	
Spinning	10ft 6in hollow-glass, 1½lb test	Fixed-spool	5lb	5lb	Small Mepps	Swan shot	None	None	Summer	Rivers, weir-pools, lakes, pits	
Plugging	10ft 6in hollow-glass, 1½lb test	Fixed-spool or multiplier	5lb	5lb	Small plug	Often none	None	None	Summer	Rivers, lakes, pits	
Fly	9ft hollow-glass, AFTM 6	Fly	DT6F	6lb nylon tapered cast	10-8	None	Large wet or dry fly	None	Summer	Rivers, small streams, weir-pools	
Freeline	10ft 6in hollow-glass, 1½lb test	Fixed-spool	4lb	4lb	12-6	None	Bread, lobworm, cheese, crayfish, slugs	None	All season	Rivers, small streams	

free allowing the flake to sink gently into the waiting mouth of a fat chub.

Freelining slugs for chub is one of the most enjoyable ways of fishing. The angler travels light with just a shoulder bag and a landing net, seeking out the chub in small streams and those rivers where they can be spotted.

The basic equipment is a 10-11ft hollow-glass rod, a fixed-spool reel loaded with 4lb b.s. line and an assortment of hooks from No 2 to No 4. Spare spools should carry 5 and 6lb b.s. lines. The landing net should be as light as possible—while a trout net is ideal it will be found that an extending net is needed in most areas.

Polarized sunglasses are essential for spotting chub. Take a quiet walk along the river, preferably working upstream, and pay attention to all likely looking swims. In areas which look 'chubby' it is worth your while standing by a tree or some other cover for ten minutes or so.

You will often see chub drifting out from cover, or lying on a gravel run at the end of a lily bed or a funnel of water running through reed mace, but beware, they are practically invisible.

Watch out and wait
Time spent without any kind of tackle is of the utmost value in tracking down specimens. Even if chub are scared, they will often come back, the same fish almost always showing in the exact spot the next day. When fishing you will spend much time in undignified positions and will be stung from head to foot by nettles (because big chub often choose the protection of water by nettle banks). You will kneel in cow pats and you will attract flies, but you must not wave your arms to brush them away or your prize catch will be gone.

Into the keepnet goes a near 5lb chub. Such a fish needs a large keepnet if it is not to suffer.

BREAM

The freshwater bream is common in most parts of England except the western extremities. It is also plentiful in Ireland, where the average run of fish is larger than elsewhere. It is less common in southern Scotland, and absent north of Loch Lomond.

Throughout their range, bream are as much at home in lakes as in rivers. They prefer sluggish waters and in swift large rivers tend to be found in the slower reaches. They attain the best sizes in stillwaters, but fight better when taken in faster waters such as the Thames, Trent or Great Ouse, where they turn their broad flanks to the current when hooked. Some of the best bream waters are in the Norfolk Broads waterways, and in the Lincolnshire and Fenland drain systems. Traditionally, too, the Arun, Nene, Welland and Witham are noted for bream. Some of the best specimens in the last few decades, however, have been taken from the reservoirs of Walthamstow, Tring, Staines and Marsworth, close to Tring.

Bream 'stations'

Bream are travellers, often covering large distances when following established beats, which can be likened to railway lines with stations where they stop to feed.

Small, 2-5lb fish, which gather in large shoals, need to cover several hundred yards to reap sufficient natural food, whereas big bream of over 8lb feed less often and will therefore need to travel only a short distance. It is for this reason that they are more difficult to catch.

The best method for locating bream is simple observation, based on the fact that bream have a peculiar habit of rolling at the surface as a prelude to, and during, feeding. Bream usually feed in the late evening or early morning, when you should look for their hump backs cleaving the surface. You may have to spend many hours over several weeks before you spot them, but once located, the same greedy shoal is likely to be found regularly in that part of the river for a number of years.

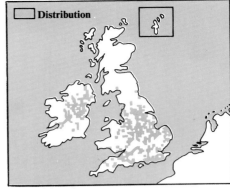

Distribution

Prebaiting for success

Prebaiting for bream pays handsome dividends, and the longer and more often, the better your chances of success. Unusual baits are not necessary; maggots, bread and worms are perfectly adequate. The choice is partly a matter of personal preference.

Big bream rarely feed close to the banks, and the average distance you need to groundbait and cast is 30-40 yards. Very often, much greater distances are involved, and to throw the groundbait so far demands a good arm and a mix that will not break up in flight. You can use a swimfeeder while you fish, but this is not common in northern waters, as threadlike algae can smother bulky rigs, rendering them useless.

Best rig for weedy waters

The fixed paternoster is by far the best rig for bream fishing in weedy waters and for long range fishing. It consists of an Arlesey bomb, $\frac{1}{2}$-1oz, depending on distance required, tied to 3ft of line. A swivel is tied at the other end, and on the same ring of the swivel you tie a shorter line, 6-9in long, which carries the hook. The reel line is attached to the same ring at the opposite end of the swivel.

The fixed paternoster casts long and accurately because the ledger weight is at the extreme end of the rig. It also sits well on top of soft weed and mud, as the hook is on a short link set well up the line.

Hook sizes depend on the bait—maggots and small worms on hooks 16 to 10, and bread and large lobworms on 10, 8 or 6. A long-shanked, eyed hook holds bread far better than a short-shanked hook, while for worms and maggots, a short-shanked spade-end, forged hook is ideal. Whatever hook you use, it should always be honed to a fine point, and the barb reduced slightly to give better penetration.

Big bream are rarely found in snaggy swims, much preferring the freedom of

Left *This 9lb 3oz bream is carefully returned to the muddy waters of a Cheshire mere from where it was caught.*

FISHING FOR FRESHWATER BREAM

Methods	Rod	Reel	Reel Line	Terminal Tackle	Hooks	Leads/ Weights	Bait	Groundbait/ Attractor	Time of Season	Habitat	Distribution
Float—Slider	13ft match rod	Fixed-spool	3lb	Single hook	18-14	Split shot bunched 15in from hook	Maggot, casters	Loose hookbait samples	Summer, autumn	Lake, mere, reservoir, slow river	Widely distributed except for parts of the North-West and Northern Scotland
Float—Fixed peacock quill (slow-sinking 'on-the-drop')	12-13ft match rod	Fixed-spool	3lb	Single hook	12-8 / 18-14	Split-shot bunched under float	Bread or worm / Maggot, caster	Loose hook-bait samples/ cloudbait	Summer, autumn	Lake, mere, reservoir, canal	
Float—Avon	13ft match rod	Fixed-spool, centrepin	4lb	Single hook	16-10	Split shot in two bunches: one in mid-water, one 9in from hook	Bread, worm, maggot	Hookbait and fairly stiff groundbait	Summer, autumn	River with fairly strong current	
Ledger— Paternoster	11ft rod with 1¼lb test curve	Fixed-spool	4lb	Single or double hook	18-8	¼-1oz bomb	Maggot, caster, bread, worm	Breadcrumb, bran, stale bread	Summer, autumn, winter	Lake, mere, reservoir	
Ledger—Link	11ft rod with 1¼lb test curve	Fixed-spool	4lb	Single hook	18-8	¼-1oz bomb	Maggot, caster, bread, worm	Breadcrumb, bran, stale bread	Summer, autumn, winter	Lake, mere, reservoir	
Ledger— Rolling bullet	11ft rod with 1¼lb test curve	Fixed-spool	4lb	Single hook	18-8	¼-1oz bullet	Maggot, caster, bread, worm	Loose hook-bait samples plus bread groundbait	Summer, autumn	River	
Ledger— Swimfeeder	11ft rod with 1¼lb test curve	Fixed-spool	4lb	Single hook	18-12	Included in swimfeeder	Maggot, caster, sweetcorn	Fill feeders with hookbait	Summer, autumn, winter	Lake, mere, reservoir, river, canal	
Spinning	9-10ft spinning rod	Fixed-spool	4lb	Small, silver Mepps spinner	Spinner	None	Spinner	None	Very early season	Lake, mere, reservoir, river	
Fly fishing	9-10ft reservoir rod	Fly	No 7-9 (sinking)	4lb leader	Wet	None	Polystickle	None	Summer	Lake, mere, reservoir	

Bite indicators for the four ledgering techniques.
Paternoster-ledger: swingtip or quivertip
Link-ledger: various butt indicators

Ledgered rolling bullet: rod top, quivertip or touch (holding the line between your fingers—always the most sensitive indication)
Ledgered swimfeeder: swingtip, quivertip or butt indicator.

open water. Nor are they renowned for their fighting abilities, so it is not necessary to use heavy lines. Nylon of 4lb b.s., and occasionally 3lb when the fish are particularly finicky, is adequate.

Rod and reel
A good bream rod is an 11ft 4in, two-piece, hollow-glass model, with a 1¾lb test curve. It is right for long-range fishing, for you need the length to pick up the long line when striking. For the same reason the rod should not be sloppy, but neither should it be stiff or you risk breaking on the strike. As for reels, the distances involved narrow your choice to one—the fixed-spool.

Bite indicators have been a source of many, sometimes heated, arguments among experienced anglers. Some swear by one that acts at the butt end of the rod, while others prefer a swingtip or quivertip.

Accurate casting is essential. Not only are you endeavouring to place a bait in a relatively small area, but there is always one particular spot in a bream swim which produces more fish—a hotspot within a hotspot. Only experience teaches you how to find it. Every time you cast, note where the bait lands, and after a while you will know which spot produces most bites. Accurate, long-range casting takes practice. Straining for distance will not lead to accuracy—you need to develop a consistent, relaxed technique.

Bream bites
Bream are capable of giving many types of bite—from ½in twitches to fast pulls, but the more usual response is a slow, steady lift that straightens the swingtip or pulls the butt indicator to the butt ring. Strike just before it reaches the ring.

The range involved requires a powerful determined strike, with the rod sweeping back over the shoulder. Your reflexes should be attuned to the resistance of a big, slab-sided bream. If the strike is not under control, and you do not ease off at the moment of impact, a broken line is inevitable.

Your first big bream
When you first hook a big bream, you encounter almost solid resistance, and will be glad there is some stretch in the line to act as a shock absorber. This is followed by several powerful thuds. All you can do, on a 4lb line, is hang on to the rod and wait, which will not be long, because the bream is not built for sustained fighting. You can soon move it into open water and bring it to the net, but always be ready for the odd fish which will fight like a tench. To give line before breaking point is reached, set the slipping clutch.

Twilight and dusk are good times to seek bream, which take advantage of the failing light to enter the shallower marginal waters in search of food. Sometimes they give themselves away by gently moving the marginal reeds, and a bait presented on the edge of the margins will often take fish.

CARP

The wild carp is an adaptable fish, which is capable of living in a wide variety of habitats in Britain. Generally, however, it favours shallow lakes and ponds, rich in aquatic vegetation, and still, sluggish, or slow-moving rivers and canals. Since Britain is at the northernmost limit of the area in which carp reproduce, it follows that, in general, the distribution and occurrence of the species are greater in the south of these islands than in the north. The most northerly wild carp fisheries in the British Isles are Brayton Pond, near Aspatria in Cumbria, and Danskine Loch, in Scotland.

Adult wild carp typically inhabit warmer environments, such as shallow areas of ponds and lakes, or slack eddies in rivers, usually where there is aquatic vegetation. On rare occasions, they have been noted in swift mountain trout streams, and netted to depths of nearly 100ft.

Basic carp fishing

Next to presenting bread crusts on a greased line, perhaps the most effective of all carp fishing methods—and there are many—is to 'freeline'. The secret behind this most sensitive presentation is to choose a bait large and heavy enough to be cast accurately without the addition of shots or float, and simply to offer it on the bottom on a completely 'free line'.

Good freelining swims are close to beds of surface weed such as broad leaf potamogeton or lilies, alongside fallen trees or where brambles trail into the water, on the top of a shallow, gravel bar, or wherever carp have been seen moving even very close in alongside marginal rushes or sedges. In short, almost any area within 20 to 30 yards of the bank. Beyond that distance freelining techniques can cause problems for the inexperienced.

Care must be taken to ensure that most of the line lies perfectly flat along the bottom, or 'line bites', where a fish swims into a 'hanging' line, might occur.

Good, heavy, baits are lobworms (try two on the hook), breadflake, luncheon meat, small whole freshwater mussels straight out of the shell, and various pastes such as tinned cat food, or sausage meat stiffened with wholemeal flour. Use hook sizes 2 to 6 depending on baits, and tie direct to 8-10lb b.s. line. Where there are no weeds or snags or where the carp average on the small side, line strength can be reduced to 6-7lb. In each case use an 'all through action' rod.

Carp bites

Bites are usually bold when freelining because the carp simply feels minimum resistance as it sucks in and makes off with the bait, so allow some 'slack' or a 'bow' in the line to hang down from the rod tip and watch it carefully where it enters the water. After a preliminary 'twitch' or sometimes without any prior warning the line will suddenly and confidently rise up through the water. Wait

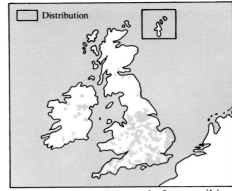

Distribution

for it to fully tighten before striking hard and far back. This is most important when using big hooks for they do not penetrate the carp's rubbery mouth easily. To help penetration, flatten the barb with a pair of forceps and really sharpen the outside edge between point and barb with a carborundum stone. It is worth the extra few minutes, because a powerful carp can be lost within seconds.

Learn to walk slowly, quietly, and not to make any sudden arm movements around a carp water, and you will even hook fish which confidently swim within mere feet of where you sit.

Carp baits

Tinned pet-foods make good carp baits when stiffened with rusk or groundbait, and the addition of a small amount of flour keeps these baits intact in the

The powerfully muscled body of the common carp, evidence of the fighting qualities of this much-sought-after but elusive fish.

FISHING FOR CARP

Method	Rod	Reel	Line	Terminal tackle	Hooks	Lead Weights	Bait	Groundbait Attractor	Habitat	Time of season	Distribution
Antenna float or betalight float	Fibreglass or carbonfibre, 11ft 6in, 1¼lb test	Fixed-spool	5-8lb	Single hook below antenna/ betalight float	4-10	Balanced split shot	Naturals, particles, some pastes, specials	Usually same as hookbait	Usually stillwaters, occasionally moving water	All times, especially winter	Widely distributed in southern England and the Midlands, becoming scarce further north
Slider float	Fibreglass or carbonfibre, 12-13ft, 1¼lb test	Fixed-spool	5-7lb	Single hook below slider float	4-10	Balanced split shot	Naturals, particles, pastes, specials	Usually same as hookbait	Usually stillwaters	All times, especially winter	
Link ledger	Fibreglass or carbonfibre, 11ft, 1¼-1½lb test	Fixed-spool	6-12lb	Swan shot or bomb link with single hook	2-8	¼-2oz bomb or variable swan shot	Naturals, particles, pastes, specials	Usually same as hookbait	Moving and stillwaters	All times	
Paternoster	Fibreglass or carbonfibre, 11ft, 1¼-1½lb test	Fixed-spool	6-12lb	Arlesey bomb, single hook	2-8	¼-2oz bomb or variable swan shot	All types	Usually same as hookbait	Moving and stillwaters	All times	
Swimfeeder	Fibreglass or carbonfibre, 11ft 6in, 1½lb test	Fixed-spool	6-10lb	Swimfeeder, single hook	4-8	Swimfeeder	Natural particles, usually maggots	Usually same as hookbait	Moving and stillwaters	All times	
Freelining	Fibreglass or carbonfibre, 11ft, 1¼-1½lb test	Fixed-spool	6-12lb	Single hook only	2-8	No weight	Usually paste specials, some naturals	Usually same as hookbait	Stillwaters	Usually summer and autumn	
Freelined floating bait	Fibreglass or carbonfibre, 11ft 6in, 1¼-1½lb test	Fixed-spool	6-12lb	Single hook only	2-6	No weight	Crust, air-injected worm, some specials	Few samples, same as hookbait	Stillwaters	Usually summer	
Ledgered floating bait	Fibreglass or carbonfibre, 11ft 6in, 1¼-1½lb test	Fixed-spool	5-8lb	Arlesey bomb or link with single hook	2-8	¼-2oz bomb	Crust, air-injected worm, some specials	None	Usually stillwaters, occasionally moving water	Usually summer and autumn	
Margin fishing	Fibreglass or carbonfibre, 10-11ft, 1½lb test	Fixed-spool	8-12lb	Single hook only	2-8	No weight	All types	Usually same as hookbait	Stillwaters	Mostly summer	

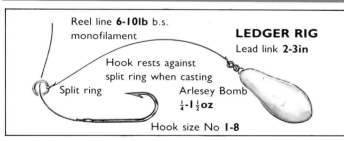

Reel line **6-10lb** b.s. monofilament

LEDGER RIG
Lead link **2-3in**

Hook rests against split ring when casting

Split ring

Arlesey Bomb
¼-1½oz

Hook size No **1-8**

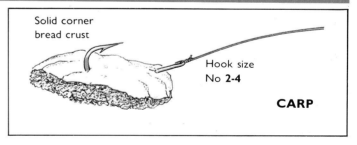

Solid corner bread crust

Hook size No **2-4**

CARP

water for long enough to be useful.

Carp will take maggots, casters, worms, beetles, snails, slugs, caterpillars, caddis, shrimps, wasp grubs, leeches, mealworms, freshwater cockles, mussels, small crayfish, silkworms, and dragonfly larvae. All of these will catch carp.

Particle baits such as sweetcorn are successful because carp are attracted to large numbers of small food items and readily become preoccupied with feeding on them. Once samples of the particle bait are already in your swim, it is only a matter of time before the hookbait is taken. A problem with small baits on carp tackle is that the fish seem to learn quickly how to avoid those hooked seeds which act differently.

Float fishing can be particularly useful with particle baits. The method gives an indication of where the hookbait is,

and loose bait particles can be scattered around the float. It also minimizes the danger of hooked bait being taken down the throat, especially if a sensitive lift method is used. But on heavily float-fished waters, carp no doubt see the line. Float fishing then becomes pointless and you have to revert to ledgering or freelining.

In 1952, Richard Walker broke the British rod-caught carp record with a 44lb common carp from Redmire Pool —a record that still stands. At that time, the norm in carp tackle was to use a cane rod of about 10ft and a centrepin reel or, if you were fortunate, one of the early fixed-spool reels.

The beginner should start with a 10 or 11ft rod with a fast taper. The reel will be a good-quality fixed-spool model with at least 8lb b.s. nylon.

Bread still catches plenty of carp if

Above left *A simple and sensitiver ledger rig.* **Above** *One of the classic carp baits, the free-lined floating crust.*

used intelligently, and the modern carp specialist uses it in all its varied forms because it is cheap and easy to obtain. But the most serious drawback of bread is that almost all other species of fish find it attractive and will remove it from the hook before the carp find it. Swans, too, can be a nuisance.

Usefulness of worms
Worms are useful baits, and are particularly good when stalking carp and casting to feeding fish. They can be made to float by injecting them with a small amount of air, using a hypodermic syringe with a fine needle, and can then be floated or ledgered. Lobworms and redworms are the best.

TENCH

The tench is a member of the carp family and is found in lakes, canals, ponds (including the village duck pond), meres, gravel pits, lochs and rivers. Although the species abounds in muddy-bottomed lakes, ponds and canals, in these waters they tend to err on the side of quantity rather than quality. Generally, gravel pits and lakes produce the larger specimens, and the bigger the water, especially if it is clear, the better.

Irish tench

The big Irish loughs produce many large tench, and every spring numerous specimen fish are taken from the famous Power Station reach at Lanesborough to where they migrate from Lough Ree to spawn. Canals, too, hold tench in large numbers, and the bigger specimens are mostly found in those waterways where boat traffic is not heavy. Although normally associated with stillwaters, tench are also found in rivers. Here, although tench are caught in summer, the best times are often when the water is high and coloured—even in winter.

Tackle selection

Choice of tackle depends on local conditions and the ability of the angler. For freelining and ledgering a fairly powerful hollow-glass rod of $10\frac{1}{2}$-11ft with a test curve of about $1\frac{1}{2}$lb is suggested. For float fishing, a similar rod with an extra few inches may well be desirable. Most tench waters have a fair share of weed for at least part of the summer, which, particularly if there are other submerged snags like trees, means that you cannot afford to fish too fine. In snaggy conditions you will need line of at least 5lb b.s., or even 7 or 8lb in really difficult spots. If you are fortunate enough to locate your tench in snag

and weed-free reservoir-type waters, you can drop to 3lb providing you have experience of handling bigger fish. For hooks, the choice is wide, depending on the rest of your tackle and bait—anything from a single maggot or grain of sweetcorn on a No 16 up to a juicy mussel 'foot' on a No 2.

Other essentials are an umbrella, a large landing net, a reliable torch for night fishing, and an eye-shade or polarized sunglasses (or both) for use in bright sunshine. Accessories such as bite alarms, bite indicators, swingtips, and rod rests should be chosen by the individual.

Tench rods

Tench rods range from 9ft to 13ft. Each has its own application, although there is no need for an armoury of rods at the outset. Soft-actioned rods are preferred to rigid pokers, but some anglers prefer the opposite. One soft-actioned wand that weighs but a few ounces is ideal for tench fishing from a boat, while for bank fishing something much longer is needed, especially for use with a float. Whatever the length or action of the rod, it should be applied to a suitable line. The soft-action rods are not likely to break a fine 2lb b.s. line; while heavier rods would be too hard on lines of breaking strain under 6lb b.s.

Reliable baits

In these days of fashionable specialist baits—high protein, magic, seed, particle, 'secret', cereal and others—it seems odd to suggest that a loaf of bread and a tin of worms are still effective baits for most tench fishing. But they are, because tench become wary of certain baits as the season progresses, and it often pays to change. In the early days of the season, sensible-sized hookbaits are just as likely to be taken as single

maggots or casters. More big tench have been taken on small crust cubes (which, at $\frac{3}{8}$in square, are huge compared with a single maggot) than any other bait. Worms such as brandlings are also excellent, especially when used in advance as groundbait.

On certain waters, freshwater mussels used whole (without shells, of course) or in pieces, have probably accounted for as many big day-time tench as any other bait, while trout pellets as groundbait, and hookbaits made up of soaked brown bread and softened pellets, have proved an excellent combination in recent years, even becoming 'standard' baits.

Soaked maize

Soaked maize, left until it has fermented and developed an unbearable smell, will undoubtedly attract tench into a given area. The maize itself is not the best of hookbaits, however, because it never really softens, and hooked fish tend to break away. Instead, it is better to fish a sweetcorn hookbait. Soft paste made from maize meal and allowed to 'go off' is also very effective when used with soaked maize.

Canned sweetcorn is particularly good for tench and carp. Maggots and casters, redworms, black slugs, snails, caddis, grubs, freshwater mussels—and innumerable other baits, natural and manufactured—are also good. Although all will take fish many of them are of little value except, perhaps, as talking points among anglers. With few exceptions most 'oddball' baits are less likely to produce specimen tench than the tried and tested alternatives.

From time to time there are reports of big tench taken on unusual baits not intended for them, but there are seldom subsequent catches on the same bait. One well-known angler once hooked an enormous tench on a piece of dead fish

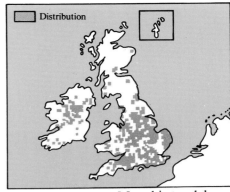

Distribution

'LIFT' BITE

Main line 3lb b.s.

Float lifts out of the water as tench lifts bait

'Tell-tale' shot

No. 12 Hook

Far left How the lift bite is registered by the float. As the tench takes the bait its head rises and raises the shotted line. **Left** A freshwater mussel hooked so the barb is exposed and can be set home at the instant of the strike.

FISHING FOR TENCH

Method	Rod	Reel	Line	Terminal tackle	Hooks	Leads/Weights	Bait	Groundbait/Attractor	Time of Season	Habitat	Distribution
Lift method	12' Glass fast taper	Small fixed spool	3-5lb	Single hook below peacock quill float	10-12	One only swan shot	Crust, flake, cereals, sweetcorn	Light groundbait and hook samples	June to October	Stillwaters, slow moving canals etc.	Widely over UK and Ireland
Simple ledger	10-11' progressive action	Medium fixed spool	4lb	Single spade hook	8-14	Swan shot link ledger, stop shot	Worms, paste, cereals	Medium groundbait	June to October		
Long range ledger	10-11' progressive action	Medium fixed spool	5lb	Single spade hook. Nylon 6lb shock leader	6-12	1 ounce bomb, stop shot	All baits	Heavy groundbait (catapult)	June to October		
Freeline	10-11' progressive action	Medium fixed spool	4lb	Single spade or eyed hook	6-12	No lead	Worms, paste, balanced-crust	No groundbait, hook samples if possible	June to October		
Stalking	9½' lightweight glass or carbon	Small fixed spool	3-5lb	Single eyed or spade hook	10-12	No lead	Worms, mussels, brandlings	No groundbait	Early season usually		
Swim feeder	10-11' progressive action	Medium fixed spool	6lb	Single hook, blockend feeder	12-16	Feeder only	Maggots	No groundbait	June to October		
Boat fishing	9½' lightweight	Small fixed spool	3-5lb	Single spade or eyed hook, quill or balsa float	8-16	Bulk-shotting high up on terminal	Maggots, particles, small worms	Hook samples only	June to October		
Drifting float	12-12½' fast action	Small fixed spool	3-5lb	Single hook, top-bouancy float	8-16	Bulk-shotting high up on terminal	Maggots, particles, small worms	Hook samples only	June to October		
Night fishing (1)	12-12½' general float rod	Medium fixed spool	4-6lb	Betalight float, single eyed hook	10-14	Balanced shotting	All small baits	Medium groundbait and hook samples	June to September		
Night fishing (2)	9½ or 10' general ledger rod	Medium fixed spool	6lb	Single hook	6-10	Single swan shot or loaded link ledger	Paste, lobworms, flake, crust	Medium groundbait	June to September		

intended for an eel, but as he had eel-fished that spot for many years previously with chunks of dead fish as hookbaits, he knew he had not discovered anything revolutionary! This fish had learnt to avoid the usual baits and, having changed its diet completely, had grown enormous. It is perhaps this change of diet that produces the odd specimen in a water where they are thought not to live.

Ledgering

Ledgering is a very successful method of tench fishing, especially in meres and gravel pits. The various techniques include the use of a blockend filled with maggots, a swimfeeder with bread or worms, straightforward ledgering with an Arlesey bomb or sliding link ledger, and freelining.

Sliding float

In deep water of 12ft and over, a sliding float is necessary. For a slider to perform properly the diameter of the bottom ring should be such that only lines of less than 6lb b.s. can pass through. Line strength should be 3-5lb. The float should have a long antenna and the shot loading should consist of about six AAA's and a No 1.

Importance of side strain

Tench are doughty and powerful fighters. You must prevent a hooked tench from swimming back into a tangled mass of weed, for once there you will be lucky to eventually net it. Exert side strain to keep the fish clear. This entails holding the rod low and putting opposite pressure on the fish, which will be forced to make greater efforts to escape; this time more quickly and using up more energy.

Make float changing simple

Several situations call for float fishing and it is not always possible to select the ideal rig immediately. Quick changes are necessary from time to time, so a separate float attachment kept permanently on the line is often advisable. This makes float changing simple with shotting adjusted without dismantling the whole tackle.

Above *The hook barb needs to be removed very carefully from the thick rubbery lips of such a specimen-sized tench.*

Rigs and tackle are not alone in accounting for success in tench fishing. As in all serious angling, locating the fish is all-important. Many really big tench are found in weedy shallows and, during the day, their paths can be plotted by the string of bubbles they send up to the surface while feeding.

BARBEL

Barbel are indigenous to the swift flowing waters that run to the East Coast of England. They are common in the Thames, Yorkshire Ouse, and Derwent, as well as in the Kennet, Swale, Nidd and Wharfe. They do not naturally occur in the slow flowing lowland rivers of East Anglia and are not found in any rivers that flow to the south or west.

Once the angler hooks his first barbel he will find himself equally hooked on barbel fishing. The sheer power and strength of this stubborn fighter has to be experienced to be believed. Salmon anglers who have inadvertently taken barbel all agree that, weight for weight, there is little to choose between the two species for endurance and power.

Barbel can be caught by a variety of methods, on many baits, and at all hours.

Baits for daytime barbel

To catch these holed-up, daytime fish is not easy; stealth and delicate bait-presentation are needed. Small baits, such as maggots, are often best, and to present them effectively fine tackle and small hooks are needed—but a 3lb b.s. line and No 16 hook are of little use for heaving a 9lb barbel from dense weed.

Bait and tackle

Barbel will also take such traditional baits as wheat, hemp, barley, maggots, silkweed, and all manner of 'secret' pastes concocted by the angler. When they are fastidious it is essential to use comparative tackle, hooks and light baits to tempt them. This spells out the paradox of barbel fishing. The angler has not only to locate his fish, but also to seek them with hooks and lines that are not so heavy as to scare them away, but strong enough to subdue and land a powerful fish.

Ledgering by day or night is by far the most effective method, and the beginner will be well advised to start this way. Essential tackle is an 11ft hollow-glass rod with a test-curve of 1½lb, combined

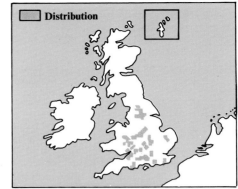

with a reliable fixed-spool reel holding line between 6 and 9lb b.s., depending on conditions. A lead attached to a 6in link and a small swivel is preferable to a lead running direct on the reel line. The distance the link ledger is stopped from the hook depends on the current, the type of bait, and the amount of weed in the swim. Usually this distance will vary between 12 and 18in, but when fishing the gaps in streamer weed you may find that it needs to be doubled.

The beginner should concentrate on well-proven meaty baits such as sausage or luncheon meat. Use hook sizes between 10 and 4, depending on the size of bait. Avoid meat baits with a high fat or gristle content; the lumps can prevent the hook penetrating. The most effective method of detecting barbel bites is to hold the rod and feel for them with line held between thumb and forefinger. At the same time, watch the rod top for movements. At night a beam from a torch on to the rod tip is a major asset and it does not appear to scare fish. But it must not be flashed on and off into the water.

For the novice perhaps the most important matter is the identification of barbel bites on the ledger, for they can vary enormously.

Left *A nice barbel caught from the River Wensum in Norfolk. Though not indigenous to the slow-flowing waters of East Anglia, barbel have been successfully introduced there to provide angling sport.*

FISHING FOR BARBEL

Methods	Rod	Reel	Reel Line	Terminal Tackle	Hooks	Leads/ Weights	Bait	Groundbait/ Attractor	Time of Season	Habitat	Distribution
Ledgering for big fish—8lb plus—snaggy swims	10ft 6in- 11ft 6in hollow glass: 1.75-2.25lb test	Mitchell 300 fixed-spool	10lb b.s.	Running link ledger	No 4-10 Sundridge Specimen, James Carp	Arlesey bombs on link, swan shot on link	Meaty luncheon meat, lobworms, sweetcorn	Regular trickle of free hookbait offerings, open blockend feeder	Summer, autumn, occasionally in winter (dusk and night-time preferable)	Rivers—for example, Thames, Kennet, Stour, Avon, Swale, Nidd	East Coast rivers, Home Counties, Yorkshire, Somerset
Ledgering for medium-size fish in less snaggy swims	10ft 6in-11ft 6in hollow glass: 1.25-1.75lb test	Mitchell 300 fixed-spool	5-7lb b.s.	Running link ledger	No 6-12: as above	As above	As above	As above	As above	As above	As above
Float fishing —trotting— in more open stretches	11ft-12ft hollow-glass: 1.25-1.75lb test	Mitchell 300 fixed-spool 3½-4in diameter centrepin	4-7lb b.s. (only in clear conditions)	Kennet Trotter 3 or 4 swan shot	No 8-14: Sundridge, Lion D'Or	Split shot, swan shot	Maggots, tares, hemp, casters, luncheon meat cubes, sweetcorn	Free offerings, plus bait dropper in fast swims	Summer, autumn, very occasionally in winter (daytime)	As above	As above

PERCH

While the perch is widely distributed throughout the whole of the British Isles—although less widespread in Scotland—its presence in the North and West is in large part due to its being introduced there for purposes of angling or food, or out of sheer curiosity.

The perch is perhaps one of the most popular freshwater species in the British Isles, especially with the young angler. The reason for this is that perch are voracious eaters and will willingly take bait, especially worms, placed quietly under their noses. For the young angler the capture of two or three perch, even if they are only 6in long, can enliven an otherwise fishless day. Though perch of this size are rarely of interest to the experienced angler, to the novice they offer good sport and the opportunity to develop a wide range of angling skills.

Big perch tackle is fairly straightforward. A general purpose 10-11ft rod, teamed with a fixed-spool reel, is suitable for most stillwater perching; a glassfibre blank with a test curve in the 1-1½lb range is ideal. The action should be on the stiffish side if really long casting is essential, but if you are going to fish gravel pits at reasonably short range, up to 40 yards say, and the water is relatively snag-free, a softer Avon-type rod is more fun to use. On the other hand, if you are going to fish large lakes at long range in the depths of winter, a rod of 11-12ft is best.

Choice of line

Perch are pretty bold fish, rarely tackle shy, so if there are snags, merely play safe and use a line of 4–5lb b.s. Go up to 8lb if, for example, you hope to catch a 3lb perch from the inside of a sub-

merged obstruction. A three-pounder is capable of making short but powerful spurts. In snag-free waters, 3lb b.s. line is a good general choice.

Keep your terminal tackle as basic as possible. If you do not have to use a lead, simply freeline. A fat lobworm can be swung out 15 yards without difficulty, adding a swan shot will give you another five, and with two swan shots you should attain 25-30 yards. Using two worms will also increase your cast a bit. Hook sizes will usually range from No 4 to 12, depending on the size and type of bait; use eyed hooks which have medium shanks.

Keep the bait on the move

It is important to keep the bait on the move to get the most enjoyment from big perch fishing. Search every inch of the water with your roving bait, be it a lobworm, livebait or deadbait. Cast to the desired spot and watch and feel your line as the bait sinks for any sudden movements: sometimes perch bite in mid-water. But the time to be really at the ready is when the bait is about to reach the bottom and for a few seconds afterwards. About 40 per cent of big perch have come at this time.

Even when the bait has touched bottom do not place the rod in the rests, but hold on for a minute or two, then give the worm a couple of tweaks. If nothing happens, rest the rod, then tweak the bait every four or five minutes, retrieving a foot or so of line each time. In this way you keep the bait active and cover a large area, searching about 15ft of water with each cast.

When the rod is on the rests, leave the bale-arm of the reel open and allow the perch to trundle off a couple of yards before you strike. If it is calm, just watch for movements on the line. In rougher conditions, use an on-line bait indicator.

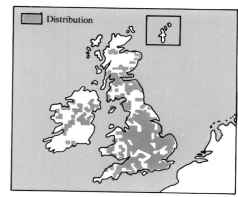

Hanningfield lure

Veltic   Ondex

Above A perch fly and two spinning lures known to attract this fish. **Below** Not a common sight for the angler, a 2½lb perch.

Below Large perch need to be fished for at long range. This rig enables the bait to be cast considerable distances.

TERMINAL RIG (LONG-RANGE) FOR STILLWATER PERCH

5-7lb b.s. reel line

Ledger stop

Swivel

10in

18in

¾in-1oz Arlesey bomb (sliding)

DACE

The dace is common throughout England and Wales, except in the extreme West.

Baits for dace

Dace will take most baits offered to roach at one time or another, according to prevailing circumstances. Bread baits, including paste, crust, crumb and flake, are popular, and cereals such as wheat, hemp, or tares also account for large bags, especially in winter, when insect life is less easily found by the fish. Many anglers like to groundbait the swim with hemp, while using elderberry on the hook. This is worthwhile, as the fish hang on to the bait a little longer, giving the angler fractionally more time to synchronize his strike with the disappearance of the float.

In summer, maggots, caddis grubs, woodlice, earwigs, or freshwater shrimps and worms are all good dace baits, and the angler must experiment to see which best suits existing conditions and the whims of the fish on a particular day.

Almost any float or ledgering method can be employed, according to preferences and the water fished, but the sparing use of groundbait is always useful for attracting shoals to the vicinity.

The free-lined worm

Perhaps the most effective and skilful way of taking good dace in shallow waters is to fish a worm unencumbered by weights of any kind. The worm simply rolls downstream, the angler feeding off line as required. Bites are registered by a swift movement of the line, sometimes also seen at the rod tip. A swift answering strike should secure one fish out of every three.

Forget small hooks and ultra-fine lines, for most likely you will be presenting your baits beneath undercut banks, in or around snags, and down richly weeded runs—everywhere the current takes them.

Fly fishing methods

Fly fishing for dace is a most enjoyable method, especially when working small streams where few other anglers are about. If possible, it is preferable to wade because this gives better line control as the fly runs swiftly down the stream. Often, almost any small fly will suffice, but if the angler is able to identify the insects on the water and present a good imitation of them, he will be even more certain of takes.

The fly can be fished upstream or down, according to conditions or to the angler's skill and preference. Both methods are productive, but require swift reflexes from the angler. The fly can be fished wet or dry, and some anglers like to attach a single maggot to the fly for dace. Sometimes this not only improves the number of takes but also provokes the fish to take firmly.

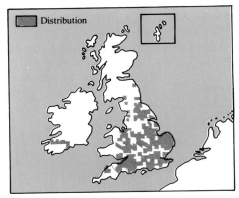

Above *A specimen 10oz dace caught by trotting maggot bait downstream, an ideal method for surface-feeding fish.*

FISHING FOR DACE

Methods	Rod	Reel	Reel Line	Terminal Tackle	Hooks	Leads/ Weights	Bait	Groundbait/ Attractor	Habitat	Time of Season	Distribution
Float: Avon	13ft hollow-glass	Centrepin	2lb	1lb b.s. hook length	14-18	Balanced shot	Maggots, casters, flake	Loose samples	Fast-flowing rivers	All year	Widespread in England and eastern Wales but not found in Scotland, West Wales and all but South-West Ireland
Stick	13ft hollow-glass	Centrepin	2lb	1lb b.s. hook length	14-20	Balanced shot	Maggots, casters	Loose samples	Fast-flowing rivers	All year	
Waggler	Fast-taper 13ft hollow-glass	Fixed-spool	1.7lb	1lb b.s. hook length	18-22	Balanced shot	Maggots, casters	Loose samples	Slower, larger rivers	All year	
Porcupine quill	13ft hollow-glass	Fixed-spool	2lb	1lb b.s. hook length	16-20	Balanced shot	Hempseed	Loose samples	Steadily flowing rivers	Summer and autumn	
Link-ledger	10ft 6in hollow-glass or split-cane	Fixed-spool	3lb	1lb b.s. hook length	12-18	SSG on link	Maggots, casters	Loose samples	Small streams and rivers	Autumn and winter	
Feeder-link	8ft quivertip	Fixed-spool	3lb	2lb b.s. hook length	12-18	Blockend or open-end feeder	Maggots, casters	Samples in feeder	Large rivers	Autumn and winter	
Fly	9ft, 6 or 7 AFTM	Fly	Double-taper No. 6 Floater	3lb b.s. cast	12-16	—	Dry or wet fly	—	Streams	Summer	

RUDD

The rudd is widely scattered throughout England, particularly in the South-East. It becomes less common in the North and West, and in the extreme West and North it is uncommon or even rare. The rudd does not occur in Scotland or west Wales but is very common in Ireland, where it is traditionally known as roach.

It is no mean fighter either. Size for size, the rudd fights better than the roach, which is hardly surprising because size for size it runs heavier. The rudd is a lake and pond fish, which thrives well in a stillwater habitat. However, it is also found in limited numbers in slow and sluggish rivers, or in the almost still reaches of older canals.

In such waters it prefers these slow reaches and pools and rarely mixes with roach populations found in the faster reaches, except when it moves in shoals between one fairly still water region and another.

Overgrown chalk pits also produce shoals of rudd and where such populations are well balanced with good pike, perch or even wild bird predators, the resident rudd do well. In other waters they are prone to become too profuse.

Rudd are shy, sensitive fish that must never be underestimated. To catch good, specimen rudd, the experienced and successful angler has familiarized himself with the precarious life cycle of the species, its movements, habitat, and feeding patterns from hour to hour.

Fishing for rudd

Rudd frequently provide a fair bag and the early season lake angler can look forward to a peaceful day when the rudd are obliging.

Surface and middle-water fishing methods are clearly indicated, and if shoals of rudd are seen well off-shore the angler must shot-up a fairly heavy tackle to provide long casting. Rudd feeding well off the shoreline are not unduly shy, but most anglers prefer to take no chances.

A useful strategy is to cast well beyond

Left *Ireland's rudd are well known for their size. This catch includes specimens of 2lb 5oz taken from Lake Cloonfree.*

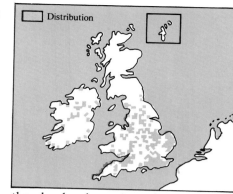

the shoal, where the splash of tackle hitting the surface will not be noticed. The tackle is then drawn slowly towards the angler and into position over the shoal. Runs are often signified by a determined lateral and oblique movement of the float as fish take the bait along with them, rather than diving with it.

Bubble float

In these situations a bubble-float partially filled with water often provides casting weight, permitting light shotting. Alternatively, a controller lying flat on the surface rather than being cocked like a float, allows swift bite detection on finer tackle than might otherwise be required.

When shoals of rudd do venture close inshore, great care is necessary to avoid alarming them. Fish hooked must be drawn aside from the shoal without allowing them to splash on the surface. This means employing side strain with the rod tip low until the fish can be landed.

FISHING FOR RUDD

Methods	Rod	Reel	Reel Line	Terminal Tackle	Hooks	Leads/Weights	Bait	Groundbait/Attractor	Time of Season	Habitat	Distribution
Long-distance ledgering	13ft, 1lb test	Fixed-spool	2lb	Running link	10-14	$\frac{1}{4}$-$\frac{1}{2}$oz bomb	Bread maggot, worm	Golden crumbs and hookbait	Late summer/winter	Stillwater	Ireland, South-West Southern, and South-East England
Short-distance ledgering	10ft/soft action	Fixed-spool	3lb	Freeline	10	None	Bread, worm	Mashed bread	Early summer	Stillwater	Ireland, South-West, Southern, and South-East England
Surface-crust fishing	12ft	Fixed-spool	3lb	Freeline	8-10	None	Crust	Samples of hookbait	All seasons at night	Stillwater	Ireland, South-West, Southern, and South-East England
Bubble-float fishing	13ft	Fixed-spool	2lb	Single hook	8-10	2 No 6s	Flake	Samples of hookbait	Summer	Stillwater	Ireland, South-West, Southern, and South-East England
Short-distance float fishing with a small sinking bait — small quill or pole float	12ft	Fixed-spool	2lb	Single hook	16-20	2 dust shot	Maggot, caster, sweetcorn	Hookbait	Summer	Stillwater	Ireland, South-West, Southern, and South-East England
Fly fishing	Trout fly	Fly	Floating line	2lb trace	10 and 12		Small wet or dry flies and nymphs	None	Summer	Stillwater	Ireland, South-West, Southern, and South-East England

CHAPTER 2

TACKLE

FLOAT RODS

Rods for float fishing should be 12-13ft long, able to handle lines of 3-5lb b.s., and have a slow action. Other types of coarse fishing rod may be used: the specimen hunter, for example, may find a light carp rod best when float fishing for tench or carp in weedy conditions and with the expectation of a big fish. The beginner will often use a glassfibre spinning rod because it is cheap, adaptable and sturdy. But the term 'float rod' is usually applied to the longer rods used for general and match fishing.

These two uses have resulted in the development of two distinct kinds of float rod: slow-action rods, which bend along much of their length when playing a fish or casting; and fast-action rods, usually rigid to within 25 per cent of their length with the action concentrated in the tip.

General-purpose float rods

General-purpose float rods are slower in action than match rods and have stronger tips, usually made of glassfibre and 2½-3mm in diameter. The tip of a match rod is nearer 2½mm in diameter to allow their use with lines of 1½-2lb b.s. In addition, the match rod is usually stiffer in the butt to give quicker striking. Fish control, however, is more difficult with a stiffer rod but as a rule, matchmen are not pursuing large fish. There are exceptions to this, such as on the Severn where matches are won with good sized chub and barbel. These fish demand a stronger rod than that used by the average match fisherman.

Match rod development

Due to the changing demands of match fishing, the match rod is constantly being developed. Different areas of fishing call for different actions so there are variations in the type of rod in use.

Most float rods today are made of tubular glassfibre, though carbonfibre rods are now popular.

Rods for float fishing are usually equipped with cork handles fitted with sliding rings for holding the reel. This keeps the weight to a minimum.

With a threaded tip ring fitted, the float rod may be used with various

screw attachments, such as a swingtip for ledgering. Care should be taken, however, to ensure that the tip of the rod will be able to stand up to the casting weight.

A rod of this description is also suited to long trotting, when float tackle is allowed to trot down with the current of a river or stream and the fish are hooked and played some way downstream from the angler. Specimen hunters tend to use the longer, lighter ledgering rods—those designed by Peter Stone, for example—since they are capable of casting tackle long distances and controlling heavy fish by absorbing their powerful struggles.

Never buy the cheapest rod unless it is recommended. Tackle quality and cost go hand-in-hand. Buy wisely.

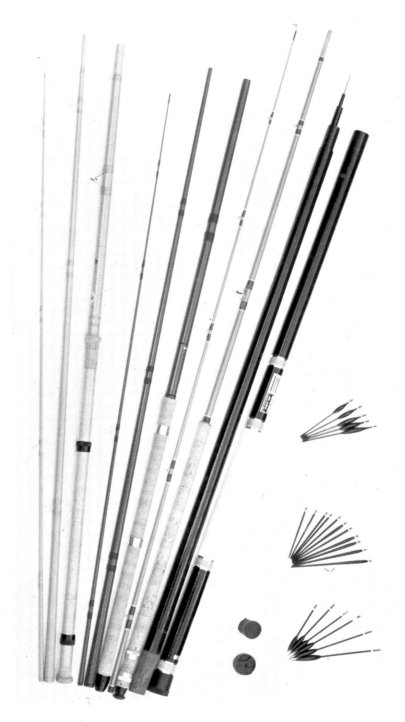

Right *A small selection of the huge range of float rods available. For the beginner a length of 12ft is recommended.*

Above *Two ledger rods in action on the River Swale in Yorkshire. Barbel have been introduced into this Northern river.*

Right *These ledger rods show how the length of the butt end can vary to suit the angler's preference in spread of rodrest.*

A ledger set-up. With tiny 'twitch' bites, shorten the bobbin drop to about 4in. Watch the line closely at the point where it enters the water.

'TWITCH' BITE DETECTION

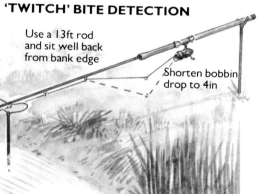

Use a 13ft rod and sit well back from bank edge

Shorten bobbin drop to 4in

Watch line where it enters water

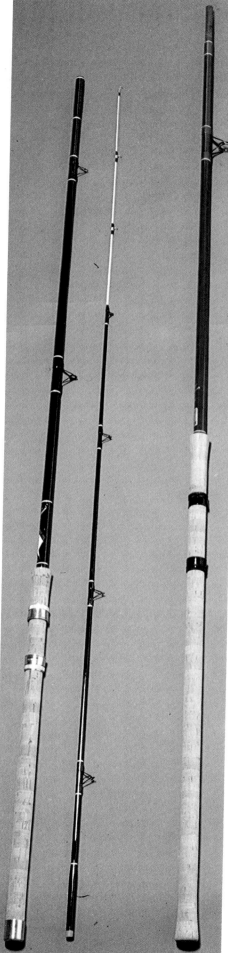

LEDGER RODS

Present-day ledger rods vary from 9ft to 11½ft, the longer rods being used more by the specimen hunter and the shorter kinds usually by the competition angler. They are also used with various types of bite indicators, although some rods have a built-in bite indicator called a quivertip, which consists of a finely tapered piece of solid glass which, because of its small diameter, is very sensitive. This type, known as a quivertip rod, is usually between 9½–10ft in length.

Rods of 9ft–10ft are usually employed by match anglers for ledgering in conjunction with a swimfeeder.

Specimen hunter's rods

The longer type of ledgering rod is more often used by specimen hunters who usually rely on fine tips and bite indicators on the line to hook fish. Quiver tip rods are used for shy-biting fish such as roach, while the longer rods are used to cast and to strike at fish at long range. A rod with a test curve of approximately 1–1¼lb is necessary due to the drag and stretch of the line, but with steep-taper rods the test curve can be less to give better bite indication, while the relatively strong butt and middle will pick up a line rapidly.

The best length

For general purposes a rod of 10-11ft is suitable for match ledgering. A stiff rod of 9½ft is the best all-round length. The rod should be fitted with graduated stand-off rings with a screw-in tip ring which will accommodate any of the various attachments for bite indication —swingtip, quivertip, springtip and others. With this type of rod, lines of 2-4lb b.s. are normally used, while the larger rods used by specimen hunters can require the use of lines up to 10lb b.s.

Many of the lighter carp rods made today can make excellent ledgering rods, as they are primarily designed for fishing on the bottom of the lake or gravel pit for carp, unlike specially designed ledgering rods. The tips are rarely used, however, for bite indication, and this should be considered when selecting a ledger rod.

SPINNING RODS

The design of spinning rods has altered considerably over the past 50 years. The original rods were heavy and long, and made for salmon spinning. They were usually of greenheart (a special type of hardwood), or built cane. The centrepin reel used with these rods required them to be slow in action to assist the revolving drum to accelerate evenly and allow line to flow off without jamming.

With the introduction of the fixed-spool reel, rod action could be improved. They could be faster in action, as well as lighter. The fixed-spool reel could cast lighter baits and, because the spool of the reel did not revolve, the line did not jam or overrun, making casting easier.

Spinning rods may usually be classified by the weights they can cast and the line strengths the rod can handle, their basic function being to cast a lure and to control a hooked fish.

SPINNING OVERHEAD CAST

The weight factor

As a general rule, the lighter the lure or spinner to be cast, the lighter and shorter the rod. In general, also, the lighter the lure, the finer will be the line used with it. This is because the heavier and thicker the line the more weight is required in the lure to overcome the drag of the line, which is to be avoided especially when long casts are needed because of disturbance to the water.

Most rods designed for use with the lighter spinning lure (up to ½oz) are 6-8ft long and are teamed with fixed-spool reels and relatively light lines of 4-8lb b.s. Rods for the heavier lures are more often 8-10½ft long and may be used with fixed-spool or multiplier reels loaded with lines up to 20lb b.s. These heavier salmon spinning rods are very often used with two hands when casting and so have naturally been referred to as double-handed.

Baitcasting rods

In addition to the standard patterns of spinning rods, there is a special type which originated in the US and is known as a 'baitcasting' rod. This rod, designed to be used in conjunction with a multiplier, features a pistol-grip, cranked handle to allow the fisherman to cast and control the reel using one hand. It is made with a one-piece top 5-6ft long, and the reel is mounted on top of the rod. This arrangement enables accurate casting but has the disadvantage that long-distance casts are not possible.

Heavy-duty spinning rods

The heaviest patterns of rod are required for spinning with deadbaits for salmon and large pike in very unfavourable water conditions. The deadbaits can weigh up to 4oz, and lines up to 20lb b.s. are needed.

A rod capable of handling heavy lures and leads should be 9½-10ft long and fairly strong, with a test curve of 1½-2¼lb. This type of rod is very often used with a multiplier, for heavy spinning. The handles are usually 24-28in long.

Above left *The correct spinning action for the overhead cast. A sideways cast can be made in a similar manner.* **Left** *Spinning the River Esk for salmon.*

FIXED-SPOOL REELS

The first fixed-spool reel was patented by Alfred Illingworth in 1905. It incorporated all the basic principles of the modern reel, which still hold good today. The line spool was fixed with its axis at right angles to the direction of casting. When line was released, as long as the tackle provided the necessary inertia to pull it off, it simply spilled over the edge of the spool with practically no unnecessary friction, and without requiring the spool to revolve. Hence the modern name—fixed-spool.

Now it is possible to buy fixed-spool reels with a wide variety of retrieval ratios suitable for every possible kind of fishing. All have adjustable clutch mechanisms, a reciprocating reel movement which provides even laying of line, and in some cases a crosswind action to prevent the line from jamming.

The modern fixed-spool reel is a masterpiece of engineering design. It has banished one of the angler's oldest problems, that of casting to the required spot, and has doubled, or even trebled, the distances over which the average angler can hope to cast accurately. At the same time, it has reduced the problem of tangled line to a minimum.

Despite this, we still occasionally hear the reel's critics bemoaning the fact that it has taken the skill out of casting. Even if this were wholly true, it would be no more a cause for regret than the fact that the washing machine has taken the drudgery out of washing day.

To be effective, such a reel must be properly used. Most manufacturers' instructions today refer to the loading capacity of the various spools, which varies with the b.s. of the line required. Many manufacturers provide a spare spool, and since most spools are quickly detachable the angler can change spool and line in a moment.

Loading the spool

When loading the spool it must be borne in mind that the rotary action of the bale-arm around the spool imparts twist to the line, and that over a hundred yards of line this becomes considerable, especially when medium-weight lines, which are fairly springy, are employed.

This twist in the line is largely responsible for the manner in which the monofilament lines often tend to spring off the spool. To prevent twist it is recommended that the line be pulled off the manufacturer's spool not by letting it turn on a pencil as you wind, but over the flange of the manufacturer's spool in much the same way as the line spills over the edge of the fixed-spool itself. Since pulling line off and laying it on both impart twist to the line, the tactic is to impart opposite twist to the line as the bale-arm lays it on to the spool.

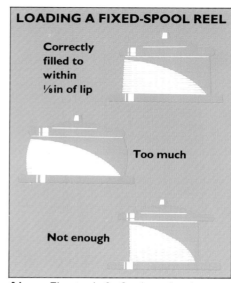

LOADING A FIXED-SPOOL REEL

Correctly filled to within ⅛ in of lip

Too much

Not enough

Above *The spool of a fixed-spool reel must be loaded as shown here. Too much line will encourage it to spill over and tangle; an under-filled spool creates unwanted friction as the line is cast.*

When the slipping clutch is set, this must be done so that if a dangerous strain is put on your line, the clutch will slip before the line breaks. This also implies that you must select a line b.s. suitable for the rod you intend to use. If, for example, your line is of 20lb b.s. and you set the clutch at, say, 18lb, you have a margin of safety of roughly 2lb. However, if you are using a rod of a ½lb test curve there is considerable danger that you will already have strained, damaged, or even broken your rod before the clutch will start to slip. To allow this to happen is clearly absurd, and so lines must be selected to suit the rod. If you must use heavy lines on a light rod you would be better to set the clutch to give when the rod is entering the test curve position, or somewhat before.

MITCHELL 300A

Tension nut

Bale arm

Unskirted spool

Spool release button

Bale arm trip

Ratchet

The working parts of a high-class modern fixed-spool reel. Always clean and lightly oil it after every fishing trip.

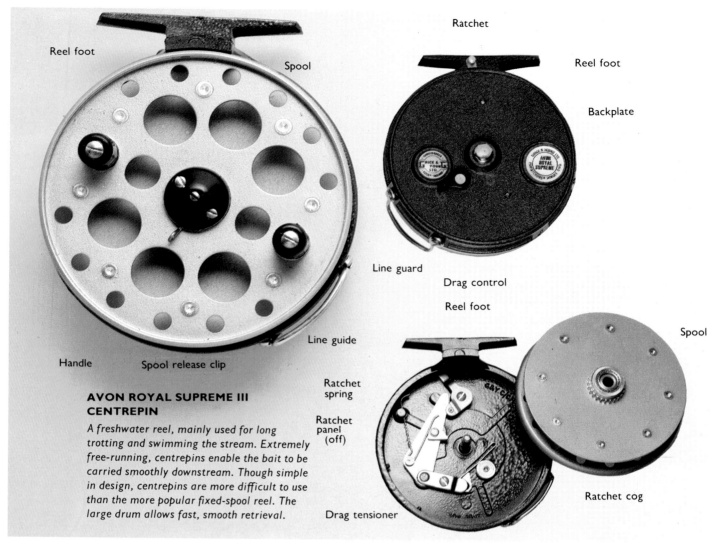

Ratchet

Reel foot

Spool

Reel foot

Backplate

Line guard

Drag control

Reel foot

Spool

Handle

Spool release clip

Line guide

Ratchet spring

Ratchet panel (off)

Drag tensioner

Ratchet cog

AVON ROYAL SUPREME III CENTREPIN

A freshwater reel, mainly used for long trotting and swimming the stream. Extremely free-running, centrepins enable the bait to be carried smoothly downstream. Though simple in design, centrepins are more difficult to use than the more popular fixed-spool reel. The large drum allows fast, smooth retrieval.

CENTREPIN REELS

A centrepin is a reel acting as a line reservoir with its axis at right angles to the rod. Good centrepins consist of a flanged drum, machined to very fine tolerances, which revolves freely on a precision-engineered steel axle. Many models have appeared over the years, ranging from the cheap and simple kind in Bakelite (an early plastic) to the comparatively expensive models manufactured from stainless steel or enamelled metal. Wooden models have also been produced, but are now not so common. The centrepin is simple in construction, and—by virtue of this—reliable, as well as being easy to operate and to maintain. Once the use of the centrepin has been mastered many anglers prefer it to the fixed-spool reel. There is certainly more satisfaction in using it properly.

Trotting

The centrepin is used mainly for 'trotting'—allowing the river's current to carry float-tackle smoothly downstream, allowing the bait to cover long stretches of water at one cast. It is with this method that the free-running centrepin drum is put to best advantage. To

recover line quickly, the drum is given a series of taps with all four fingers in a practice called 'batting'.

The diameter of the reel can vary, but most are between 3½in and 4½in. The drum's diameter will be almost as large, and the larger the drum the more rapid will be the line recovery. Most centrepins have a line guard and optional ratchet, while some also have a drag mechanism. An exposed smooth rim, which allows finger-pressure to be applied to control the line when casting or playing a fish is a valuable feature. Many of the older centrepin reels are now very much in demand for their fine, free action.

Although the centrepin is still used—and indeed has made a come-back in recent years—its popularity suffered greatly when the fixed-spool reel was introduced over 40 years ago. This reel permits almost effortless long casting, because the drum is parallel to the rod. To achieve similar distances with a centrepin is a satisfying accomplishment. Nevertheless, the centrepin is still unrivalled in two circumstances: in water where the fishing is virtually under the rod end and there are likely to be big

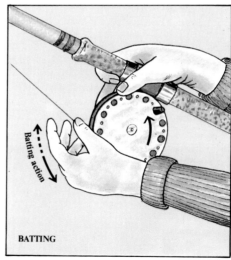

BATTING

Above *Recovering line when using a centrepin is called 'baiting'.*

fish which go off at high speed, such as carp; and where the fishing is close-in.

The centrepin scores in both conditions due to the perfect control which can be exercised by the thumb on the drum of the reel. A point in favour is that the alternative—using the slipping clutch of a fixed-spool reel—was not designed for use with fine lines.

NYLON LINE

Nylon monofilament line, the kind used by most anglers, is manufactured by first drawing the nylon into a thread while in a semi-molten state and then straightening out the molecular chains by drawing it out a second time. Its value to the angler lies in its great strength, fineness, and resistance to kinking. All these qualities are supplemented by nylon's natural elasticity.

Elasticity

It should be mentioned that the elasticity which aids strength also has a definite disadvantage in that a strike is softened by the line stretching, especially if it is of low breaking strain. This must be borne in mind and a strike over long distance made correspondingly forceful if the fish is not to be missed. Braided nylon, which stretches less, is sometimes used in sea fishing to overcome this difficulty.

Manufacturers claim that their clear nylon lines are virtually invisible in water, but even so, camouflaged varieties in blue, green or brown can be bought. Some enthusiasts even dye their lines themselves to match water conditions.

Rewinding

When nylon is retrieved onto the spool under pressure, as when playing a large fish or drawing a heavy specimen up through perhaps 30 fathoms of heavy sea, it winds back very tightly, especially with a multiplier reel. After fishing, the line should be wound at normal speed onto another reel, for if left on the first it can distort the spool and ruin the reel. It is also worthwhile to wind off your line occasionally and then wind it back onto the spool, making sure that it is distributed evenly. When tying hooks directly to your nylon, be careful to remember that one of the properties of nylon is that the old-fashioned 'granny knot' will not hold. A good knot for tying hooks to nylon is the half-blood.

As with nylon line's elasticity, its resistance to decay has a serious drawback. Hook lengths, 'bird's nests' and odd lengths of unwanted line are frequently thrown away or left at the waterside after fishing. These coils and loops can easily become entangled in birds' feet, especially as they will often investigate the remnants of bait that anglers also leave nearby. Birds are even hooked occasionally on discarded tackle. The consequences of careless jettisoning of line are all too often fatal for birds and so it should be taken home and disposed of.

Line in reserve

It is always advisable to have a good reserve of line on the spool in case a fish should make a long run, taking a good proportion of your line. A fish can easily be lost through lack of line on which the angler can play it. Backing lines, available from tackle dealers, are used to pad out the spool, on a fixed-spool reel to within $\frac{1}{8}$in of the rim.

Far right The results of throwing away unwanted nylon. This bird's leg became trapped and it died a nasty death. **Right** The final moment of a catch – not the time for the nylon to break. **Above right** The strength of nylon monofilament comes from its molecules joining under tension and infra-red light. **Below** How to load the spool of a centrepin and a fixed-spool reel.

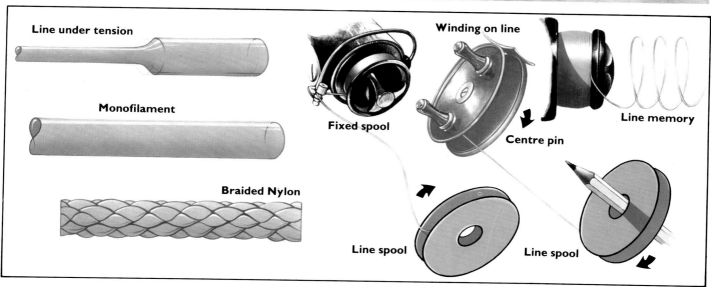

Line under tension
Monofilament
Braided Nylon
Winding on line
Fixed spool
Centre pin
Line memory
Line spool
Line spool

SPLIT SHOT (actual size)	SSG	AAA	BB	1	3	4	5	6	7	8
Number per ounce	15	35	70	100	140	170	220	270	340	450

Above Some of the lead weight shapes available commercially for the coarse angler. **Left** Shown same-size, the range of split shot, which originated from the size of charge in 12-bore cartridges. **Below far left** The plummet and how it is used to determine depth. **Left** Six ledger leads: coffin leads (top) and bombs, the well-known Arlesey bomb in the centre.

PLUMMET LEAD – to test float depth

LEAD AND SHOT

Leads have become an indispensable item in every freshwater angler's tackle box and are used to perform a variety of functions. In float fishing they provide casting weight and, if the right amount of lead is selected, they cock the float enabling it to 'ride' the water with the required amount left above the surface.

Arlesey bomb

By far the most successful modern lead is the Arlesey bomb, designed by Richard Walker for casting baits 50 yards into Arlesey lake. Streamlined in shape, it is easily cast and the swivel in the top, through which the main line runs, creates minimum resistance. This swivel also ensures that if the tackle becomes twisted as it flies through the air, the twists in the line come out as the tackle sinks. The line also runs easily through the eye of the swivel no matter what the direction of pull.

The fold-over or half moon lead is occasionally used in small sizes to replace split shot, but has more value as a casting weight for spinning and does not allow the line to become kinked by the strain this technique puts on it.

Coffin leads were designed to hold to the bottom in fast water—a job they performed very well. The length and shape of coffin leads, however, requires at least 1in of line running through it and this sets up considerable resistance to the taking fish. To overcome this difficulty, a swivel may be placed at one end of the lead held in place by tapping it with a hammer. The line is then passed through the swivel. This reduces resistance while enabling the angler to keep the bait in one place in a fast current.

Plummet

The plummet is another form of lead with a particular application. It is used by the angler to discover the depth of the water in which he intends to float fish.

The depth of the swim is ascertained by attaching the plummet, pushing the float up the line some 5ft, then casting into the swim. If the float sinks, push it farther up the line. If it lies flat it must be pushed down. When it has been adjusted correctly, the bait rests on the bottom when the plummet is removed. When the bait is presented off the bottom, it is vital that the angler knows the depth of his swim so the bait can be fished at the depth that he considers necessary or the depth fish demand.

Lead shot

No matter what its size, or how packed, it is the quality of lead shot that counts. The lead must be soft enough to open and close easily to make alteration of terminal tackle a quick and simple operation. Shot should be soft enough to be pinched onto the line.

HOOKS

Hooks are the most important items of an angler's tackle and yet, all too often, they are not chosen with enough care. Admittedly the range of hooks available is bewildering to the beginner, but in order to enjoy consistent success a reliable hook is indispensable.

Kinds of hooks

Freshwater hooks fall into three categories: eyed, spade-end and ready tied to nylon. The first are tied to the line by the angler, who can use a variety of knots. The important thing is to be sure the knot holds, as this can easily be the weak point in your tackle which will fail when most needed. Spade-end hooks, as the name suggests, are flattened at the top end and are whipped to nylon. Ready tied hooks are bought already whipped to a short length of line, nowadays nylon.

There are many variations as to bend, length of shank and so on, but these are mainly variations on the three main kinds of hook. Double and treble hooks are mounted on plugs and spinners for pike, perch, chub, trout, and salmon. Stewart tackles comprise two single hooks set a couple of inches apart.

The basic requirements

The essential requirements of a hook are the same for all kinds. It should be well-tempered and thin in the body (or 'wire'); the point and barb should be sharp; the barb should be set close to the point and not stand out at too great an angle from the body.

The thickness of the 'wire' is very important. The weight of a thick hook can cause a bait, especially a light one such as maggot or caster, to sink too quickly when 'freelining'—using no float but allowing the bait to sink naturally down to the fish. An additional disadvantage of a hook that is too thick is that it can burst a bait instead of entering it cleanly.

Barbs

The barb is most often the trouble-spot in a hook. Most are cut too deep (stand out too far from the body), which causes weakness at that point. This, coupled with the common fault of the barb being set too far from the point, means that undue force is required to drive home both point and barb, sometimes causing the line to break. If the strike is less forceful, a hook of this sort will not fully penetrate the fish's skin, particularly if it is a hard-boned and tough-skinned species like the pike, perch or barbel. A big, deeply-cut barb may look effective but is not.

The eyes on eyed hooks should be examined. The size of the eye will depend on the gauge of the hook but always try to pick one which will just take the thickness of the line you intend to use.

Shanks

The length of the shank is important where some baits are concerned. For crust, paste, lobworms and sweetcorn a long shank is best; for maggots a short one. For casters, the variety with a long shank, known as a 'caster hook', is favoured. It should be remembered, however, that the longer the shank relative to the eye, the smaller will be the angle of penetration. This means that the hook will penetrate more easily but to a lesser depth. With short-shanked hooks it takes a stronger strike but the hook will drive home deeper.

Hooks to nylon should always be treated with caution. First, see whether the whipping reaches the top of the shank. On some hooks it is too short, thus causing the hook to turn over when making contact with a fish and preventing proper penetration.

Sizes and patterns

The size of hooks is indicated by even numbers on a scale from 2–30, the lower the number the larger the hook. A number 2 is about $\frac{3}{4}$in long, a 12 is $\frac{3}{8}$in and a 20 is $\frac{1}{8}$in. Hook sizes, unfortunately, are not yet standardized. The 'Goldstrike', for example, is one size bigger than most other brands.

Choice of hook pattern

The angler will sometimes use a different pattern of hook to suit particular circumstances. The 'Crystal' is a combination of curved and angular, which requires little force to drive home but which, because of its sharp bend, is weakened and not recommended for strong, fighting fish such as carp or tench. The 'Round Bend' has a curve with plenty of 'gape', and is preferred for use with lobworms by many anglers.

The famous 'Model Perfect' hook, which was developed by Allcocks, had a round bend and an off-set point with wonderful holding power. Many modern hooks are based on the design of this classic hook.

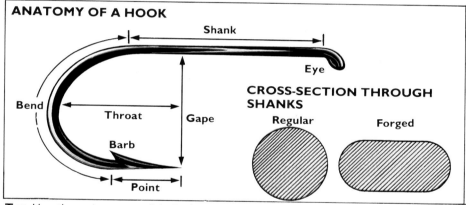

ANATOMY OF A HOOK

Shank · Eye · Bend · Throat · Gape · Barb · Point

CROSS-SECTION THROUGH SHANKS

Regular · Forged

Top How the various parts of the hook are described. **Right** Always keep your hooks sharp by using a specially made stone. **Below** Watch for these common faults when buying hooks. Any fault may mean the loss of a fish.

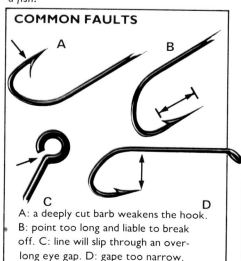

COMMON FAULTS

A · B · C · D

A: a deeply cut barb weakens the hook. B: point too long and liable to break off. C: line will slip through an over-long eye gap. D: gape too narrow.

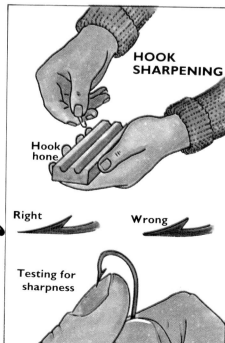

HOOK SHARPENING

Hook hone

Right · Wrong

Testing for sharpness

FLOATS

Peacock quills are the 'Jack of all trades' of float-making and are used in pieces. An average peacock quill can be used to make anything from two to six floats, all for a few pence. To make a very versatile float all you need is a length of peacock as straight as possible and around 4–8in in length, a piece of welding rod or thin cane—depending upon whether you want the float partially self-cocking or not—a used ballpoint refill, a razor blade, pliers, waterproof glue and emery paper.

The first job is to clean up the quill, rubbing down with emery paper or fine 'wet and dry' sandpaper. You will see the quill is thicker at one end; after cleaning, carefully insert the piece of cane or welding rod into this thick end —use welding rod if you want the float loaded or partially self-cocking—so that the quill and cane are as straight as possible. Then separate the cane and quill again, add glue and then place them back into position. The cane or rod should protrude from the quill about $\frac{3}{4}$in.

The next job is to cut the ballpoint refill into small pieces about an inch long. Slide a suitable piece on to the cane or rod and again glue it in position, leaving a quarter inch of the tubing protruding beyond the cane at the bottom. When the glue has set, heat this bottom 'overhang' and then tightly squeeze it with either pliers or a pair of forceps to flatten it, so making a tab. When the plastic has cooled and hardened, all that remains to do is to make a hole in the centre of the tab with a fine piece of wire or a needle and then to trim the tab with the razor blade.

Paint finish

Finished off with a lick of paint, this simple float is very useful on stillwaters such as ponds or canals. The dimensions of the float as described can be varied to give you a range of floats.

The cane or welding rod at the bottom is essential in making the float as it gives at least one part which can be handled without damage. The ballpoint tubing, too, makes a very tough base, not liable to corrode as wire does. Simply pass the line through it and it can either be locked on with shot or used as a simple slider. The base can also be loaded with lead wire if required.

The versatility of these floats can be increased by using a set of float corks. Ream out the holes in the corks carefully—a round file is suitable for this— so that they just fit over the peacock and can be pushed down to the base of the quill. When this is done, the simple float is transformed into a bodied waggler or

SIMPLE PEACOCK QUILL FLOAT

Rub down quill with emergy or wet-and-dry paper

Cane or welding rod glued into bottom

Cane base inserted into balsa body

$\frac{3}{4}$in   4in

Balsa is tapered and 'shouldered' at top

1in

Quill cut with a very sharp knife

Quill glued to shoulder

a small zoomer for occasions when extra distance is required.

A little extra effort, to mark the bodies of your homemade floats with the amount of shotting they will take, is well worth the trouble. It saves a lot of time on the bank. Once more the tough base is useful here in avoiding damage to the quill when pushing on the weights.

The peacock quill float just described is fine for stillwaters, such as canals, but for fishing big rivers with delicate baits such as wasp grub or bread flake, a

SHOTTING ARRANGEMENT FOR FLOAT

Float rings

No 4 swan shot

BALSA AND GOOSE COMBINATION FLOAT

2 No 4 swan shot

Finished float painted to suit

Left A simple means of making a sensitive peacock quill float. Above A goose quill and balsa combination creates a useful float. Opposite top How to make the flattened end of the peacock quill float.

better float can be made from a combination of goose quill and balsa wood. To make it, first cut off the top inch or so of a goose quill—this is not quite as simple as it sounds for it is surprisingly tough and care is needed to make sure it is cut straight. Then obtain a 4in length of $\frac{3}{8}$in balsa wood, and taper it from one end to the other with the thick end just rubbed gently with rough sandpaper to give it a round 'shoulder' instead of a rough edge. When it is roughly shaped, give a smooth finish with 'wet and dry', and finally, glue the goose quill to the top of the 'shoulder'.

Before tapering the balsa, however, drill a small hole into the future base— the thin end—insert a small piece of cane, about $\frac{1}{2}$in long, and glue it in place. For strength the cane should be inserted as far into the balsa as it protrudes outside—like this it provides a strong place to which the line can be attached without damage. Balsa is so soft it can easily be drilled using any sharp pointed object carefully worked round; but if you want to save yourself trouble you can buy balsa which has already been drilled.

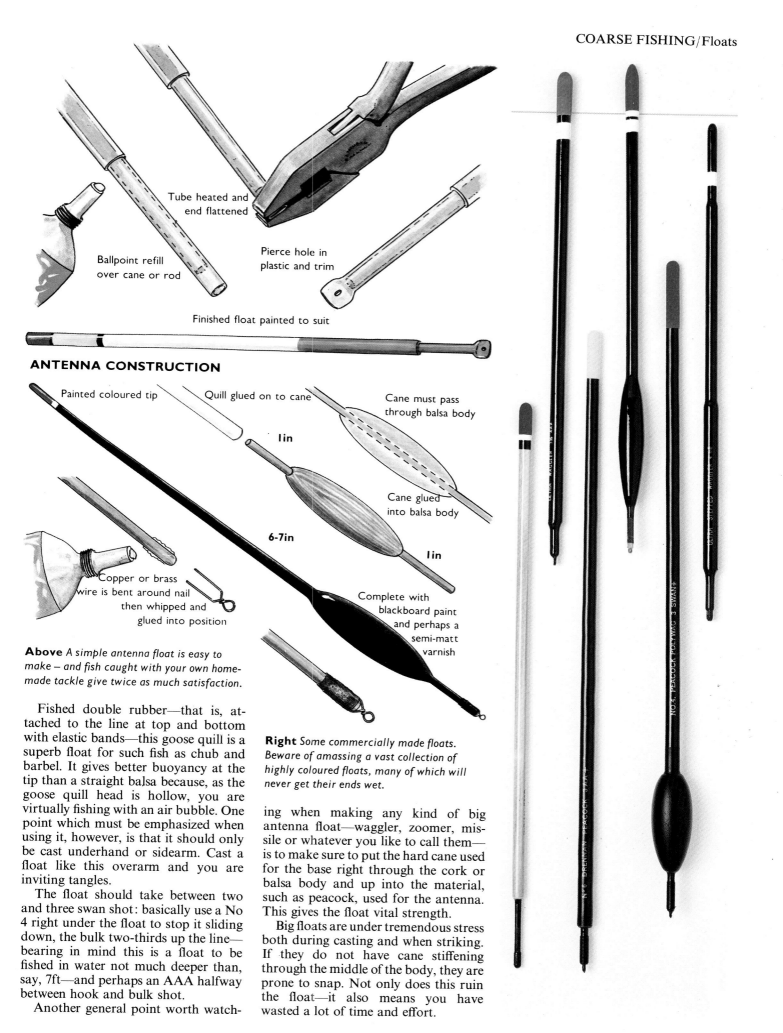

Tube heated and end flattened

Ballpoint refill over cane or rod

Pierce hole in plastic and trim

Finished float painted to suit

ANTENNA CONSTRUCTION

Painted coloured tip

Quill glued on to cane

Cane must pass through balsa body

1in

Cane glued into balsa body

6-7in

1in

Copper or brass wire is bent around nail then whipped and glued into position

Complete with blackboard paint and perhaps a semi-matt varnish

Above *A simple antenna float is easy to make – and fish caught with your own home-made tackle give twice as much satisfaction.*

Fished double rubber—that is, attached to the line at top and bottom with elastic bands—this goose quill is a superb float for such fish as chub and barbel. It gives better buoyancy at the tip than a straight balsa because, as the goose quill head is hollow, you are virtually fishing with an air bubble. One point which must be emphasized when using it, however, is that it should only be cast underhand or sidearm. Cast a float like this overarm and you are inviting tangles.

The float should take between two and three swan shot: basically use a No 4 right under the float to stop it sliding down, the bulk two-thirds up the line—bearing in mind this is a float to be fished in water not much deeper than, say, 7ft—and perhaps an AAA halfway between hook and bulk shot.

Another general point worth watch-

Right *Some commercially made floats. Beware of amassing a vast collection of highly coloured floats, many of which will never get their ends wet.*

ing when making any kind of big antenna float—waggler, zoomer, missile or whatever you like to call them—is to make sure to put the hard cane used for the base right through the cork or balsa body and up into the material, such as peacock, used for the antenna. This gives the float vital strength.

Big floats are under tremendous stress both during casting and when striking. If they do not have cane stiffening through the middle of the body, they are prone to snap. Not only does this ruin the float—it also means you have wasted a lot of time and effort.

35

SPINNERS

A spinner is an artificial lure with a blade or body which rotates quickly about a straight line axis consisting often of a wire bar. Spoons, in contrast, have a wobbly retrieve and do not usually spin.

The basic kinds of spinner are artificial minnows, wagtails, fly spoons, and barspoons. It is unfortunate that the last two incorporate the word 'spoon' in their names, for they are in fact spinners with a straight axis around which the blade spins.

Artificial minnows

Of all the kinds of spinners, artificial minnows most closely represent fish, both still and on the move. The body, made of either wood, plastic or metal, is round in cross section, minnow-like in profile, and has a hole along its length through which a metal bar or wire trace passes. At the tail is a treble hook and at the head a swivel which can be attached to the reel line or, if fishing for pike, to a wire trace link swivel. Generally, the swivel at the head has a smaller overall diameter than the hole through the middle of the lure so that on the take the fish tends to blow the lure up the line, giving itself nothing to lever against as it tries to throw the hook.

The head of the minnow has a pair of vanes which cause it to rotate. Some makes have adjustable vanes so that the spin can be reversed, and line twist reduced.

A variation on the minnow theme is the quill minnow, a superb lure for fishing for trout in hill streams. The whole body of the quill minnow rotates, often including the bar wire through its middle, so that the swivel has to work well to avoid line twist, and an anti-kink vane is usually necessary.

Wagtail movement

Wagtails look more lifelike when moving than when still. They usually have a head complete with eyes, spinning vanes, a swivel and tube-like body hidden inside two long rubber flaps which are pointed at the tail end, close to the treble hook. The name comes from these loose, flapping strips of rubber. All this detail disappears, however, when the whole body rotates quickly and, other than in body softness, the wagtail probably differs little from the minnow.

Fly spoons

Fly spoons, as their name implies, have traditionally been used for game fish, but are very effective for chub and perch on small streams. They are small, twinkling lures, most of which spin rather than wobble, and are essentially spinners for short casts on light tackle of 2-6lb b.s. monofilament lines.

Many fly spoons are constructed with a spinner blade attached at only one end to a split ring connecting two swivels. A treble hook is attached to the other end of one swivel and the reel line to the opposite end of the other swivel.

Barspoons

Barspoons are in fact more correctly classified as spinners since they have a straight axis of wire around which the blade, attached at one end, rotates with a strong vibration. Weight is added to the bar, just behind the spinning blade, and this weight can be made to look like a body and can be painted different colours. Barspoons are among the most versatile of lures and all except the very heavy ones are retrievable even when you are fishing in very shallow-water.

A change in the blade shape has given rise to some classic lures: the Vibro has the end away from the bar pointed quite sharply, and the result is a spinner which vibrates very strongly. The kidney spoon has a kidney-shaped blade which gives a pulsating spinning action.

Right *A few of the huge range of spinners.*

Intrepid Flectolite

Abu Drop Flex

Mepps Aglia Longue

Mepps Black Fury

Normark Vibrax

Daiwa

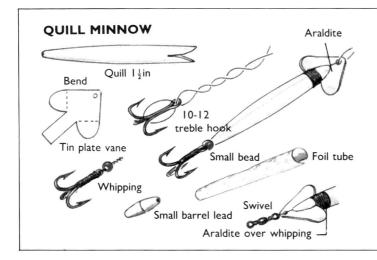

QUILL MINNOW

Araldite

Quill 1½ in

Bend

Tin plate vane

10-12 treble hook

Small bead

Whipping

Small barrel lead

Foil tube

Swivel

Araldite over whipping

WAGTAIL

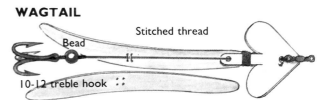

Stitched thread

Bead

10-12 treble hook

Left *For the quill minnow, a goose quill is used, to which is glued and whipped a piece of metal cut in the right shape. A triple hook with a bead at its eye is whipped to Alasticum wire and threaded through the quill. A small barrel lead is* drawn down the quill and a swivel is attached, and the body of the minnow covered with foil.

Above *Wagtails look unnatural when seen out of the water, but in action they work in a lifelike manner.*

An impressive array of plugs stored neatly in trays ready for selection. Dry them after use and never put them back wet and dirty.

Having fallen to a colourful lure, a pike is drawn to the waiting net. Remove the hooks with forceps without injuring the fish.

PLUGS

The best description of a plug is a cross between a spinner and a deadbait. In shape it resembles a dead fish with hooks ready-set. In use it is retrieved in much the same way as a spinner. But a plug possesses advantages that neither spinner nor deadbait have—it can be made to work with innumerable variations on a straight retrieve at any of many chosen depths. The astute angler can impart sharp, darting, erratic movements, and the series of vibrations produced in this way will travel several yards. The vibrations serve to stimulate the urge to hunt: so much so that a plug may be savagely attacked when a seemingly enticing livebait has been completely ignored in the same swim.

Kinds of plug

Floating plugs are light, usually made from wood, and have a V-shaped wedge inserted in the nose. There are models made to represent mice, and one has broad arms, or sweeps, that vibrate backwards and forwards during the retrieve; they are intended to represent a surface-swimming fish in distress—rather in the fashion of one with swim-bladder trouble.

They should be cast close to the bank, under overhanging trees and bushes and retrieved alternately fast and slow, causing them to dive a few inches under the surface, then pop up to the top. The bow wave caused by this sudden dive is probably the lure's main attraction.

Floating divers are the most versatile of all plugs. They have lightweight bodies with a medium-sized diving nose (or lip) set into the head. After being cast, they will lie on the surface, only diving when the angler commences the retrieve. The faster the motion, the deeper they will dive—short, hard turns on the reel and then a few seconds with the handle stationary, produce a series of swoops and rises that few fish can resist. They have an added advantage in snaggy waters. By stopping the retrieve when an underwater obstruction is reached, the plug is allowed to float up, and can be coaxed gently past the danger area before continuing with the normal dive and rise action.

Sinking plugs

Sinking plugs are for very deep gravel pits and reservoirs where the lure has to sink some way before it can be fished usefully. In order to find and keep the 'taking' depth, the count-down method should be used. After the lure has hit the water, the angler counts from, say, one to six, then starts his retrieve. On the next cast, he may count to seven, then eight on the following casts—and so on until a fish is taken. This will probably be the taking depth, and future casts should be allowed the same time before retrieve begins.

Few plugs in this category have a diving vane, all are heavy, and some models have a metal ball sealed into a cavity in the body. When the retrieve begins, the action of the plug under the water causes this ball to rattle, making vibrations that are highly attractive to predators.

Deep divers

The last selection of plugs, the deep divers, are easily recognized by the extra large metal vane set into the head. This broad lip sets up drag against the water when the retrieve starts and causes the plug to dive quickly, at a sharp angle. As with sinkers, the count-down method is the best when exploring a water.

The colour range of plugs displayed in a tackle shop can be quite staggering. But action is more important than colour in a plug, and generally those with green, yellow and a little red coincide with the natural colours of fish and appear to be the most acceptable to feeding predators.

Unfortunately, the vibrations produced by a plug can, on occasions, make predators bolt for cover. However incomprehensible the response is, it calls for an immediate switch to spinner or deadbait.

Plugs fall into four general categories that coincide with the depth at which they should work. There are surface lures, floating divers, sinkers, and deep divers. Their shape, especially at the nose, often gives a clue to their working use.

SWIMFEEDERS

Swimfeeders and blockends are perforated plastic cylinders, approximately 2-3in long and 1in diameter. Swimfeeders are open at both ends and when ledgering are used mainly for groundbaiting with cereal or cereal mixed with samples of the hookbait—maggots, casters, worms, and in recent years, sweetcorn. Used in rivers by bream and chub fishermen, a swimfeeder is particularly effective. Blockends have closed ends and are usually packed with either maggots or casters.

The shape and size of both blockends and swimfeeders is important. A blockend with cone-shaped ends, for example, will cast farther and more easily, resulting, in some situations, in a bigger and better catch. A large feeder is usually better than a small one when attempting to hold a large shoal of chub or bream in a swim, but when seeking specimen roach in a small, shallow river a small feeder is probably best.

Early swimfeeders

Experiments with blockends began several years ago when two Oxford anglers, Fred Towns and John Everard, ran a length of nylon through the centre of a small plastic container of the type in which screws and nails used to be sold. Holes were made with a small file heated over a gas or electric ring, and swan shots attached to the end of the nylon. The line was then passed through a swivel which was tied to the other end of the nylon.

With this new-style feeder, casting was found to be both easier and more accurate, with less resistance in running water. Another important feature of this feeder was that the weight was adjustable. If insufficient weight is used in rivers a feeder will roll, which in most situations defeats its object. By adding or subtracting shots, the weight could be adjusted to just hold the bottom, or roll at whatever speed is necessary.

In running water, feeders are fished either stationary or allowed to roll along the bottom. In fast water, the stationary method is usually adopted to avoid the contents being scattered. Only in water of moderate flow—and then not in every situation—should the feeder be allowed to roll or move.

Accuracy is essential

In stillwaters, cast the feeder into the same spot every time: if you do not, the contents will be scattered around like a rolling feeder in rivers. Accurate casting is essential. It is also important when casting to keep the line straight, especially in a side wind. As the feeder is punched forward, bring the top of the rod down to eye level then, as the feeder hits the surface, quickly thrust the top under the water to a depth of 3ft. The feeder is allowed to sink on a slack line. Should it sink on a tight line, it will fall out and away from the swim.

The loaded bait-dropper is a very handy means of placing attractive hookbait particles near the hook. It is lowered to the bottom of the swim when a trip wire opens the lid and releases the contents. The match angler usually starts by putting down several droppers full of hookbait samples. Once the fish

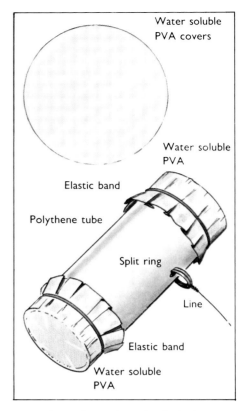

move into the swim, the bait-dropper should be used with caution, for it may scare the fish.

Concentrate your loose feed by using a blockend feeder in strong currents, or an open-end feeder on medium to slow waters. These can be stopped 12in from the hook by a split shot fished on a separate link via a pair of swivels, or even fixed paternoster-fashion. Try to place tackle consistently into the same area so that a concentration of bait particles builds up there.

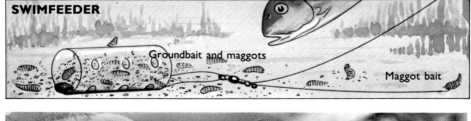

SWIMFEEDER
Groundbait and maggots
Maggot bait

Left The swimfeeder releasing maggots near the hookbait. Below left Filling a bait-dropper. Below How the baitdropper works. When it touches the bottom the pin operates to open the container and release the contents into the swim near the hook. A very useful accessory.

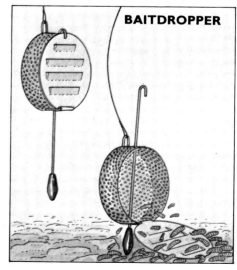

BAITDROPPER

CATAPULTS

The fishing catapult is available in various designs, both good and bad. The good points should be checked carefully before the item is purchased. It naturally follows that the bigger the model the greater will be the force that can be applied as the bait is released. Weak, spindle-type forks of wire or thin plastic will soon bend and snap, and they should be rejected. Look for a heavy plastic, one-piece moulding, preferably with a shaped hand-grip that is well below the fork. If the handle is too short, there is a risk that you will receive a painful blow on the hand each time you let go of the pouch.

Right shape for accuracy

Too big is better than too small, and this particularly applies to the spacing of the forks themselves. A large U-shape, with the ends of the forks turning slightly outwards, will give the greatest accuracy. The elastic should be secured through holes at the fork ends, either by a large knot (which makes for easy replacement) or by crimped metal tubes. The elastic should be soft and able to return to its original length after stretching. Before buying elastic, flex it once or twice to ensure that its pull is within your capability. The cup into which the bait is placed should be rigid and have a large, well-shaped flange at the rear which enables you to keep a firm grip when it is pulled back.

Know its limitations

While most anglers are well aware of what a catapult can do, it is sensible to know its limitations before starting to use one. It cannot place large amounts of groundbait at any one time, nor can it manage very heavy baits such as saturated and stiffened cereals with any degree of accuracy. It will not cope with extremely light cereal baits—the spring of the elastic and forward propulsion make it break up in mid-air and scatter over a wide area. It is most successful with pellet and grain baits, which include maggots, casters, hemp, wheat, tares and so on. These should be kept damp or, in the case of cereals, wet. This will provide the weight and 'cling' needed to keep the bait intact.

Judging the speed of the current

To place the bait accurately, the angler must be able to judge the speed of the current where the bait is finally to land. If this is against the opposite bank, then check the speed of the current against the bank you are fishing from. Many anglers make the mistake of estimating the speed of the current from the faster-flowing mid-river swims, which results

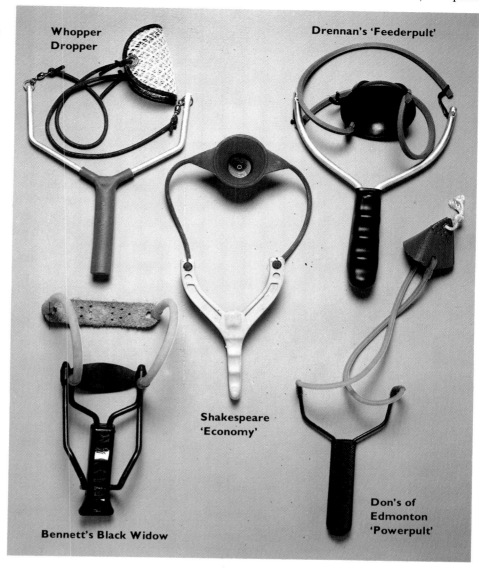

Whopper Dropper

Drennan's 'Feederpult'

Shakespeare 'Economy'

Bennett's Black Widow

Don's of Edmonton 'Powerpult'

A selection of catapults for anglers, part of today's coarse fishing accessories and widely used for match and pleasure fishing.

in the groundbait being placed too far upstream.

The purpose, once the cup of the catapult is loaded, is to drop the bait into the swim by means of a gentle curve through the air. Firing the bait straight will cause a big surface disturbance and make the groundbait break up. The curving type of delivery applies especially if the opposite bank is tree-lined; by lobbing the bait through the air, it will drop through the overhanging branches and fall naturally into the swim.

Safety first

A final word of warning concerns the temptation to hold the catapult at face level and to sight along the elastic and through the fork. Should the elastic break or pull free (and this happens) the result can only be face or eye injuries. It is essential to keep the cup with its load well down below the face and to keep the forks on a level with it. Then if anything should break, only the body will receive the impact.

The bait thrower is a simple tool usually consisting of a short stick with

a metal cut-away cup mounted on to the end. Groundbait is loaded into this cup and the thrower held in the hand with its high back facing the angler. A quick forward flick and the bait is propelled out into the swim. This is a straightforward way of throwing heavy groundbait over a considerable distance, governed by the length of stick that is used. In general terms, the longer the stick of the bait thrower the farther the bait will travel.

Bait throwers

A bait thrower can easily be made from a small tin, its top completely removed. The side of the tin is cut away with a pair of tinsnips, leaving the high back which stops bait from spilling over the angler during the throw. The tin is secured on to a length of $\frac{3}{4}$in dowling, 2-2$\frac{1}{2}$ft long, and the tin itself given two or three coats of paint to prevent rusting.

LANDING NETS AND KEEPNETS

Watching the expert angler swinging small fish directly to his hand, a beginner might be misled into thinking all fish can be landed like this. A quick glance at the bankside equipment, however, should dispel the thought at once. There will certainly be a landing net made up, in position, and ready to hand. This is because the fine lines (of about 1lb b.s.) necessary to take shy fish are capable of dealing with fish up to several pounds when gently played, and *while in the water*. To attempt to lift them bodily places the dead weight directly on the fine line, and if this doesn't break at once, there is every chance of a light hook hold giving way.

The beginner, already having spent large sums on the basic rod and reel, and attracted by a host of highly coloured floats and gadgets (which catch more anglers than fish) may be tempted to do without a landing net. But floats can be home-made for next to nothing and it would be wise to save money on floats and to buy a landing net, which is as essential as the rod, reel, line and hook.

A landing net comprises a bag-like net; a triangular or circular metal frame, which can be folded for easy storage and transport; and a 4ft handle with a screw thread at one end for attaching frame and net.

The net and frame can usually be purchased for the price of a few days' bait, and for both a minimum width of 18in is strongly recommended. A 1in diameter cane or even a broom-handle can be fitted with a brass screw fitting at one end to provide a serviceable handle at little cost. Such a net will see the novice through several years of his apprenticeship in the art of fishing. It

Right *Always use a landing net for any sizeable fish. It takes the strain off rod and line.* **Below** *Slide a fish steadily over the rim of the waiting net (**a**). Never plunge the net into the water and try to scoop the fish out (**b**).*

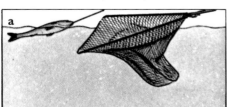

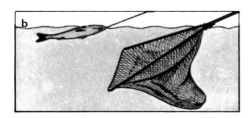

will cope with roach, rudd, dace, bream and tench, as well as the odd jack pike.

The extending handle

One valuable refinement is an extending handle which is very useful when fishing from banks several feet above the water's surface, or when fishing over extensive reed fringes. These handles are usually telescopic and can be obtained in metal or glassfibre. They should be matt-painted in dark green to prevent glare, and it is essential to test the locking device to ensure that the handle will not close or extend except when needed.

Keepnets vary a great deal according to their specific function. The match angler's net is likely to be about 8 or 10ft long, with hoops of at least 15 or 18in. His specimen-hunting counterpart will probably use a far larger net which may be anything up to 12ft long with hoops up to 3ft in diameter to accommodate larger fish.

However big the net, it cannot do its job if it is badly placed in the water. If the net is not properly extended, 10ft of netting is of little value, and hoops of 2ft diameter are useless in 18in of water. They are usually attached by a screw fitting to a bank stick conveniently placed to allow the angler easy access to the open end. They can also be prevented from collapsing with the aid of mesh-spreaders which attach to the rings and hold them apart.

The ring at the neck, into which the bankstick is mounted, is important. Many models have a very small ring, which makes it more difficult to slide a fish into the bag of the net. Choose the net with the biggest plastic-coated ring

possible, so that if a fish is dropped against it there will be less risk of injury. Some rings have a dent or curve so that a rod can be rested across the net while the angler unhooks a fish—an advantage if the net is firmly fixed in the river bed.

Maintenance

Regular maintenance is needed if a keepnet is to remain efficient. Although mesh may be advertized as 'rot-proof' it is still liable to strain, especially if a large weight of fish is lifted awkwardly. Check the base of the net for signs of fraying, and replace it at once if need be.

Remember that fish naturally face the current, so the net should lie parallel to the bank, the mouth facing upstream.

Below *Take care not to snag the keepnet when retrieving. Small hooks can be hard to extricate from the closely woven mesh.*

ROD RESTS

Until recently a rod rest was a length of stick with a forked end, often cut from a hedge by the water and sometimes referred to by the term 'idleback'. Its best use was as a support for the rod while the angler ate a snack, but today any attempt at ledgering or laying-on is certainly pointless without a firm base on which the rod can be securely cradled.

Strength, lightness, adaptability and simplicity are the four essentials of a good rod rest. Strength sufficient to penetrate deeply a hard bank or gravel pit edge so that the rod will be firmly held, especially in a wind, suggests the use of a metal support. But when one considers that two sets (four rests) may have to be carried, lightness prohibits the use of thick steel or iron bars.

The best models

Various kinds of thin, light alloy rod rests are available in the shops, but most are likely to bend if full body pressure is applied to drive them into the ground. Better models are thick, hollow, well pointed, and without a seam or join along the side through which water can seep and leak over tackle or the angler.

One or two models, made from a hard metal and shaped into a 'T' or 'I' section, have recently appeared on the market. They are remarkably strong and by virtue of their shape are easy to mount into the bank. But they do cost a lot more than the average rest and are just as likely to be left behind as their cheaper counterparts. One suggestion for the forgetful angler is to paint a part of the rest a bright colour to act as a visual reminder.

Telescopic rests

Adaptability includes adjustable length and several angles of use apart from the upright position. Telescopic rests that can be held open to the required length by a thumbscrew are popular, but rather more delicate than the one-piece variety. Unfortunately, they tend to collect water and mud in the hollow section, to the detriment of rod bags or hold-alls.

There are a few rests that have adjustable heads, but most have vertical grips for holding the rod. A model with an inclined head is available, which can support a rod with the tip pointing downwards for swing-tip ledgering.

Simplicity is essential at the head. The rod should sit lightly but firmly in the support, and there should be a gap so that the line can run smoothly when a fish takes. The usual 'U' and 'V' shapes are particularly likely to trap a line below the rod, and more than one good run has stopped short because of this.

Setting rod rests demands a little thought. They should be well spread, giving maximum support to the rod itself. Mounted too closely together the rod will vibrate in any reasonable wind, leading to false bites registering at the indicator or float tip. Where the bank is extra hard, preventing a good vertical push into the ground, try to set the rests at right angles to each other. Sufficient shaft can then be buried to give support.

Finally, there should be adequate soft plastic or rubber padding around the arms of the head so that the rod will not be chipped when set down or accidentally knocked. Electricians' waterproof tape can help where protection is thin, but it should be renewed every season.

Right *A rod rest for roach pole laying-on.*
Below *Rod rests must support the rod and allow line to be pulled-freely through.*

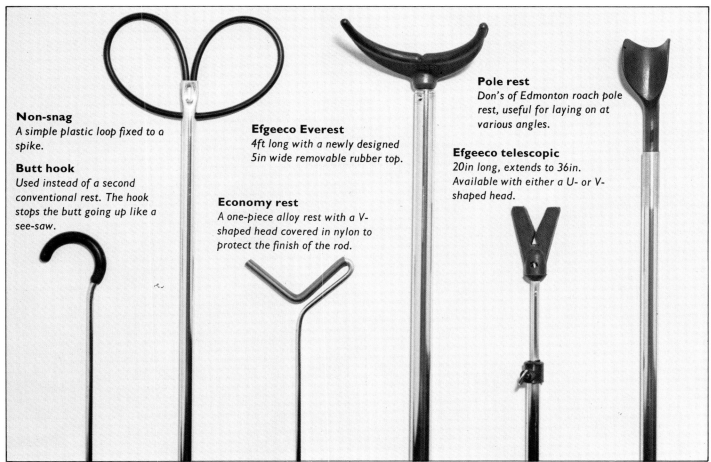

Non-snag
A simple plastic loop fixed to a spike.

Butt hook
Used instead of a second conventional rest. The hook stops the butt going up like a see-saw.

Efgeeco Everest
4ft long with a newly designed 5in wide removable rubber top.

Economy rest
A one-piece alloy rest with a V-shaped head covered in nylon to protect the finish of the rod.

Pole rest
Don's of Edmonton roach pole rest, useful for laying on at various angles.

Efgeeco telescopic
20in long, extends to 36in. Available with either a U- or V-shaped head.

DISGORGERS AND FORCEPS

Of the many tackle items that the angler will invest in, disgorgers, forceps and pliers will be the cheapest, most essential, and generally the most easily mislaid. These simple pieces of equipment enable him to remove a deeply embedded hook and are vital to fish life and fisherman alike. They are important time savers too. There is a bewildering array on sale.

Of course there are times when a fish bolts the bait with such speed that throat or cheek hooking is unavoidable, but many such cases could be avoided if proper attention were paid to the rod, with the angler close at hand and not several yards away from it. A small hook is another cause of deephooking.

It is in the realm of pike fishing where most unnecessary disgorging is seen. Reasons for it include bad timing of the strike ('Give him a few seconds more to make sure he has really taken it'), and the use of fancy dead-bait rigs that are reminiscent of gorge tackle.

If all reasonable precautions have been observed and the angler is still presented with a deeply hooked fish, quick action with the correct unhooking aid will prevent a death.

Disgorgers

Many anglers wrongly believe that one type of disgorger will release a hook from any fish. At least two types will be required depending on where the hook has lodged and on the type of hook being used. Where the hook is deep inside the mouth, but still visible, then the straightforward flattened 'V'-shaped disgorger, with a long handle, may be used to ease the barb back through the skin. Where the hook is deep and cannot be seen, a disgorger with some sort of loop or ring will be necessary. This can be slid down the line to the bend of the hook.

Several of the ring and guide types are

Forceps are very efficient for removing a treble hook from a pike's toothy jaws without harming the fish or fingers.

available, but most fail in practice either because they do not slip easily onto the line, or more generally because they jam at the eye or spade of the hook. Only one type will slide onto the line and ride easily onto the bend of the hook, and that is the simplest design of them all—the open wire loop or 'pigtail'.

Simply sliding the disgorger down the line and blindly stabbing with it will, in many instances, push the barb deeper into the flesh. The easiest method—and the safest for the fish—is to support the creature with one hand gently but firmly behind the gills. If it is too large, lay it along the bank with the head raised against a tackle box or rod handle. Hold taut the line leading into the mouth, put the disgorger onto the line, slide it down and ease it over the eye or spade of the hook and onto the bend. Press directly downwards until the hook moves freely and withdraw from the mouth—still supported in the disgorger—taking special care not to catch it against the tongue.

The disgorger is ridiculously easy to lose, but there are two things you can do to reduce the number that you mislay. One is to tie the handle by a piece of thin, strong line to your jacket lapel or

through a buttonhole. The other is to paint the whole object either bright red or yellow, preferably with luminous paint. This also makes the business end easier to see inside a fish's mouth.

Forceps

Within the last few years, medical artery forceps have become popular as a means of releasing a deeply-embedded hook, and several firms have produced them specifically for the angler. They are useful, but like most pieces of equipment, they have their limitations.

Some fish have a relatively small mouth opening even though the actual mouth cavity is quite large. The width of a pair of forceps, particularly when they are open, can block the view of the mouth, and if they are opened widely, can cause actual damage. It is all too easy to grasp a portion of flesh, together with the hook, and tear it in the process of unhooking. For fish with bony or leathery mouths, therefore, artery forceps are an efficient means of freeing most hooks.

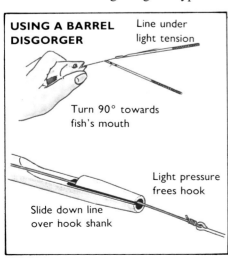

USING A BARREL DISGORGER

Line under light tension

Turn 90° towards fish's mouth

Slide down line over hook shank

Light pressure frees hook

CHAPTER 3
BAIT

BREAD, PASTE AND CRUST

Bread is not only an old-fashioned bait but also a very successful one. In recent years, and on many waters, it has been neglected, perhaps because its uses are not fully understood. Four different baits can be made from a white loaf—flake, crust, balanced crust and paste. The first two of these come from a new loaf, the fourth from an old loaf, the third from both.

Paste must be made from an old loaf, four days old at least. The loaf is prepared by removing the crusts then cutting it into slices an inch thick. Take one slice and dip it into a bowl of water, removing it almost immediately. Placing it into the palm of one hand, knead it into a paste with the other hand. Keep kneading until all the lumps have disappeared and it is soft.

Place a piece on the hook, cast and retrieve. If it remains on the hook during the retrieve it is too hard; if it flies off during casting it is too soft. Adjust it accordingly.

Hook sizes suitable for breadpaste range from 4–20 depending on the fish sought. For roach, bream, dace and grayling, 14–20 are right; chub, bream, tench and sometimes large roach need size 10; 8 for chub and barbel; 4 or 6 for carp.

Casting with paste

Because paste is a very soft bait if properly mixed, great care must be taken when casting. While overhead casts can be made without paste and

Above *Flake must be moulded firmly round the hook shank, leaving the bend and point exposed.* **Left** *Breadpaste moulded to the hook. Again, it is important to leave the barb free.*

hook parting company, in most situations a sideways cast is preferable. To ensure that the paste remains on the hook, the cast must be a smooth one: the least jerk and the bait will either fly off or dislodge itself from the hook.

Crust

Crust must come from a newish loaf, not more than two or three days old. The loaf should be kept in the shade, because once hardened the crust is useless. Depending upon the species being sought, sliced and unsliced loaves can be used. For roach, dace and grayling, a cut loaf is best: where larger pieces are required for such species as chub and carp, an uncut loaf is necessary.

The best way to cut the crust from an unsliced loaf is to insert the point of a sharp knife into the side of the crust.

Cut through the crust in the shape of a square. When you pull the square of crust away from the loaf, a chunk of the soft flake beneath it will also come away.

Opionions differ as to which side up the crust should lie. To make the bait hang crust side down take the crust and the hook, push the hook into the crumb side, out of the crust, then back through the crumb until both bend and part of the shank of the hook protrude. The opposite actions will make the bait hang with the crust up. About half the shank with the point and barb should always protrude from the crust. A hook slightly larger than the thickness of the crust must be used. If the hook is completely buried, the wet crust is liable to fall or cast off.

Flake

Flake is the name given to the crumb of new bread. The crumb of a two-day-old loaf is difficult, if not impossible, to place on the hook. When removing the crumb from the loaf a light touch is essential. Take hold of the crumb and lightly pull it from the loaf: it should be like a sponge with one edge sealed between thumb and forefinger. With the other hand take the hook, push the shank into the 'sponge' and gently pinch the crumb over it. Both the bend —or part of it—and the point of the hook will be exposed. The two sides of the crumb must be joined together with the minimum of pressure.

Left *A good, castable bait, balanced crust is very attractive to carp.* **Far left** *Another very effective bait, floating crust for carp or big chub.*

MAGGOTS

The maggot is the most popular coarse fishing bait used in Britain. Almost all our freshwater species may be taken on it, major competitions have been won on it, and it has also accounted for some record fish.

Maggots are small, easy to buy, transport and use. Not so long ago they were cheap, but prices have risen steeply. Maggots now cost at least £1 a pint. They are sold this way because pint beer glasses were once used to scoop them up for sale.

The maggot is the larva, or grub, of the fly. The maggots of the bluebottle, greenbottle, and common housefly are the ones which are used by the angler.

Coloured maggots
To increase the attractiveness of maggots to fish, they may be dyed a variety of colours, and indeed can be bought coloured orange, yellow, red or bronze. Tackle dealers supply colouring agents for dyeing them orange or bronze, Auromine O for yellow, and Rhodamine B for red.

How to use dyes
It must be pointed out that serious doubt has recently been cast on chrysodine as a colouring agent. These dyes may be used in one of two ways. First, the maggots can be coloured by raising them on foodstuffs treated with a small amount of the dye. The second method is best for maggots that have already been cleaned, as they are when bought. For this, sprinkle dye on them and stir well, then leave for one to four hours according to the depth of colour desired. Next, add bran or sawdust on which they will deposit excess dye. Lastly, sieve them to remove the bran, and they are ready for use.

The 'annatto' is a special colour-fed maggot whose yellow colour comes from the dye used to colour butter. Gozzers and other extra soft maggots produce the best results with this dye. Annatto is bought in roll form and must be cut into slices and mixed into a thin paste with water before use. The best time to introduce annatto is when the maggots are about half-grown. Spread the paste on the meat and replace in the bran. When the maggots stop feeding they are ready for use.

Lastly, if buying maggots from a shop, be sure they are fresh and do not include remnants of last week's stock. They should be shiny and wriggle vigorously.

Maggot breeding
Breeding maggots is big business. Millions are sold every week by tackle dealers all over the country. Professional breeders use bluebottles for mass production of the ordinary maggot. The common housefly's maggots are known as 'squatts', and being smaller than the bluebottle larvae they are used as 'feeders' thrown in to attract fish. Maggots from the greenbottle are called 'pinkies'. These are also small and used as 'feeders', but may be used on the hooks when circumstances require very fine tackle.

Right The maggot must be hooked at the blunt end of the creature to allow it to retain its attractive wriggling action. **Below** *Maggots can be coloured by edible dyes, but care should be taken when handling them. It has been recently suggested that some dyes may cause harmful skin diseases.* **Below right** *The angler must keep his maggots and groundbait handy and within easy reach to avoid unnecessary movement. The time element too is important in match fishing and the time you spend hooking bait is time wasted.*

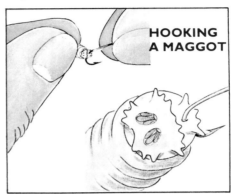

HOOKING A MAGGOT

CASTERS

The chrysalis, or pupa, of the fly is known to anglers as a caster. At this point in its life-cycle (from egg to grub, or maggot, to pupa, to fly) it is an excellent bait. First made popular by match anglers in roach waters, some experts consider casters to be the most important new bait adopted in recent years. Although the maggot remains the most popular general bait, the time may be near when the caster will have replaced it. As well as roach, chub and dace are partial to it and it has accounted for bream, gudgeon and tench. When first introduced to a stretch of water the fish may be uninterested but, once sampled, every caster is likely to be taken. Casters can be purchased from a tackle shop or bait dealer and kept in a refrigerator for about a week.

Removing floaters

By putting the casters in water any floaters can be removed as they appear. You will find that the casters vary in colour. Casters of a uniform dark red colour—the favourite—can be achieved quite simply. On the evening before use, wrap all the casters in a wet towel and leave in a bucket overnight. Next morning all the casters will be the same colour.

The choice of hook size will be governed by the size of the caster. The biggest you can use will probably be a 14, but generally a 16 or 18 will be necessary. The hook must be buried in the caster. Hold the caster between thumb and forefinger and, with the hook in the other hand, pierce the head of the caster with the point. Turn the hook very gently into the caster and, with

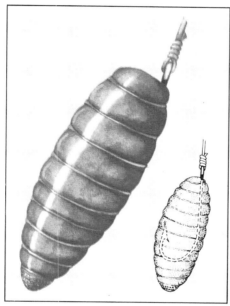

some of the shank still showing, lightly tap the top of the shank until the hook sinks into the caster.

Casters may be fished singly, or in twos, threes and fours. In deepish, fast flowing water, casters are best introduced as groundbait. Where there are plenty of fish and they start to take, you can put as many as two dozen casters in every cast.

This bait can also be used in combination with other small bait, such as worm tail, hempseed or tares. When groundbaiting the swim with a mixture of hemp, it is essential to make sure the casters are fast sinkers. Floaters drift with the flow and could attract fish out of the swim.

Big fish bait

Casters are not just small-fish bait—fairly good bream, chub and barbel

Above left A selection of hookbaits and groundbaits is wise, for the angler may find the fish difficult to tempt on just one bait. Alternative baits are always recommended.
Above The change from maggot to caster (or chrysalis) is fairly quick. As a bait, the caster probably has more nutritional value and is therefore more instinctively and eagerly taken by the fish. Left How to hook a fragile caster without splitting the case.

have been caught on casters. But big fish require larger hooks with more than one caster placed on the hook. As a rough guide, a 10lb barbel might take a bunch of five casters on a size 12 hook. But an 11lb 8oz barbel has been known to take a small bunch of maggots with a single caster on the tip of the hook.

When fishing deep water at long range, a quantity of casters can be mixed with a cereal groundbait to resemble a 'plum duff' with crunchy casters worked into the groundbait ball. Thrown into the top of a swim by hand, the ball will drop quickly to the bottom before breaking up—an ideal groundbaiting method when ledgering casters. Little and often is always a good maxim when groundbaiting with casters because it is easy to over-feed the swim so the fish lose interest.

When fished singly, casters need fine and delicate tackle. An easy-casting rod is advisable when fished far off—too vigorous a cast will flick the bait off the hook. Quality casters are thought to be a good roach bait on any canal or river. With the approach of autumn they can be unbeatable on some waters.

Casters work best on clear waters, so when a river is coloured it may pay to revert to the maggot.

WORMS

There are three kinds of earthworm that are of interest to anglers—the lobworm (the largest), the redworm and the brandling—and they can all be kept in stock.

The numbers you keep depend very much on the fishing you intend to do. Nowadays few anglers keep stocks of the smelly brandling. When it is hooked, the smell it gives off stays on the angler's hands for hours afterwards. Modern anglers (particularly matchmen) prefer the small, lively redworm which, when hooked, wriggles and writhes most enticingly. The lobworm tends to be favoured by specimen hunters and is relatively easy to gather on a dewy, summer's night.

There are various ways of cultivating a stock of worms. The easiest is to create a worm-patch, and this can be developed in a shady part of the garden where the worms would tend to gather of their own accord. This method is particularly good for the encouragement, nurture and collection of lobworms.

The ingredients

A worm patch is made by simply forking in garden refuse, stable manure, vegetable scraps, lawn mowings and various plant material from the garden. Earth collected from molehills makes a good soil medium for a wormery as does stable or farmyard manure.

Right The three kinds of worm used by anglers. **Below right** For use as bait, worms must be fresh and lively. One dead one in a box will soon kill all the others. **Below** A worm should be hooked so that it can still wriggle enticingly.

The compost heap will be better contained by building a framework of wood or corrugated sheeting. To stock the heap, a supply of brandlings or redworms can be collected or purchased from a dealer.

Hooking the worm

It is important to hook a worm correctly, for this ensures that it stays on the hook and that it will wiggle naturally to attract the fish. A whole worm can be hooked anywhere along its length. If necessary, pierce a long worm several times and feed it along the hook. Tails or pieces of worms should present no problem and stay on the hook. In general do not try to cover the hook, for a worm is a very tempting bait and, if lively, will probably wriggle enough to expose part of the hook anyway.

Apart from using a single hook, there is the two-hook rig known as Pennell tackle, and the two- or three-hook Stewart tackle. These multiple-hook rigs are best when the whole of a big lobworm is used.

BLOODWORMS

If someone were to describe a freshwater bait that took hours to discover, entailed wading and sifting through thin, black mud, needed careful preparation and eventually required the finest hooks and line to present it, they would no doubt be referring to the bloodworm. But, despite these many problems, this tiny bait has an enormous success rate. In fact, it is such a killer that it has been banned from use in angling matches in the past and remains banned in many areas.

COMMON BAIT WORMS

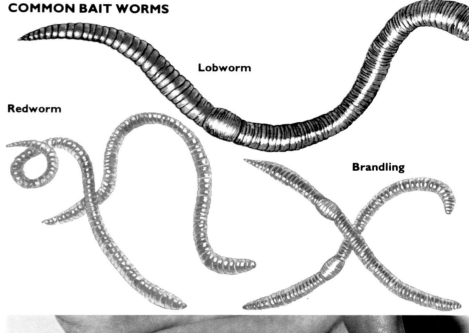

Lobworm

Redworm

Brandling

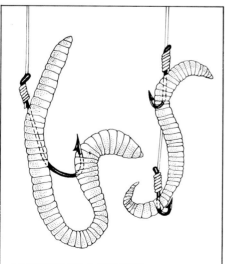

HOOKING A WORM

If using a single hook (left) make sure that it pierces the body of the worm twice, or alternatively, you can use two hooks (right).

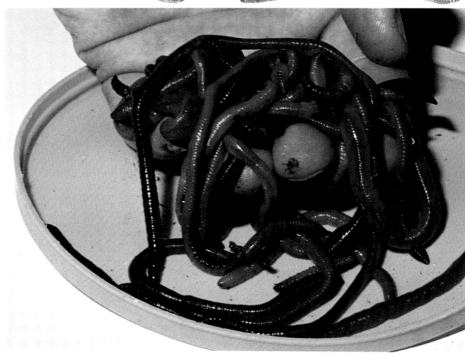

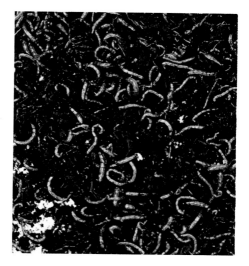

Collecting bloodworms

The largest bloodworms will be found in stagnant water. Those that inhabit running water are somewhat smaller in size and are referred to by the angler as 'jokers'. The traditional instrument used for their capture is a long firm pole some 5ft in length. To one end of this is fastened a thin strip of pliable aluminium at least 1½ft long. This strip can be bent into various angles to suit the depth of water that is being searched, and the scraper is sliced through the top surface of mud a short distance out from the bank, with an even motion that traps the worms by folding them over its leading edge. After each sweep the worms can be gently slid off the scraper into a tin or plastic box. The whole action is rather like scything grass and takes practice to perfect. Polarized sunglasses can be a great help in allowing the angler to see and follow the contours of the bottom.

An easier, though more messy, method is to net bloodworms with a shrimping type of frame using a nylon stocking as the net. More worms will be collected by this method, but with considerably more mud and slime attached.

Once enough have been collected, they must be carefully washed to rid them of mud and slime, using nylon for a sieve and sifting out the worms under running water. Washed clean, it is possible to separate them into hook and groundbait sizes.

What you will then be left with is a tangled mass of worms, twigs, leaves and weeds. Sorting out this little lot will take hours and so the Northern professional scrapers have perfected a way of ensuring that only live, neat bloodworms are separated. The simple process involves half submerging a good sized maggot riddle in a dustbin lid with about 2in of water in it. The whole gooey mess is then spread on top of the riddle and within five minutes every living bloodworm will have found its

Above left Bloodworms are not true worms but the larvae of gnats. *Above* Mealworms are the grub stage of a beetle that is found in flour mills. *Above right* This match fishing contest, part of the 1981 World Angling Championships, held on the Warwickshire Avon, was won by anglers using bloodworms as bait.

way through the mesh into the water below. Pour the water into a fine sieve and you will be left with thousands of clean, bright red beauties; simple once you know how.

Storing lively bloodworms

They should be stored separately in moist, black garden peat which has been crushed and broken until it is a fine dust. Not only will this keep the larvae alive and active, but also provide a binding medium for those that are going to be used as groundbait. The peat forms a black carpet across the bottom of the swim which is, in itself, an attraction. If hookbaits are kept for any length of time, they should be packed into damp moss and stood in a refrigerator where they will normally remain useful for several weeks.

Hooking bloodworms is an art. Naturally, only the smallest hooks, sizes 20–22, will be fine enough to match the small bait. Hooks should be mounted on ¾lb or, at the most, 1lb b.s. hook links. The easiest method of hooking is to lay the bloodworm on to the thumbnail, then pierce one end of the worm with the point of the hook and gently ease it over the barb.

Need for small floats

The float is a very important item in bloodworm fishing. Often the bait will be taken 'on the drop' and, if the angler is counting on small fish to make up his weight in a competition, he will be fishing a mere 12-18in below the surface. This means that the float must be small, require only few small shot to cock it,

and that these shot be mounted into, or immediately below, its body. Above all, that part which shows through the surface must be as thin as possible so that the smallest touch on the bait will produce an immediate response.

Tight-line tactics

A tight-line tactic pays excellent dividends with bloodworm fishing, and the roach pole is probably the best instrument by which to apply it. Its easy style of casting will also prevent undue strain on the bait, which is so delicate that it will usually be thrown off the hook by a long-distance cast.

When a long pole is being used to present the bait, a barbless hook is by far the best for the job as it causes minimal disturbance to the outer skin of the worm, thus preserving the natural colour and juices that fish find so attractive.

MEALWORMS

Mealworms make an excellent bait. The long, straw-coloured grubs, segmented and rather similar to a centipede in appearance, are the larvae of a large beetle found in granaries and flour mills. They can occasionally be purchased at pet stores, where they are sold as food for insectivorous birds and mammals. Although they are expensive, they can be stored for a very long period in a ventilated tin of fine bran or oatmeal. If an even temperature is maintained, they will often go through the chrysalis stage, adult insect, and breed, allowing a succession of baits from the one purchase.

Mealworms should be mounted through a middle segment rather than one near the tail end, which is delicate and likely to break off during the cast.

Even if there is no acceptance of a mealworm bait on or just below the surface, it should be allowed to sink and lie on the bottom for a short time before being retrieved gently.

SEED BAITS

Seed baits are apparently baits of fad and fashion. Those in current vogue with non-specialist anglers are sweet-corn, tares and as an enticer or feed-bait, hempseed.

Most seeds will tempt fish and most are prepared for the hook in a similar way. It pays to soak seeds overnight in cold water after first washing the hard grains. Then they are placed in a sauce-pan and again covered with water which is brought to the boil and left to simmer gently for a particular length of time, decided by the kind of seed.

Correct timing is very important. Under-cooked seed baits are too hard for any fish to mouth. Over-cooked, they become too mushy to use at all. So do not just put them into a pot and leave them. They must, as in all *cordon bleu* culinary arts, have close attention.

Hemp

Can hempseed pollute a water? Of course it can, as can any substance deposited in excess over long periods. Massive mounds of rotting hemp have been found at the edge of waters, left there by anglers who took too much with them. It is best to take any surplus home and not risk spoiling a swim for other anglers.

Acclaimed by the match fisherman

Throw loose seed baits into the eddies of a weir to attract fish. A self-cocking float will allow your hook bait to follow the loose particles as they swirl in the current.

and other anglers as a 'superbait', banned by some clubs as unsporting, condemned for years as a water pollut-ant, suspected of drugging fish—con-troversial hempseed has been all of these.

Good quality hemp, available at a reasonable price nowadays from most tackle dealers, is big, black, and should be free from dust or husks. A pound is ample for a normal day's fishing. Before use it should be washed carefully in cold water, immersed in a clean pan of cold water and then brought to the boil. To emphasize its blackness a large lump of household soda can be added, together with two teaspoonsful of sugar to hide any acidity. Having boiled, allow to simmer and carefully watch until one side of the seed opens and a white kernel protrudes slightly, showing that it is fully cooked. Boiled beyond this point it will disintegrate and become totally useless.

Now sieve the seed and wash it under a cold tap until thoroughly cool, other-wise the cooking process will continue. Finally—and vitally important—store the seed in an airtight, watertight box, keeping it sealed until it is required. If you fail to keep hemp wet it will float on the water, bring fish up to the surface and eventually, as it carries downstream, take them with it out of the swim.

Hooks for hemp

Hooks for use with hemp should be small—from size 10 downwards—and made from fine wire. Special hooks,

Water-resistant glue can be used to attach difficult-to-hook seed baits to the shank.

with the back of the bend flattened to allow a single hemp grain to be easily mounted were available at one time; some anglers today flatten their own with a small hammer and a fine punch. The effort taken to do the job is amply repaid with time saved in re-baiting the hook while fishing.

Hooking hemp

Select a large seed, hold it between finger and thumb, then squeeze it and push the bend of the hook into the open side through the white kernel. Gently done, this should hold the seed on the hook. If the seed drops off, it will indi-cate that the hemp has been overcooked. With each cast it will probably be necessary to re-bait the hook, a tire-some procedure that, as will be seen later, can be avoided by the use of artificial hemp or alternatively a suit-able substitute.

At every cast to the head of the swim, throw in no more than 8-10 loose grains, aiming them right on the tip of the float. Once they hit the water, tighten any slack line between rod tip and float and prepare yourself for some of the fastest bites imaginable.

Beans

Haricot beans—small and hard skinned —make an excellent bait after being soaked for at least 24 hours, then boiled gently. They can be improved by being stewed in a pan of milk for a further half hour after they have been boiled.

Tinned buttered beans can be expen-sive if used in bulk. It is far better to use the haricot beans as groundbait, reserv-ing the butter beans for the hook. The tin should be opened the day before they are required and the liquid content thrown away. The beans should then be soaked in a mixture of sugar and water or honey and water, at a ratio of one teaspoonful to the pint, before being drained and packed.

Any hookable seed can be tried. One never knows how a hungry fish will react.

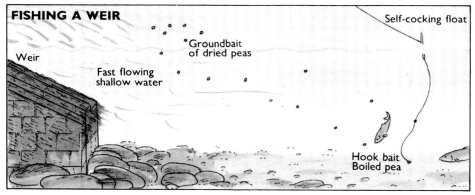

FISHING A WEIR

Self-cocking float

Groundbait of dried peas

Weir

Fast flowing shallow water

Hook bait Boiled pea

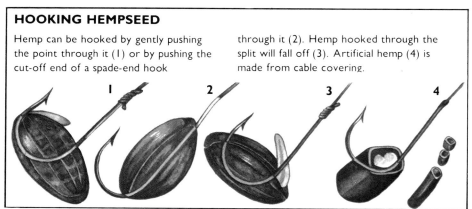

HOOKING HEMPSEED

Hemp can be hooked by gently pushing the point through it (1) or by pushing the cut-off end of a spade-end hook

through it (2). Hemp hooked through the split will fall off (3). Artificial hemp (4) is made from cable covering.

1   2   3   4

SWEETCORN

Sweetcorn's greatest attractions are its availability and its convenience. In its ready-to-use, canned form, it can be put on the hook without any preparation. Alternatively, you can buy fresh or frozen corn which is just as good after a little preparation. Whole corn-on-the-cob needs cooking and de-cobbing, while frozen loose corn needs boiling for a few minutes to soften it. But if you intend pre-baiting with large quantities, you can make a significant saving by buying bulk and boiling up as required.

Nevertheless, the canned corn is still the most popular form, but do give the environment a thought before taking cans to the waterside. It is more convenient and less antisocial to open the can at home and empty the corn into a plastic bait box or other container. In fact, there are now a few environmentally conscious clubs that ban cans of all types on the river banks and punish

Right *Single grains of sweetcorn make excellent baits for tench, roach and chub.*
Below right *How to hook various seedbaits.*

infringements with instant expulsion.

Sweetcorn keeps quite well, but in hot weather treat it like maggots and keep it in the shade if possible. Drain off the 'juice' and give the corn a quick rinse under the tap before putting it in your bait box, for it becomes sticky and slimy in hot weather. Removing the juice does not detract from its effectiveness as a bait. Corn can be frozen after use, too; it is expensive, so do not waste. With care, it can even be re-frozen.

Sweetcorn grains range in size from that of a match-head to that of a large pea. So all manner of bait sizes and hooks can be used—from a single small grain on a No 18 to six or seven large grains hiding a No 4 or No 2 carp hook. Compared with other particle baits, few grains are needed to cover the hook.

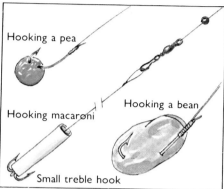

Hooking a pea

Hooking macaroni

Hooking a bean

Small treble hook

It pays to use eyed hooks or spade-ends with a prominent spade. These help to keep the corn on the shank. With whipped-to-nylon hooks there is always a risk of the corn sliding up the line, resulting in false bites and snagged hooks. Some anglers favour gilt or gold hooks, but the author has found them no better and uses bronzed, eyed hooks.

How much as loose feed?

The big question with corn is how much free bait to introduce into a swim. This is a very controversial subject, and the views of experts vary, particularly when it comes to 'educating' carp and tench in stillwaters. The general plan, however, is to encourage big fish to feed intensively over a small area.

In larger lakes and pits, scatter corn finely over wide areas to accustom the fish to it, then select a hotspot of a few square yards and carpet it with corn. But in both large and small lakes, you will have to modify these general guidelines to take account of the fish population, both of the species you are after and the unwanted species that also like corn. How much modification is a matter of choice.

Like many other baits, sweetcorn suddenly became popular and was the 'in' bait for a number of seasons with tench and carp anglers. But never make the mistake of assuming that a single bait is the total answer to success. The experienced angler always has at least two, probably more, baits with him for that day when the 'in' bait goes out.

Specimen-sized tench can be attracted to take sweetcorn. Take a tin with you on a tenching trip but do not leave it there.

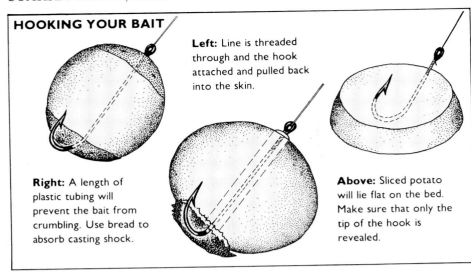

HOOKING YOUR BAIT

Left: Line is threaded through and the hook attached and pulled back into the skin.

Right: A length of plastic tubing will prevent the bait from crumbling. Use bread to absorb casting shock.

Above: Sliced potato will lie flat on the bed. Make sure that only the tip of the hook is revealed.

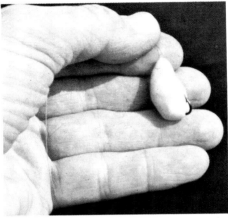

CHEESE

For most purposes Cheddar cheese makes an excellent bait—but it must be fresh. On occasion, softer cheeses such as Stilton or Danish Blue are also very good.

Understanding wives and mothers do not object to anglers removing small pieces of stale cheese, but taking the fresh Cheddar may raise a few eyebrows. Removal of the Stilton or Danish Blue is apt to put a definite strain on any relationship.

The thoughtful angler makes his own arrangements to purchase cheese before he goes fishing. But however you obtain it, it is well worth trying this versatile bait.

Fresh Cheddar can easily be moulded into a putty-like consistency. This should be done as and when needed, the cheese being flattened between the finger and thumb and then folded around the hook and shaped firmly.

For chub or barbel, walnut-size pieces on sizes 4, 6, or 8 are about right. In slow or sluggish waters this can be used on the bottom without using any weights. In faster water, however, it is necessary to use a ledger lead such as an Arlesey bomb to hold the bait down, once in position. A few smaller lumps of cheese should be thrown into or upstream of the swim at intervals during fishing. Groundbait should also be liberally laced with cheese powder as this helps to hold shoals in the area of the hookbait.

For roach or dace, pieces the size of peas on size 10–14 hooks are used. In suitable swims a ledger might be used but the favoured practice is to swim the stream with standard float-fishing tackle. Again bites are usually positive. Though durable, cheese is soft enough to allow good hook penetration when the time comes to strike.

The much softer cheeses, such as Stilton and Danish Blue, when mature,

Above How to hook small whole potatoes and single slices. In both cases the barbs only must protrude. Above right Squares of cheese make good baits for chub and roach. Cold water however makes cheese cubes go hard and brittle. Right Mix soft cheese with bread paste to make an attractive bait.

are sometimes too soft to be moulded on to the hook. If so, mix the cheese well with a good stiff bread paste. The cheese imparts sufficient flavour to the paste to provide a tasty bait for many species.

Cubes of cheese

As an alternative to moulding the cheese on to the hook, it is possible to cut it into small cubes of a size to suit the hook. The hook is then either pressed firmly into the cube or threaded through it. In either case the hook point must be very close to the surface of the cube, even protruding. Some smaller cubes are thrown into the swim as attractors.

The versatile cheese slice has gained a lot of friends over the last few years. You can use either the white or yellow variety, cut into slivers, to fish running water where it dances and shimmies through the swim in a most attractive way. It attracts bites from all species of fish—the roach in particular being susceptible to a thin strip of tasty cheese lowered tantalizingly below a lightly shotted stick float.

Different shapes cut from the slices sink and fish quite differently from any other bait, and bites can come at any time during the bait's introduction to the water. A big chub, for example, may appear from nowhere to grab a halfpenny-sized strip of cheese almost as soon as it hits the water.

Sliced cheese is equally effective when used in conjunction with a bread punch. On stillwaters this is an advantage because the shapes don't come into contact with the angler's hands. Lay the

slice on a flat surface, press in the punch, and insert the hook lightly. During summer months, crucian carp are spellbound by punched cheese, and very often a tench or two show up.

During the winter, most kinds of cheese lose their impact because the cold water makes them rock hard. This is the time to turn to the various cheese spreads. A little messy to hook during the summer, these soft, creamy cheeses make an ideal winter bait. They are just hard enough to stay on the hook during casting but sufficiently soft to tempt fish.

POTATO

Cooked potato, presented in a variety of forms, is favoured as a bait for large carp but is also attractive to bottom-feeders in general and sometimes tench, bream, chub and barbel. The occasional larger roach will take a potato but one of the bait's advantages to the carp fisherman is that smaller fish will usually be deterred by its size and will leave it to the specimens. The attractiveness of potato to large carp is perhaps attributable to its curiosity value and, despite a notorious cautiousness, they will investigate a potential food not normally found in their natural environment if careful groundbaiting is used to allay their suspicions.

To hook a potato, thread the line

through it, using a baiting needle. Better, sink a short piece of plastic tubing through the bait and pass the line through it. This will prevent the line cutting into the potato with the force of the cast, which often has to be a long one. Then tie on a suitably sized hook (some use a barbless model or cut the barb off the regular kind) and pull the hook back into the potato gently so as to prevent fragmenting when casting.

GROUNDBAITING

Groundbaiting is carried out to attract fish into a swim and get them feeding. There are various methods of groundbaiting, depending mainly upon the type of water, the rate of flow, and the species of fish sought. When fishing fast flowing water, and barbel or bream are the quarry, a ball of groundbait which sinks quickly should be thrown in slightly upstream so that when it hits the bottom and breaks up, the particles drift along the bottom and through the swim. Bream usually swim in large shoals, feeding on the bottom, and large amounts of groundbait are often needed to concentrate the shoal in the swim. A large bucketful of groundbait is generally the minimum required for a day's fishing.

Baiting up a swim several days in advance can pay dividends, particularly when bream, tench or carp are sought. This can draw a big shoal of bream into the swim and hold them there until fishing starts, even though their usual tendency is to be on the move.

A ball of groundbait can be used to land a quantity of loose maggots on the bed of a deep swim. In strong flowing water, such as a weir stream, bank clay can be worked into the mixture for this purpose. It is then moulded in the shape of a cup, the cavity filled with maggots, worms or another bait, and the top closed over. A strong flow, coupled with the action of the wriggling bait, will soon break up the balls, sending the hookbait samples trickling along the bottom to bring fish close.

Groundbaiting from a boat

When fishing from a boat, groundbait can be dropped over the side or lowered to the bottom in a meshed bag weighted with stones. An occasional tug on a cord attached to the bag will release and circulate particles of the groundbait through the mesh and into the swim.

When ledgering, it is essential to get

Above right Double groundbaiting means keeping two swims going, one close in, the other some distance away. **Right** Water flow must be taken into account when throwing in your groundbait.

the groundbait in the right place, and then to fish the baited hook in the middle of it or as close as possible—on the downstream side.

Groundbaiting is frequently done with the use of mechanical devices, such as bait-droppers, swimfeeders and catapults. One sure way of landing loose maggots, or other hookbait samples, on the bottom, is to put them there by means of a bait-dropper, of which there are various kinds on the market. The loaded bait-dropper is lowered to the bottom of the swim, when a trip wire opens the lid and releases the contents.

Cloudbaiting

A form of groundbaiting which is effective in many types of waters, particularly for surface and mid-water species, is cloudbaiting. This means clouding the water by introducing minute particles which the fish will search through, looking for more substantial food.

After taking note of the rate of flow of the water, the angler regularly throws

Groundbait must be placed close to the hookbait. Fish will be attracted to the area and find the baited hook as they forage among the loose particles.

small balls of cloudbait into the swim. This is done upstream, so that the cloud drifts down and through the area being fished. The float tackle is cast out immediately after, following the groundbait closely through the swim.

Drip-feeding

For roach, dace and chub fishing on a small, secluded river, regular swimbaiting can be made by the use of a 'drip-feed'—a tin with a few holes punched in the bottom, which is filled with maggots and hung from a bridge or overhanging branch. The steady trickle of maggots over a long period will entice fish from some distance away into the swim.

As match fishermen know, regular groundbaiting of the swim is very important no matter what hookbait is used. Without it, the angler is fishing on a hit-and-miss basis. This is why, when ledgering, groundbaiting the swim manually is sometimes employed at the same time as offering the hookbait samples in the swimfeeder.

Care must always be exercised when groundbaiting a swim where specimen fish are the quarry. On a river, the introduction of a large quantity of groundbait will invariably attract shoals of small fish.

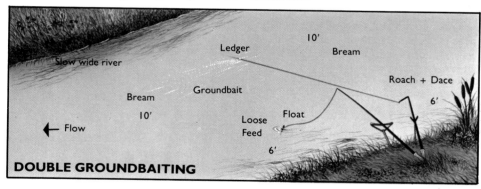

DOUBLE GROUNDBAITING

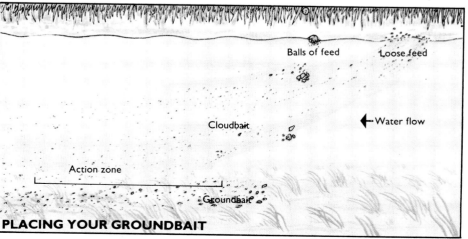

PLACING YOUR GROUNDBAIT

CHAPTER 4
SKILLS

FLOAT FISHING

Float fishing is probably the most popular form of coarse fishing. There are a great number of different types of float and different methods of float fishing, but too many anglers, having found that one tactic and one float work reasonably well, stick to this method without considering other methods. Rather than just settling for the most convenient method, the angler should try to achieve the best possible presentation of the bait in each situation. He should go for the most effective method. This might not be the easiest, but it is the angler with the techniques and ability to do this who will more often than not catch the most fish.

The waggler

The large antenna float—the waggler—seems to be the float most abused by lazy anglers. Certainly in the past few years, it has been responsible for winning a lot of matches. Yet is this because this is the most effective float, or because it is being used when it shouldn't be?

This is not as contradictory as it sounds. People are winning matches with the waggler, but it is possible that with other floats, such as a stick, they would have won with even more fish. And while a waggler is comparatively easy to fish, it will not allow the angler to get the best out of every swim.

The reason for this is simple. The waggler does not allow the same degree of control over the presentation of the bait as a double-rubbered float. When the waggler is being properly used it is fished attached by its bottom end only and has a lot of tip showing above the water. This is because it is fished with a shot dragging the bottom and the float must not be sensitive enough to be dragged under.

Even so, despite its size, try to hold it back against the water flow, so that the bait is presented in a slow, attractive manner, and what happens? It merely goes under because of the drag of the line between rod tip and float—unless you have achieved a degree of expertise and control of the float possessed by very few anglers. In contrast, a stick or balsa, fished double-rubber, can be held in the stream so that the bait just trickles along.

This is not to say that the waggler

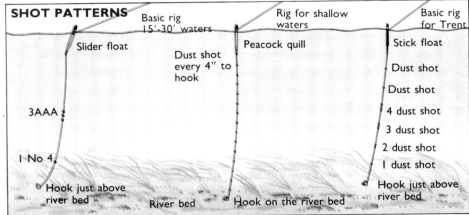

SHOT PATTERNS

Basic rig 15'–30' waters — Slider float — 3AAA — 1 No 4 — Hook just above river bed

Rig for shallow waters — Peacock quill — Dust shot every 4" to hook — Hook on the river bed — River bed

Basic rig for Trent — Stick float — Dust shot — Dust shot — 4 dust shot — 3 dust shot — 2 dust shot — 1 dust shot — Hook just above river bed

Top Float fishing is the first skill the beginner will learn. It is the basis of all coarse fishing styles. **Above** *Three kinds of shotting pattern for different float fishing methods. There are many others.*

cannot be a very useful float in certain circumstances. In difficult conditions, rough water and fierce downstream wind, for example, or when the fish are biting freely three or four rod-lengths out—when it has the edge in speed—it can be ideal. In other circumstances, on rivers such as the Ribble, which has an uneven flow, other floats, such as the Avon balsa, are more successful. When fishing within easy sight of the float and

in good light all one needs in normal float fishing is just enough float visible to be detected at the first twitch indicating an interested fish. But the angler's reactions must be fast on the strike.

The Avon balsa

The size of the balsa is important. It must be big enough to carry sufficient weight to allow you to pull back on the rod without it dragging into the bank too quickly. A float which can carry about two or three swan shot serves the purpose. Shotting is simple: all you need is a small shot, say a No 4 (directly under the float to stop it sliding down the line under the pressure of striking), the bulk shot roughly halfway between the float and the hook, and the tell-tale which goes 1ft to 18in from the hook. The purpose of the tell-tale shot is to regulate the presentation of the bait. The tell-tale's size will depend on the strength of the flow.

The method with this rig is to cast out to the area you wish to fish—with this rig the under-arm cast is a must if tangles are to be avoided—and then to mend the line, that is to lift the line and swinging it upstream if it threatens to put drag on the float and bait, until the float settles. Then lift the rod tip high so that the line goes directly to the float tip without touching the water.

If you choose a float with plenty of bulk and weight-carrying capacity, it will strip line from the reel at the pace you dictate and carry on the current far more smoothly than a waggler. Furthermore, if you check the line on the rim of the spool with your fingertip, you can slow the float right down or even momentarily stop it—something you can't do with a waggler.

There's no doubt that this pays off. If you have studied the swim, you should know what part of it may produce a fish; you can then slow up the float when it is approaching the area, relaxing again when it has passed downstream.

Advantages of float fishing

Float fishing is also widely practised in gravel pits and has some advantages. A sliding float, an antenna, or in windy conditions, a long, wide-bodied float, can be used to search deep water under the bank for tench, bream and roach during the summer months. A float is also helpful when fishing deep water beyond a shelf on which a ledger rig would snag and so reduce bite indications.

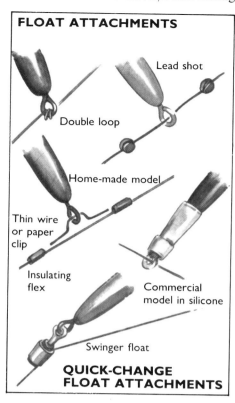

FLOAT ATTACHMENTS

Lead shot

Double loop

Home-made model

Thin wire or paper clip

Insulating flex

Commercial model in silicone

Swinger float

QUICK-CHANGE FLOAT ATTACHMENTS

Above *A variety of means of attaching the float to the line. A change of float is often needed and time will be wasted if it is spent dismantling the terminal tackle.* **Below** *Some styles demand that the bait should sink slowly. This rig, using a quill or Avon slider float, lets the hookbait sink steadily and attractively.*

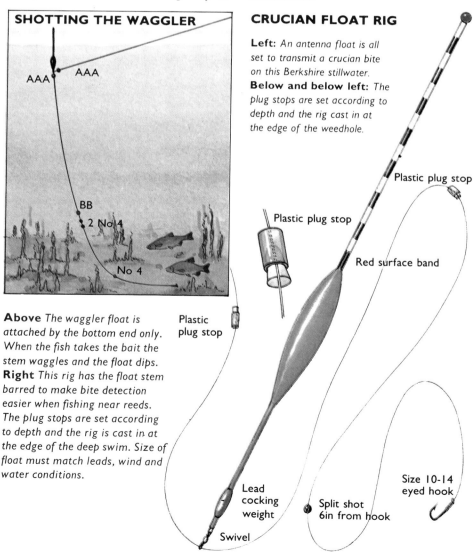

SHOTTING THE WAGGLER

AAA   AAA

BB

2 No 4

No 4

Above *The waggler float is attached by the bottom end only. When the fish takes the bait the stem waggles and the float dips.* **Right** *This rig has the float stem barred to make bite detection easier when fishing near reeds. The plug stops are set according to depth and the rig is cast in at the edge of the deep swim. Size of float must match leads, wind and water conditions.*

CRUCIAN FLOAT RIG

Left: *An antenna float is all set to transmit a crucian bite on this Berkshire stillwater.*
Below and below left: *The plug stops are set according to depth and the rig cast in at the edge of the weedhole.*

Plastic plug stop

Plastic plug stop

Plastic plug stop

Red surface band

Lead cocking weight

Swivel

Split shot 6in from hook

Size 10-14 eyed hook

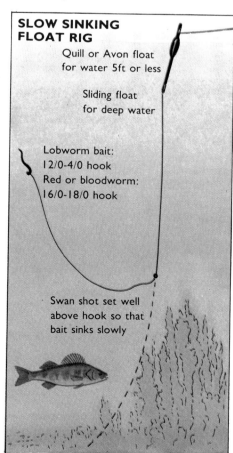

SLOW SINKING FLOAT RIG

Quill or Avon float for water 5ft or less

Sliding float for deep water

Lobworm bait: 12/0-4/0 hook
Red or bloodworm: 16/0-18/0 hook

Swan shot set well above hook so that bait sinks slowly

UNDERARM CASTING

One of the most neglected skills of many anglers is casting. It should be a smooth operation designed to use the action of the rod to place the tackle in the required spot. It is easy to find anglers who have not even mastered that basic skill, so it is little wonder that they have not explored the various alternative casting techniques.

One particularly useful skill is the underarm cast. This technique once turned an apparently hopeless peg in a national match on the Severn into a productive spot. It is also useful in casting delicate baits, such as wasp grub, which would be ripped off the hook by the force of an overarm cast. That peg on the Severn had a 6ft gap between the water and some overhanging willow branches. Quite a lot of competitors in that match would surely have given up, but one man was able to underarm cast a loaded slider float 15-20 yards into the main flow and catch fish.

'Backhand cast'

Perhaps the actual term, underarm cast, while commonly used, is something of a misnomer. The correct description should be the 'backhand cast', for in many instances the cast is more of a side sweep delivered from the back of the hand. It is similar to the action of a spin bowler in cricket involving a nice steady arm movement across the body, with a smooth sharp delivery the wrist makes as the ball is bowled.

The starting position for underarm casting is with the rod positioned across the body and the point down. The bait is held in the free hand. So, if you are right-handed, the rod is in that hand and the bait in the left, the line being tight to the rod top—not too tight, though, as you can easily hook yourself. The rod tip should be positioned on your left side—vice versa if you are left-handed—with the point near to the surface of the water.

The 'follow-through'

A smooth, sweeping action then sends the tackle on its way. The next second is vital to the action, for the rod must 'follow through', with the tip raised high and pointing directly at the spot aimed for.

As the end tackle starts to fall the rod tip is used to straighten or mend the line—either by moving it upstream or, on a stillwater, against the wind—while the line is 'feathered' off the reel with the forefinger to retard the float and allow the length between float and hook to straighten out and so enter the water smoothly.

The rod tip is now dropped and should finish up just above the surface of the water again, if the line is to be sunk.

It all sounds easy, and it is, with practice. Most probably, the first few attempts will be disastrous, but practice will make perfect and a skill that leads to improved catches will have been acquired and will never be lost.

Points to watch are the follow-through—vital for direction; dropping the rod point, and 'feathering' the line off the reel to eliminate tangles and give clean entry. Do not expect to cast as far with the underarm method as with an overhead throw if using similar tackle. You need plenty of weight in the float, but, properly placed, it will not affect bait presentation. Loaded floats, such as sliders and stick floats which carry weight in their base, are the right choice for this job.

The importance of shotting

Shotting is important. With a 'waggler' or loaded slider, normal shotting is right—the bulk shot should be about 5ft from the hook with the tell-tale shot around 18in from the hook. The stop-shot—to stop the float running down and fouling the bulk shot—should be 10ft 6in from the hook. When float fishing shallower water, the pattern of shots should be positioned in proportion.

Below left *Underarm casting allows the angler to cast from beneath overhanging trees.* **Below** *The underarm cast is made by swinging the tackle out in an arc and at the instant before it begins to drop back the line is released to allow the terminal tackle to be thrown forward into the swim.*

POLE FISHING

Pole fishing has become very popular in Britain. With this style of sport, a rod in the region of 14-28ft long is used and the line is fixed direct to the end of the rod without the niceties of reel or rod rings. The float tackle—often very small and sensitive—is fished extremely close to the top of the rod. This makes it easier for the angler to strike at very small bite indications, since he is in almost direct contact with the bait. Because of the stiffness of the pole, a shock absorber of fine elastic may be fitted between the rod and line so that, on striking, the line does not snap. This type of fishing is becoming more popular, particularly where bleak are the quarry, as the pole can be used to strike 'quickly and to place the bait very accurately.

In theory, the super-long tapered pole, with the line fastened to the end, uses a short link below the rod tip to

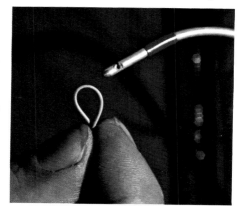

How the elastic loop, which absorbs the bite, is fitted to the crook on the tip of the pole.

convey the strike, which must drive the hook home very rapidly in this kind of fishing. In practice, there is an added bonus in the slim taper of the rod, for this produces sufficient spring to allow the careful angler to land fish well above the size of a roach that it was originally designed to catch.

The name 'roach pole' suggests that a pole can be used only for catching small fish. This is not so. Used properly, a pole can also handle big fish, such as chub, tench, bream and barbel.

Poles vary in length from 14ft to 28ft, but models made of ultra-lightweight hollow carbonfibre have been made over 40ft long. The more common hollow glass pole, however, designed to suit the average pocket, is about 18ft in length, and the assembled pole can be shortened according to the angler's needs, simply by not using the bottom sections.

When you buy a pole, you are advised also to obtain tackle specially designed for pole fishing. You *can* make do with ordinary elastic, floats, shots

Right *A modern glassfibre pole, much lighter than the traditional cane ones. But the length still makes holding a problem.*

and so on, and still catch plenty of fish, but, on the other hand, the tackle specially designed for pole fishing is neater, more streamlined, and makes pole fishing easier.

Tackle

The most important item of tackle is that length of elastic. Most poles are designed to be fairly rigid at the tip, and as a reel is not used with a pole, the elastic acts as a shock absorber when hooking and playing a fish. Our grandfathers used a length of knicker elastic fixed to the end of their bamboo poles.

Nowadays, special angling elastic is attached to the crook (or swan neck) tip, which is in turn fitted into its slot, and secured with a plastic sleeve which slides over the slot when the elastic loop is in position. The line is tied to the free end of the elastic, and carries the float, shot and hook, so it is useful to have several traces with end tackle on winders, ready for use. A ready-for-use assembly like this could consist of line, plus a float, weighted with either a celery shot pinched onto the line, or a hollow olivette lead with the line running through its centre. (A split shot is pinched onto the line to stop the olivette lead sliding right the way down to the hook.)

The vital rod tip

The rod tip, or point, is the vital part of the pole and it should follow the float and remain directly above it, otherwise the strike will be delayed fractionally by slack line, which may well mean the difference between a hooked or missed fish. It also follows that once a fish is hooked, the rod point should follow, and be kept immediately above it.

Once a fish is allowed to move away from the tip, then direct strain is placed

on the line, all spring absorption from the rod being lost. A break is almost inevitable under these circumstances, and on more than one occasion an ardent pole angler has been seen running up and down the bank, following a fish to try to prevent the loss of a match-winning fish.

Although pole fishing may be new to you, it should not prove difficult. It is simply another way of fishing with a rod and float or ledger tackle. When you first go pole fishing, try for the smaller fish—gudgeon or bleak. You will soon get used to the fact that there is no reel on the rod, and quickly learn to use the stretch of the elastic instead of the slipping clutch of a reel.

Below *A variety of pole fishing tackle, now much in demand by British match anglers following the successes of Continental matchmen.* **Below left** *Fine terminal tackle is used in pole fishing. Line of 2lb and 1½lb b.s. is usual, with hooks down to 22.*

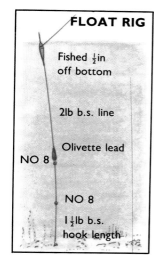

FLOAT RIG

Fished ½in off bottom

2lb b.s. line

Olivette lead

NO 8

NO 8

1½lb b.s. hook length

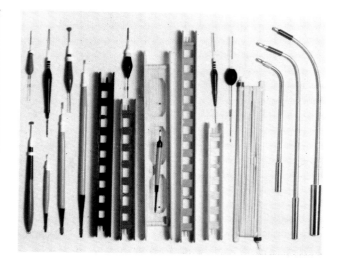

FLOAT LEDGERING

As its name suggests, float ledgering combines many of the advantages of ledgering with those of normal float fishing. The simplest and best known method of float ledgering is widely known as 'laying-on'. Anglers often resort to laying-on when fish are responding to float tackle either in midwater or near the bottom. By changing style, they are able to fish the bottom itself to seek the more wily and larger specimens.

When laying-on, the float is raised to a position on the line about a foot or so greater than the water depth (measured with a plummet). When the tackle is cast into position the float fails to cock because the weights or shotting, lying in a heap on the bottom, exert no pull on the line. The line is then tightened with a turn or so of the reel, drawing the float towards the bank and at the same time taking up the slack between the float and the shotting. The shotting straightened out, the shots exert a downward pull on the float, which cocks somewhat obliquely.

This is a far finer presentation of the original tackle than simply float fishing with the bait on the bottom, because the float is now set well away from the bait. The line runs obliquely and is less likely to cause shy fish to become suspicious of the bait when it is well presented.

Modifying the tackle

Although a simple change to laying-on from normal float tackle can be very effective, you can improve your tackle with several modifications. The shotting can be rearranged to provide a

Right *Another simple float-ledger rig which combines float fishing with a ledgered bait.*
Below right *Two specimen roach caught by John Wilson using the laying-on style.*
Below *A swan shot ledger with an extremely sensitive peacock quill float which lies flat on the surface.*

more immediate reaction to bites or the float can be changed to suit the slightly different balances of forces now operating between float, shots, and current or wind. The combination of float and shotting should be varied to suit the widely varying water conditions met by the angler. Laying-on is just as effective with a light porcupine quill and a single shot in stillwaters as with a heavy cork or balsa-bodied antenna float with several shots in a light stream.

In the proper hands, laying-on tackle can be extremely sensitive and very effective. Bites are normally signified by a light trembling of the float, which eventually slides under, giving the angler ample time to tighten on a good fish. Good bream, roach and other species often succumb to laying-on techniques, and the method is particularly suited to fishing in slow and sluggish waters or in the stillwaters of lakes and ponds.

Below *A simple ledger rig constructed from swan shot and a nylon loop. The size of shot is exaggerated in this drawing.*

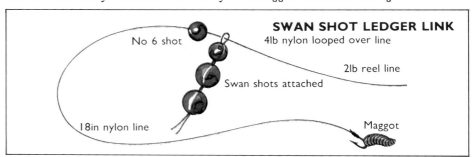

SWAN SHOT LEDGER LINK
No 6 shot
4lb nylon looped over line
2lb reel line
Swan shots attached
18in nylon line
Maggot

FLOAT LEDGER RIG

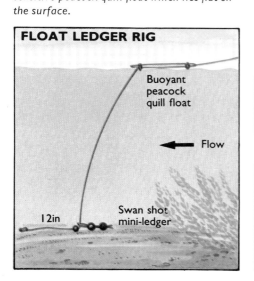

FLOAT LEDGER RIG
Buoyant peacock quill float
Flow
12in
Swan shot mini-ledger

LEDGERING

Once, ledgering was considered a crude and clumsy way of fishing, only resorted to when float fishing had failed to catch fish. Now, ledgering has a separate and valued status as a means of fishing, and the varied styles and techniques have led to the capture of many large fish.

Basically the method presents the bait on the bottom of a lake, reservoir, stream or river where coarse species such as bream, barbel, carp and tench often feed.

Link ledger

The technique known as link-ledgering has become extremely popular in recent years. For this, a 4in length of nylon, doubled, with shots attached and the line passing through the loop is the simplest method to use.

In stillwaters, after the lead has sunk, the line is tightened without moving the lead or bait and the rod placed in two rod rests with about 4in of the rod top submerged (except when a rod-tip bite indicator is being used): this counteracts wind, drift, or both. Bites are indicated by one of the indicators available.

Be prepared to strike

In river fishing it is sometimes advisable to hold the rod and so be prepared to strike quickly. The rod can be supported on one knee and the line held between thumb and forefinger so that a bite can be felt. The tip of the rod must be sensitive. With practice, a take by a fish will be distinguished from the natural movement of the tackle with the current.

The tackle can be cast into one spot and anchored there, but it usually pays to cover a larger area, particularly if the water is unfamiliar, by allowing a light rig such as a link-ledger (also known as a paternoster link) to roll across the bed. Cast down and across stream and cover a stretch with repeated arcs, moving downstream. The question of bite detection is of prime importance in ledgering. There are various methods of detecting a fish, but, of course, the most important one is the rod tip.

Leads

Rigs for ledgering vary according to river conditions and the bait being used. At *all* times the weight of the lead should be sufficient to do what is required but no more. When 'rolling the bottom' the amount of weight should be such that the bait (and lead) will roll *but only just,* and much experimenting is often necessary to get this right.

For holding the bottom in very fast water—where say, six SSG (swan) shots will not hold bottom—an Arlesey (a pear-shaped lead designed by Richard Walker) flattened with a hammer is ideal. Leads like the old-fashioned 'coffin' and running bullet set up resistance and should be avoided, although the former has much to recommend it if a swivel is pushed into one end and held in place by flattening the lead at that point. The line is then passed through the swivel.

Left *Ledgering from a quiet swim well hidden by vegetation. The angler must keep alert and ready to pick the rod up instantly.*
Below *Stillwater ledgering in diagram. Not shown is cover for the angler, whose silhouette should not appear on the fish's horizon.*
Inset *A simple ledger rig constructed from swan shot and a nylon loop. The size of shot is exaggerated in this drawing.*

LEDGERING IN STILLWATER

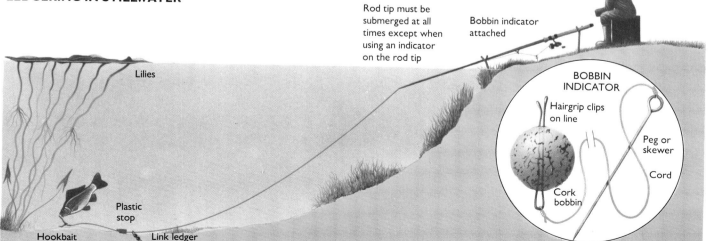

Rod tip must be submerged at all times except when using an indicator on the rod tip

Bobbin indicator attached

Lilies

Plastic stop

Hookbait

Link ledger

BOBBIN INDICATOR

Hairgrip clips on line

Peg or skewer

Cord

Cork bobbin

SPINNING

Spinning is the art of casting and retrieving a lure designed to look or act like a small fish, frog or mouse. Spinning is often a deadly method and most sea, game or coarse anglers find it necessary to use this method at times. Using a variety of spinner-spoons and plugs, anglers use it for a number of different species on waters throughout the country.

For young anglers, spinning is also one of the best methods. Armed with one or two plugs, a closed-face fixed-spool reel and a decent spinning rod, the novice will learn both to cast and to catch a sizeable fish.

When to spin?

Generally speaking, spinning is a good method for the open river where there are deep pools, or for large still-waters, gravel pits and reservoirs. One should not spin, if unskilled, in confined spaces, as retrieval will be difficult. If the river is overhung with much vegetation though it may hold good fish, bad casting will result in lost lures.

Choice of rod depends on the water more than anything else. On big rivers, gravel pits or reservoirs you may need a powerful, two-handed, stepped-up carp rod to throw biggish spoons, spinners or plugs a long way. In contrast, on small rivers, canals or ponds, short casts with a 7-8ft spinning rod of hollow glass for use with lines of 5-8lb b.s. may be adequate.

A certain amount of common sense is needed in choice of rod: big pike or salmon on a small river, for example, would need a powerful line, from 10lb –20lb b.s.

Reels for spinning

The choice of reels is legion. It is possible, though, for the experienced angler to spin directly from a top-class centrepin. With plugs you can pull off loops of line from the rod rings, while for sizeable plugs and heavy spinners you may use a multiplying reel. Multipliers are accurate on short to moderate casts, but difficult to use for light baits.

Other than for light spinning, closed-face reels are rarely used. For playing heavy fish they prove to be ineffective since the line within the housing goes through too many angles, creating considerable friction. Many open-faced fixed-spool reels are, however, superb. One with a roller pick-up and a reliable, easily reached anti-reverse switch is especially useful.

Right Spinning for perch in winter. This careful angler is keeping well out of sight behind bankside cover.

The species of fish also governs the choice of rod, reel and line. In weedy water, like the Fenland drains, you need heavy line and a powerful rod to hold the fish. The same applies to heavy fish in small waters. On the other hand, when perch or chub fishing, a MK IV carp rod, or its lighter version, the Avon, in glass or split cane, is excellent.

The wide range of rods and reels provides great versatility of spinning techniques. Lines are also varied, but a good standard line is a simple nylon, usually dyed dark in colour, and supple. Some anglers use plaited nylon, particularly on multiplying reels, but monofil generally has more stretch.

Wire traces

For fish with sharp teeth you may need a wire trace on the line. This applies particularly to pike and zander and many sea fish, but not when spinning for game fish, or coarse fish such as perch or chub.

Minimum of equipment

At the waterside, remember that you are always on the move, so a minimum of equipment is advisable. A small ruck-sack on your back is best, to hold food and waterproof clothing, and an angler's waistcoat with numerous pockets for spinners, spoons and miscellaneous items of tackle such as a spring balance, forceps for removing lures from fishes' jaws, a sharpening stone for blunted hooks, scissors and other small items, will prove useful.

Where to cast

Where to cast? First, with a sinking spinner, find out the depth of water working on the principle of retrieving

Right A spinning rig which uses a plastic vane to prevent the spinning lure from kinking the line. The Wye lead also forms an anti-kink unit as well as providing weight to keep the lure down.

slow and deep. Cast out and allow the spinner or spoon to sink with the pick-up off, and judge the time it takes the spinner to strike the bottom. As the spinner nears the bank, raise the rod top to avoid the lure running into the slope. Casting in a fan-wise fashion, each cast being some five degrees to the side of the previous cast, is also used, but this can make for boring fishing, except from an anchored boat. It is probably better to cast where you think the predator will be.

In winter, when the sky is blue, the air a shade above freezing and the frost crunches under the boots, spinning for perch is possibly the perfect fishing method. The feet and body keep warm, the tackle is at a minimum, and the only caution to be taken is that of keeping bank vibration down. A slither on frozen mud can be a disaster.

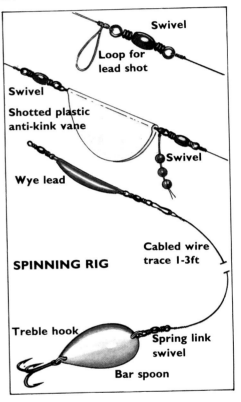

Swivel

Loop for lead shot

Swivel

Shotted plastic anti-kink vane

Swivel

Wye lead

Cabled wire trace 1-3ft

SPINNING RIG

Treble hook

Spring link swivel

Bar spoon

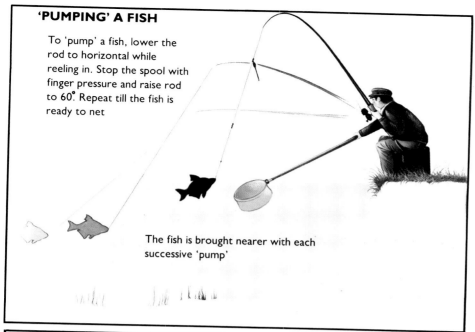

'PUMPING' A FISH

To 'pump' a fish, lower the rod to horizontal while reeling in. Stop the spool with finger pressure and raise rod to 60°. Repeat till the fish is ready to net

The fish is brought nearer with each successive 'pump'

Left The angler lowers the rod while reeling in. As he lifts it, reeling in stops. Called pumping, the cycle is repeated until the fish is netted. Below left How to control an active fish, using either a fixed-spool or centrepin reel.

increase finger pressure on the spool rim and bring up the rod to its former position. Repeat the process until the fish runs again or is ready for the net.

It is now—at the point of netting—that most mistakes occur. When the fish is played out, the net is placed in the water, ready for use. With the fish wallowing or lying on the surface, bring the rod tip down to waist level once more, and, with the other hand holding the net, draw the rod back over the shoulder, maintaining strong pressure on the spool all the time. Steady the net about 12in below the surface and draw the fish towards and over it. Do not lift until it is over the net.

Two rules of netting
Sometimes, as the fish is drawn to the net, it will suddenly find new strength and either swim off or change direction. Let it do so for it is unlikely to take line. Keep the finger on the spool and allow the rod to take the strain. Two important points must be remembered: first, as the fish comes over the net make sure that the rod is no farther back than 30 degrees to the vertical. If it is, you will not have complete control over the fish. Secondly, never move the net towards the fish but keep it still and pull the fish over it.

Problem fish
The problem of the fish that runs into weed is one that requires swift action. Some fish, especially roach and chub, however quick one's reflexes are, will manage to transfer the hook to the weed and escape. Other species, barbel and tench in particular, are not so clever and must be extracted from the weed by 'pumping'. As soon as the fish reaches the weed, use the technique described earlier, repeating the process without stopping and keeping the finger down hard on the spool. Once the fish starts to move, keep control of the situation with continual pumping, as this will, in the majority of cases, get the fish out of the weed. This technique relies on knowing how much pressure your line will take—that only comes with experience.

The clue to the safe netting of any fish is a simple one: never, never lunge the net into the water as the fish is drawn towards it. The bigger the fish, and therefore the stronger it is, the greater the danger of losing it in a moment of panic.

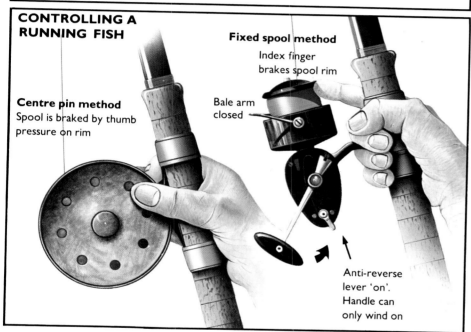

CONTROLLING A RUNNING FISH

Centre pin method
Spool is braked by thumb pressure on rim

Fixed spool method
Index finger brakes spool rim

Bale arm closed

Anti-reverse lever 'on'. Handle can only wind on

PLAYING AND LANDING

Despite thousands of words of sound advice from fishing writers on the subject of playing and landing, many fish are nevertheless lost by anglers who lack this basic skill. The most common weak spots are: little or no understanding of the slipping clutch on the frequently used fixed-spool reel, and not knowing how to coax out a fish that has run into weed (which can happen to the most experienced angler).

Slipping clutch
Before making the first cast, hold the rod in one hand and place one finger lightly on the edge of the spool. With the other hand take hold of the end of the line and pull as hard as possible. The clutch should not slip. If it does so before reaching maximum pressure the clutch is set too loose, while if the line

breaks the clutch is too tight. With the spool set correctly it is impossible for a running fish to break the line, providing, that is, that everything else is done properly. When a fish is hooked, immediately apply one finger of the rod hand to the rim of the spool. In this way, when the rod is held at an angle of between 15 and 30 degrees to the vertical, maximum pressure is brought to bear on the running fish. The line will be almost at breaking point but, if the slipping clutch is correctly set, will not actually break.

Pumping and netting
When the fish stops its run, line is recovered by the process known as 'pumping'. For this, assuming the fish is stationary or nearly so, turn the reel handle, at the same time lowering the rod until the tip is at waist level. Then

SEA FISHING

The sea holds a vast variety of fishes, many of which are sought by the saltwater angler. Britain's coastline offers every kind of sea fishing from rocks, beaches, sea walls, harbour walls, piers; while the off-shore waters attract huge numbers of anglers in charter-boats and their own vessels.

Sea fishing tackle is, of necessity, stronger and more durable than the delicate and sensitive equipment of many coarse fishermen. Jibes from 'non-sea-anglers about 'block-and-tackle' methods of sea anglers are based on an ignorance of the power of the sea and its fishes. There are times when 10lb b.s. line can be used, but in general 15-20lb b.s. is needed simply because the pull of the tide and the nature of the seabed demand that line be of a diameter to combat erosion from sand and the often-sharp teeth of fish. Playing a large cod, or infuriated conger, some 100ft below in a 3 or 4 knot tide, especially for the newcomer to sea fishing, means that a great deal of strain will be put on angler and tackle.

As with the coarse fishes, a few species have had to be omitted. You will at some time or another hook black bream, dabs, one of the colourful gurnards and from close inshore perhaps a mullet, or from brackish esturial waters a flounder. Most of the flatfish have bites that send vibrations up the line as a signal. Mullet are shy, suspicious fish that can sometimes be tempted to take bread paste fished on very light float-fishing tackle.

A decade ago, when Leslie Moncrieff popularised beachcasting with his famous lay-back style, he started what has become an artform in itself. Now, beach casters vie with each other in competitions of distance casting and the rods have become specialist weapons in the angler's armoury. In extreme cases, distance casting in competitions has become divorced from fishing.

Deep-sea fishing for large shark uses tackle that in some cases would haul a fair-sized boat from the water —if the angler's arms were strong enough. But whatever kind of sea fishing, indeed *any* fishing at all, that you decide to follow, never be too humble to seek the advice of those with experience. At sea, the skipper's decisions are always final. The sea must be treated with the greatest of respect for it can change very quickly from a pleasant rocking, lulling the angler into an afternoon snooze, to a very nasty white-horse sea. So if the skipper says 'OK, lads, reel in, I think the weather's turning', don't argue!

There is a wide diversity of fishes in the sea, and for the angler the great unknown is that when he lets his line down to the seabed or casts out from the shore he never knows whether his bait will be taken by something stronger than he is! When that sudden, mighty tug pulls the rod over in your hands and you either give line or break it, sea fishing's excitement becomes real.

Clothing for the sea fisherman must be of good quality, for the sea is a corrosive element and quickly spoils anything left wet. The rule is always have weatherproof, warm clothing with you even if it is a nice, sunny, summer morning when you set out. Britain's weather is not as reliable as some lucky parts of the world, and when you are 15 miles out in a boat that can only do 5 knots, you may well spend a couple of very cold, wet hours on the way in.

Perhaps food and sea sickness should not be discussed in the same section of this introduction. But wholesome food and warm drinks are essential to a day's pleasurable fishing at sea. Many anglers, the author is one of them, seem to feel perpetually hungry while out in a boat and that hunger must be assuaged if the day is to be enjoyed. But a hot summer's day and a cold winter's one both require adequate drinks to be available—preferably not spirits or fizzy beer.

A word here about sea sickness. There are anglers who never set foot on a boat, but who just go beach and pier fishing, and it may not be believable, but even some of them always feel sea sick! There really is no cure, but one of continual involvement in fishing at sea. The advice to the newcomer, out in a boat for the first time and suddenly feeling 'wrong', is to wrap up warmly, sit still and keep the eyes on the horizon. Sea sickness stems from the motion of fluids in the inner ear, where the organs of balance are situated, and if one can convince one's body that things are quite normal, the horizon nice and flat, the feeling may pass. The pills available from chemists do work, but must be taken well before setting out and on top of a good meal—preferably not too fatty.

Records are kept, of course, and in the official rod-caught list there are over 100 different species. These record fishes span a remarkable range in weight from the vast 851lb tunny caught off Scarborough in 1933 to the tiny $\frac{1}{4}$oz sea stickleback hooked in Poole Harbour in 1978.

The tunny record is not likely to be broken, for this species has not been seen for decades. But the huge 226lb common skate, the incredibly powerful 109lb 6oz conger, the 500lb mako shark—all these records will surely fall. It may be your turn to suddenly find the rod and fish fighting *you*, while you hang on, strength draining from tired muscles and the skipper holding you back in the boat.

Sea fishing is exciting, fun, challenging, rewarding, healthy, and really is a get-away-from-it-pastime. Added to that is the fact that, unlike the coarse fisherman, you can eat pretty well all you catch. And you will receive a royal welcome home!

That's sea fishing!

CHAPTER 5
THE FISH

SHARK

Considering the fighting qualities of the various species of shark liable to be taken in British waters, and the weight to which they go, the following types of tackle are recommended so that each would allow the fish to give the best sport: blue shark—30lb-class tackle; porbeagle—50lb-class tackle; mako, thresher and large porbeagle—80lb-class rod and reel. Each one of these tackle classes can be reduced to a lower one with increasing experience in catching shark.

The terminal tackle, because of the size of baits used and the size of sharks' mouths, should consist of large 6/0 to 10/0 good-quality hooks; attached to a biting length of 2 to 2.5mm diameter braided wire, because a shark's teeth are liable to cut through anything else. The biting length, 2 to 3ft long, should be attached to a further 10ft of slightly thinner, similar wire or longliner's monofilament nylon to withstand the abrasive action of the shark's skin.

Bait

Bait in shark fishing consists of whole fish used either singly if the fish is large,

or in number if they are small. The favourite bait is mackerel which as a shoal fish probably represents the commonest natural food of sharks. However, any other species may be used and many sharks have been taken on pouting or pollack. Various methods of mounting the bait are used with the head or tail pointing up the trace. Each method should ensure that the bait does not come off when first taken, for sharks rarely swallow the bait at once. Natural presentation is not essential, for the movement of the bait should give off the erratic vibrations of an injured or sick fish.

The off-the-bottom rule

Since sharks are usually mid-water or surface fish, the bait should be fished off the bottom. This is achieved by attaching a float, either a balloon or square of polystyrene, to the line once the depth set for the bait has been reached. The float should always be as small as possible so as not to produce resistance once the bait is taken. This off-the-bottom rule on bait presentation is not absolute, for many sharks are taken with bait on the bottom fished as

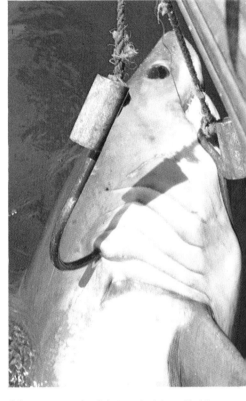

A large spent shark being double gaffed for safety. Such a fish is dangerous still.

Below *A balloon tether-float and the necessary wire trace are used in this shark rig. The balloon sets the bait at a predetermined depth.*

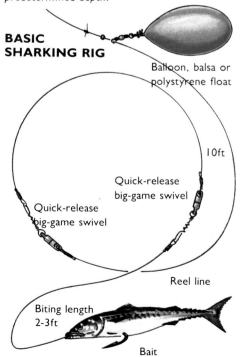

BASIC SHARKING RIG

Balloon, balsa or polystyrene float

10ft

Quick-release big-game swivel

Quick-release big-game swivel

Reel line

Biting length 2-3ft

Bait

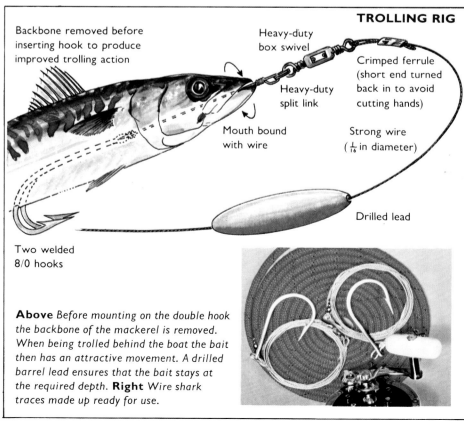

Backbone removed before inserting hook to produce improved trolling action

TROLLING RIG

Heavy-duty box swivel

Crimped ferrule (short end turned back in to avoid cutting hands)

Heavy-duty split link

Mouth bound with wire

Strong wire ($\frac{1}{16}$ in diameter)

Drilled lead

Two welded 8/0 hooks

Above *Before mounting on the double hook the backbone of the mackerel is removed. When being trolled behind the boat the bait then has an attractive movement. A drilled barrel lead ensures that the bait stays at the required depth.* **Right** *Wire shark traces made up ready for use.*

a simple but very strong flowing trace.

The methods of fishing for sharks depend very much on the area, the wind and tides, and both drifting and fishing at anchor are successful. It is an exciting, brutal sport, and at times dangerous.

TOPE

The tope is a strong, slim-bodied member of the shark family and is found all around our coasts. The fact that it frequents shallow water facilitates the use of light tackle and permits the tope to show its superb fighting qualities.

How to hook tope

Tope pick up a bait and run a short distance before pausing to turn and swallow it. A ledger rig, therefore, is the most suitable terminal tackle as it allows the fish to seize the bait and move off with it without feeling drag or pressure. The fish should not be struck until it commences its second run, unless a very small bait is being used.

One method is to use an all-wire trace of 40lb b.s. Its overall length is 4ft because anything longer causes serious problems in casting. It is joined to a shock leader of 30lb test and then to the main line. The sinker is attached to a free running swivel on the shock leader, which permits the fish to take line freely.

That essential wire

A similar trace is also used except that the short wire hook-link is followed by heavy monofilament of at least 40lb test. Tope have sharp teeth so a short-wire link to the hook is essential. Their skin is as rough as glass paper when rubbed against the grain, and as they have a tendency to roll up on the trace, light nylon will part like thread. All-wire is therefore safer, but heavy nylon is preferred since it is more flexible and fishes better.

It should, however, be changed after each fish as it becomes unreliable due to abrasion and chafing. Hook sizes will depend on the size of the bait used, but are normally 6/0 to 9/0. They should be razor sharp.

RUBBY DUBBY

Rubby dubby, a word coined in Cornwall in the 1950s when shark fishing as a sport began to expand in British waters, is a foul-smelling concoction used as a shark attractor. In America, 'chumming'—throwing chopped up pieces of fish into the water—had long been used to attract tuna and other species of giant game fish.

The best dubby is made from oily pilchards, herring and mackerel,

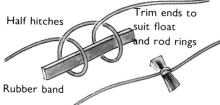

Half hitches · Trim ends to suit float and rod rings · Rubber band

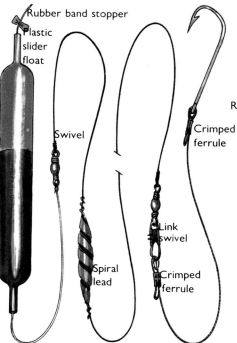

Rubber band stopper · Plastic slider float · Swivel · Spiral lead · Swivel · Crimped ferrule · Link swivel · Crimped ferrule

Above *A large tope being returned to the sea.* **Left** *How to apply a rubber stopper on the line.* **Below** *When tope fishing from a boat, either a slider float rig or a straight ledger rig is ideal depending on the nature of the seabed. When a large tope is hooked all other anglers should reel in to avoid tangle as tope often circle the boat.*

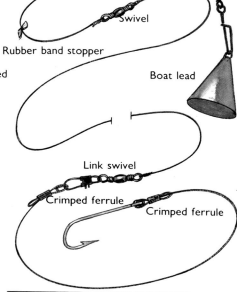

Clements boom · Swivel · Rubber band stopper · Boat lead · Link swivel · Crimped ferrule · Crimped ferrule

pounded to a pulp with a blunt instrument. Fish offal and unwanted fish are constantly added and some skippers introduce bran to thicken it up. Blood collected from slaughterhouses is also a popular ingredient but contrary to belief it does not stay in a liquid state, due to it being a coagulant. It then resembles jelly, and is a useful additive to existing rubby dubby. Occasionally it is kept separate and after a good stir ladled directly into the sea with an old saucepan.

A word of warning to those prone to sea sickness. If you are beginning to feel 'doubtful'—stay right away from the rubby dubby bin. If there is one certainty in sea fishing it is that your 'doubtful' tummy will have its mind made up for it immediately.

A tub of extremely smelly but highly efficient rubby dubby. Not for the squeamish.

COD

Big cod can be caught from all coastal waters of the British Isles, both from boats and the shore. Being a greedy fish it can be caught on a variety of baits and tackle. Kent and East Coast cod, for example, feed mainly on lugworm, while farther west squid and mackerel-strip are used as the most effective bait. To catch cod consistently one must know and understand the baits and rigs which are most effective in the various localities. Large black lugworm are best fished on a one- or two-hook paternoster rig.

Secrets of success

The paternoster allows the worm to hang clear of the sea bed in full view of the hunting cod packs. Squid and fish cuttings work well when presented on running-ledger tackle. A single-hook ledger is recommended, but many successful cod anglers fish with one or two flyers above the main hook. The argument against the multi-hook ledger is that most of the cod that take squid or fish-strip baits tend to be heavyweight fish and the combined weight of these fish—two or even three 20lb cod at one time—would make a tackle breakage almost inevitable.

In northern waters cod, or better still codling, can often be caught in vast numbers on large white-feathered hooks. These are basically an enlarged version of the standard mackerel feathers. Cod-sized feathers can be very effective, especially when each hook is tipped with a slice of mackerel or squid strip. Cod feathers can be fished by lowering to the required depth and then raising and lowering the rod tip just as with mackerel feathers.

Anglers first realized cod were attracted to white-coloured objects when hundreds of cod were found when gutted to contain pieces of plastic cups thrown from cross-Channel ferries. Experiments soon proved that white feathers and spoons gave the angler an advantage.

BASIC COD RIGS

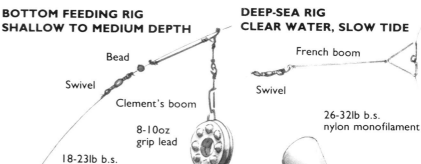

Ledger rig

Basic two-boom Paternoster

Combination Paternoster and running ledger

Buoyant rig

BOTTOM FEEDING RIG
SHALLOW TO MEDIUM DEPTH

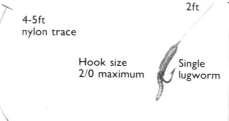

Bead

Swivel

Clement's boom

8-10oz grip lead

18-23lb b.s. nylon monofilament

4-5ft nylon trace

2ft

Hook size 2/0 maximum

Single lugworm

Hook size 4/0 or 5/0

Squid bait

Above and left *Various cod rigs.* **Right** *A squid/lugworm 'cocktail' bait, at times very killing for winter cod.* **Below** *Lawrence Emmet, a Cornish sea angler, took this 37lb cod from a western wreck mark.*

DEEP-SEA RIG
CLEAR WATER, SLOW TIDE

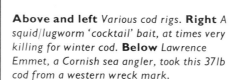

French boom

Swivel

26-32lb b.s. nylon monofilament

6ft

3lb cone lead

POLLACK DRIG RIG

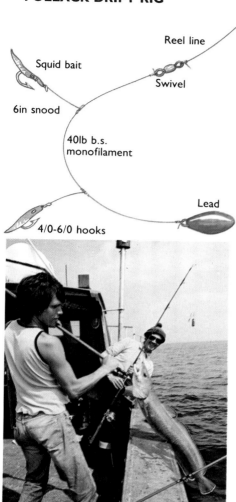

POLLACK

The pollack is a fish that, when hooked, has an exhilarating first run. With the pollack, terms such as 'power dive' seem appropriate. This member of the cod family can be one of our most sporting fishes provided it is taken over a suitable habitat and on tackle that responds to the fish's movements.

During high summer, pollack provide good sport for boat fishermen, but until mid-October those fish coming close to land are rather small. Fish that live in deepwater wrecks are present throughout the year, but the population dramatically increases from the beginning of November, when the residents are joined by migratory shoals.

Deep-water marks

Many wrecks beyond the 40-fathom line, about 20 miles offshore, hold thousands of large fish during the winter, and provide spectacular sport. Between December and March the females grow heavy with roe. A pollack weighing 18lb in December may, by the end of February, be close to the British boat-caught record weight of 25lb. There are three kinds of boat fishing: inshore, offshore, and reef and wreck. Each demands a completely different approach and to find specimens in numbers requires quite a lot of dedication.

Light-tackle pollack fishing in shallow water is exciting during the autumn and early winter. In the western English Channel from Torbay to Land's End, pollack up to 14lb are caught within a few hundred yards of land—sometimes in less than four fathoms. While specimen fish can come from any patch of rocky ground, fishing off prominent headlands, where the tide runs strongly, is the best for consistent sport.

For inshore fishing, most experts favour a 10ft fast taper, hollow glass spinning rod, matched with a small multiplier loaded with 10-12lb b.s. monofilament. It is essential to choose a

Above A 14lb pollack caught close inshore at Mevagissey, Cornwall. Above right A rig suitable for drift fishing for pollack. Right The ling, a long-bodied relative of the cod, is a fierce predator of the depths. Large ling often need to be gaffed by two anglers when being brought aboard.

soft line with a small diameter. End tackle for anchored or drift fishing is a 12ft trace worked from a single wire boom—commonly known as the 'flying collar' rig.

Obviously, some consideration must be given to the length of trace that can be handled from whatever boat you are fishing from. A fixed boom, of twisted stainless steel wire or swivelled brass, can be built into the rig. Its purpose is to keep the hook trace standing off the reel line when the gear is being lowered, for all too often a simple nylon paternoster will tangle the bait around the reel line if lowered too fast. A weak nylon sinker link of about 3ft is ideal.

Down to the fish

The rig is lowered to the reef or wreck and stopped immediately any solid ground or obstruction is felt, and the line is wound back a couple of turns. This will allow the bait to swim freely just above the habitat. Sooner or later, the weight will be held fast, but breaking out will only mean losing the lead.

The presentation of the bait is critical. A great lump of mackerel or herring can never be as attractive as a properly cut and mounted bait. An attractive bait is a diagonal lask of fish about 6in long and tied to the hook with elasticated thread, so that it is not easily torn from the hook.

LING

The ling is another member of the cod family, although at first sight one might think it more closely resembles the conger. It has a long, slimy, eel-like body but the head and back are broad and its coloration, spineless fins, bar-

bules and very small scales are telling indications that it is a member of the great family of the Gadidae.

Seeking ling

When fishing from an anchored position for ling, a simple ledger rig is very effective. As conger are found on the same ground it is advisable to use a short 6-9in wire link to the hook, for conger are likely to sever an all-monofilament trace. When fishing on the drift there is a risk of conger taking the bait. Wire is also recommended when wreck fishing as ling will be found on the bottom together with conger. If you are seeking ling, another hazard when fishing wrecks are the shoals of very large pollack. The difficulty here is trying to get a large bait down without it being taken.

Because of their predatory lifestyle, ling are best caught by using whole, small fish about 4–6in long. Pouting, mackerel, whiting or herring, on a 6/0 or 9/0 hook, are ideal. The tackle must be strong enough to cope with conger for they are found in the same habitat.

TURBOT

The turbot is a shallow-water fish, rarely taken in depths of over 40 fathoms. Records compiled over the past 20 years show that all catches were made on or close to sandbanks, in water of between 4 and 12 fathoms. The favourite environment of the turbot is around sandbanks situated in deep water, where sandeels, sprats and other immature fish abound.

Muddy or gravelly bottoms in the estuaries of large rivers, where young fish are usually present, also hold an attraction for these large flatfish. Big specimens are taken off the many wrecks off Devon and Cornwall and littering the sandy bays around the south west and west coasts of Ireland. Many small turbot up to 4lb are taken by the surf caster baiting with mackerel strips.

The species is almost entirely fish-eating, obvious from its large mouth and sharp teeth. Considering its bulk, the turbot is a surprisingly strong and rapid swimmer. Sandeels and sprats are the chief food, and in addition small flatfish, whiting and pouting—in fact, any small fry—are readily taken. Worms or crustaceans are rarely found in the stomach contents.

The record turbot (boat) is 33lb 12oz, taken in Lannacombe Bay, near Salcombe in South Devon, by Roger Simcox in 1980. The current shore fishing record is a magnificent fish of 28lb 8oz, caught by J D Dorling at Dunwich Beach, Suffolk.

Baits for turbot

Bait is important. Without doubt, sandeels are the favourite diet of the turbot and brill. These species are not alone in their weakness for sandeels, for mackerel also chase them until whole areas of the sea boil in the efforts of the prey to escape. To represent the sandeel, filleted flanks from a freshly caught mackerel make excellent turbot and brill baits. Strips an inch wide are cut the full length and the hook turned twice through one end only so that the free section moves realistically in the tide.

A main line of 35lb b.s. is advised,

Below *A very thinly cut strip of mackerel resembles a sandeel, which forms part of the turbot's diet. The long 'tail' flutters in the tide to attract feeding flatfish such as turbot, brill and plaice.*

while traces and hook snood should be 50lb b.s., for turbot laying back against the tide can quickly bite through lighter line with their sharp teeth.

Three distinct types of terminal tackle are recommended, all based on the conviction that turbot and brill respond to a moving bait.

The first is a two-hook, long flowing trace, the main line passing through a running boom with lead attached. The fish can pick up and swim away with the bait without feeling the resistance of the weight. The trace, roughly 6ft long, can be clipped to a link swivel which has been attached to the end of the main line.

In a strong tide, a sink-and-draw technique can be used with a single hook on a 6ft length of nylon on a link swivel. The weight is attached to the main line. The same rig, with a float above the lead, can be fished in a light tide.

When hooked in a strong tide the turbot will put up a doughty struggle on a balanced rig.

TWO-HOOK LEDGER RIG

Monofilament trace 6ft 50lb b.s.

Monofilament reel line 35lb b.s.

Link swivel

Bead

Running boom

Lead size enough to trot bait downtide

Below *Two specimen turbot weighing 32lb 3oz and 31lb and 4oz, caught by Derrick Dyar fishing a reef 21 miles SE of Plymouth, Devon.*

Blood loop

Hook size 6/0-7/0

Hook snood

Stop knot
Stop bead

Below *A slider float allows accurate drift fishing with the sink-and-draw style. The spiral lead helps prevent the bait spinning.* **Left** *the running ledger rig is used when fishing a sandbank while at anchor.*

Sliding float removed to fish sink and draw

SINK AND DRAW OR SLIDING FLOAT RIG

Spiral lead bent into half moon to stop spinning

Link swivel

PLAICE

Plaice do not grow to great size and the rod-caught record is a fish of 10lb 3¾oz, boated by H Gardiner fishing in Longa Sound, Scotland, in 1974. Professional trawlers frequently take bigger fish than this, often well into double figures, but the rod and line angler can usually count himself lucky if he takes fish in the 3-4lb range. For this reason a light hollow glass rod in the 20lb class is to be recommended, providing leads of over 12oz are not going to be used.

For terminal tackle a trace should be used when the tide is running, but paternoster gear is favoured on sluggish tides or slack water. If using a trace, it should be about 8ft long, either fished through a Clement's boom or a Kilmore boom.

Lugworm bait

If baiting with lugworm, a long-shanked hook, No 2 or 1, is quite large enough. Use three hooks together, as it is not unusual to take more than one fish at a time. This is often because, even if you are holding the rod when the plaice swallows the worm, no bite is detected due to them swallowing the baited hook and remaining still. It is only when you lift the rod tip that you realize that a fish has in fact taken the bait.

Fish caught like this are usually deeply hooked. If, however, a bite is felt it is usually only a light tap, tap, and should be left for the fish to gorge the bait. To avoid the temptation of striking too soon, it is best not even to hold the rod.

SOLE

Although the rod-caught record sole was a fish of 5lb 7oz, caught by L Dixon from an Alderney, Channel Islands, breach in 1980, most fish encountered when rod and line fishing are under 2¼lb, with the majority between 8oz and 1½lb, so heavy gear is completely unnecessary. As most sole fishing is

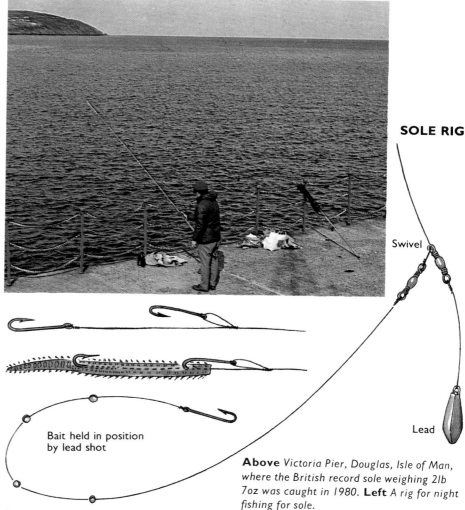

Bait held in position by lead shot

SOLE RIG

Swivel

Lead

Above *Victoria Pier, Douglas, Isle of Man, where the British record sole weighing 2lb 7oz was caught in 1980.* **Left** *A rig for night fishing for sole.*

done on quiet summer nights, the lightest possible beachcasters can be used with a line of under 15lb b.s. If the venue demands long casting, then the nylon-type paternoster rig should be used to achieve a good distance, but in other areas a stainless steel paternoster gives the best results. Soles, like all other members of the flatfish family, are attracted by glitter.

Hooks should be long-shanked to

Right *Thin strips of squid are good baits for plaice and sole.* **Below** *Typical sole habitat of sand and mud.*

make unhooking easier, as the fish usually gorges the hook. The hook should be no larger than a size 6. The best bait depends on the worm commonest in the area. For instance, if there are extensive lugworm beds in or near the fishing area, lugworm is the obvious bait; if the main worm in the area is ragworm, then this should be used.

Razorfish Mussel bed

CONGER

Above *Evidence of the massive size a conger can reach. This monster, hooked off the Eddystone Reef, weighed 109lb 6oz and holds the British rod-caught boat record.*

Conger fishing can be one of the most exciting forms of saltwater angling, whether practised from a boat or from shore. From the beginning of a trip when the bait first enters the water until the first tentative 'knock' on the line, the tension grows—for there is no way of knowing at this stage just how big a fish is mouthing the bait. Next comes the excitement of the strike and playing the fish, for this is no tame, easy-to-catch species. Even when the conger is on the surface of the water there is still the task of finally landing or boating it.

When the angler goes fishing for a species that has a rod-and-line record of 109lb 6oz from a boat, and a shore record of 67lb 1oz, it is obvious that the tackle must be suitable for a large fish.

The choice of reel is most important. A strong multiplier or large centrepin is essential. A rod that will stand the shocks from the lunges of a big fish, yet is flexible enough to play the fish out, is also necessary.

The type of line used will depend on where the conger fishing is done. In shallow water the braided lines are extremely sensitive and give a feel of the movements of the fish.

Wire traces are needed, and the stronger the better, to prevent the conger's jaws from biting through the line, and also to grasp firmly when landing the fish. A conger can twist a trace around a gaff and break 60lb wire as if it were cotton thread. The wire trace should therefore be of at least 100lb strength, and about a foot long.

As a large bait is more often used, a size 9/0 or 10/0 hook is needed. The conger is more readily hooked in the jaw with a large hook. With the swivelled hooks, sometimes sold as suitable for conger fishing, the angler may find that the fish ejects the hook with the bait or swallows the bait, together with the hook, deep inside itself.

Conger tackle

The best tackle when shore fishing for conger is a good rod, a reliable reel loaded with at least 30lb-strength line with a strong wire trace, and a hook at least 6/0 baited with an oily fish bait or squid. A running boom placed on the main line above the trace should have the lead weight attached to it by some lighter line, as this enables the angler to retrieve the remainder of the tackle if the lead gets jammed on the bottom. This is one of the hazards that conger fishermen have to endure. Wherever this sort of fishing is done—from the shore, over the reefs, or when wrecking—congers and snagging ground go together, and the angler must be prepared for many tackle losses.

Boat fishing for conger

Boat fishing for conger employs similar techniques, but the fish are usually larger. Wreck fishing almost inevitably produces the biggest specimens. It is advisable to leave the locations of these marks to the professional charter skippers who have the equipment to locate the wrecks, and the knowledge to anchor their boats in the right place for anglers to fish into them.

PREPARING A MACKEREL SOFT BAIT

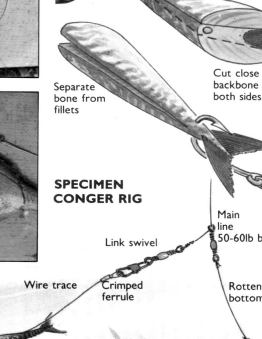

Remove head

Cut close to backbone on both sides

Separate bone from fillets

SPECIMEN CONGER RIG

Main line 50-60lb b.s.

Link swivel

Wire trace

Crimped ferrule

No 10/0 hook

Mackerel bait

Rotten bottom

Left Mackerel in a number of forms is the most effective conger-catching bait. The terminal tackle and rod must be able to withstand sheer, brute force from a fighting conger. The fight can be long and bruising for the angler. Below A rotten-bottom length of less b.s. than the reel line. When the lead is snagged it will break and avoid loss of other expensive terminal tackle.

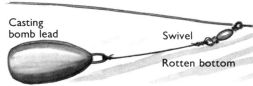

Casting bomb lead

Swivel

Rotten bottom

The boat has to be positioned uptide, at just the right distance for the baits to reach the fish. A stout boat rod, with 50lb monofilament on a heavy duty multiplier reel is recommended. You can use the same end tackle with a Clement's boom or a large swivel to which the lead weight is attached. This weight is at least 1lb and sometimes has to be heavier if the tide is a strong one. Between the end of the main line and the wire traces, use a strong link swivel which will act as a quick release if the fish is deeply hooked. You should also have spare traces ready.

The bait is either a small whole mackerel or half a very large one. A small mackerel is baited-up by taking the point of the hook into the mouth and bringing the barbed end out between its eyes. Conger seize a fish-bait head first, so the hook should always be at the head end.

When the conger takes

When a bite is felt, it is best to start winding your line in slowly until you feel the weight of the fish. There are two good reasons for doing this. First the line will be tightened ready for the next move, and second, if the fish is only nibbling at the bait, its movement away from the conger will cause an even more enthusiastic attack on it.

Get the fish clear off the bottom. In most cases in deep water there is no need to strike as the fish will hook itself as it turns towards the bottom. Very often the fish will come up quite easily. It is often possible to get the fish half-way to the surface before it realizes that something is wrong and starts to fight.

Tenacious conger

Conger demand respect. Tenacious of life, many are as dangerous after a couple hours out of the water as when fighting the angler, as is borne out by the number of commercial and sporting fishermen who have been injured handling fish they thought to be dead.

Even when thought safe in the bottom of a boat, congers will try to escape, and at least three fish—the biggest being 42lb—have been known to fling themselves back over the gunwale.

Giant conger

The largest authenticated conger ever caught weighed 250lb and was captured in a trawl off the Westman Islands near Iceland. It is probable, however, that some fish grow to as much as 350lb. So the angler has few fiercer adversaries than this brutal fighter.

Specimen conger weighing over 50lb are commonly found in wrecks, and on rocky ground. Both types of mark produce heavy fish, although most specimens are taken from wrecks. In the period 1966-72, many thousands of large eels were caught by anglers fishing off Brixham, Plymouth and, to a lesser extent, near Mevagissey.

The latter port was developed as a wreck fishing centre after 1971, and although excellent fish have been taken, its full potential for congering has yet to be exploited. Older marks include the dozens of wrecks lying under 40 fathoms of water in Lyme Bay in Dorset.

Left *Two conger rigs. All booms and swivels must be heavy duty.* **Below** *The gaff must be stout and applied firmly when bringing a large conger on board.*

CONGER FISHING RIGS

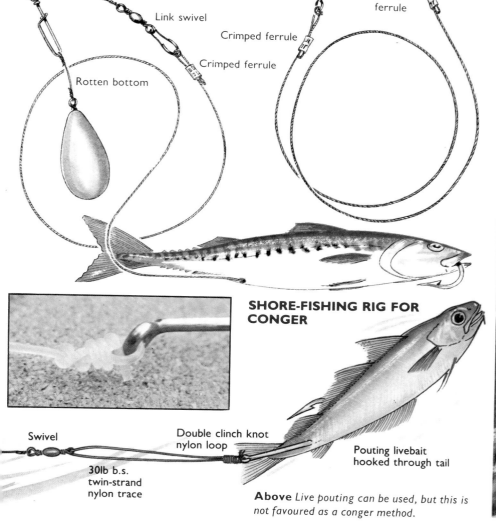

Main line 30lb b.s.

Rotten bottom

Single sliding boom

Link swivel

Main line 50lb b.s.

Crimped ferrule

Crimped ferrule

Crimped ferrule

Rotten bottom

SHORE-FISHING RIG FOR CONGER

Swivel

Double clinch knot nylon loop

30lb b.s. twin-strand nylon trace

Pouting livebait hooked through tail

Above *Live pouting can be used, but this is not favoured as a conger method.*

SKATE

Skates are massive fishes, far larger than any of the British rays and almost as heavy as any fish that swims in our seas. The angler is concerned with three species—the common skate, the white skate, and the long-nosed skate.

The white skate is the biggest of the three with a maximum weight in excess of 500lb. It grows to 8ft in length, and has a wingspan of 5ft. The common skate is altogether smaller, weighing up to 400lb with excellent rod-caught specimens less than 200lb. The long-nosed skate has similar dimensions.

The problem with all skates and rays is positive identification. There is much confusion and controversy as to the characteristics of the three British skates. The common skate, which is not at all common in some places, is often confused with the white skate. It is suggested by some fish biologists that most of the larger common skate hooked in Ireland were in fact whites. This raises the whole question of record fish: how many were really the common, white or long-nosed skate that their captors claimed? Any fish thought to better current records should be identified by experts, not left to fishermen whose judgement might be clouded by the prospect of a record fish. Many specimens need close scientific examination before a correct decision can be made and the fish authenticated.

The favourite habitat of big skate is broken ground interspersed with sandy patches and deep-water channels, par-

Below Checking the weight of a large thornback ray. The spiny tail can wound.

ticularly those with a sandy, muddy bottom. If there is a good population of lesser spotted dogfish, the chance of specimens is better.

Fishing for specimen skate—fish in excess of 100lb—requires good tackle from reel to hook. The rod should be very powerful, preferably of the type where the top joint locks into a solid screw-winch fitting on the butt section. When completely assembled, the rod should be some 6¼-7ft long.

Stretch and strength

Most skate fishing is done in water of over 15 fathoms, although in one or two exceptional places big fish have been encountered in less than five fathoms. Dacron line gives greater sensitivity when fishing deep water, but 55lb b.s. nylon has an elasticity which tolerates the sudden plunges of a hooked skate. (Wire line, though sometimes used, needs only one small kink to develop an

immediate weak spot.) The 6ft trace should also be of 55lb nylon, terminating in a 6/0-8/0 hook on 12in of stainless steel, nylon-covered wire of 100lb b.s. Skates' jaws are so powerful that they will grind their way through anything other than wire.

The Mustad Seamaster range of hooks have brazed eyes which do not open up even if the pull comes on the side of the eye instead of the top. These hooks may not be needle-sharp when purchased, and so must be sharpened with a small carborundum stone, for parts of the skate's mouth are very hard. The hook is secured to the wire with brass crimps, then to the nylon trace with a stainless steel locking attachment rather than a swivel, since a swivel can fail you.

The lead should be on a Clement's boom, which allows the fish to move off without feeling resistance from the weight. Which size of lead to use

COMMON SKATE RIG

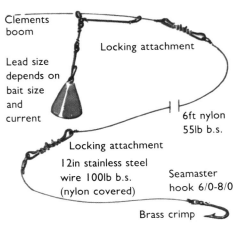

Clements boom

Locking attachment

Lead size depends on bait size and current

6ft nylon 55lb b.s.

Locking attachment

12in stainless steel wire 100lb b.s. (nylon covered)

Seamaster hook 6/0-8/0

Brass crimp

RUNNING LEDGER RIG FOR THORNBACK RAY

Clements boom

Matchstick stop

Lead size depends on bait size and current

Reel line 26lb b.s. nylon monofilament

15-20ft

Locking attachment

2/0-4/0 hook size

Nylon trace 3lb b.s. 7ft

TWO BAITS FROM ONE HERRING FILLET

4/0 hook

Herring fillet sliced diagonally

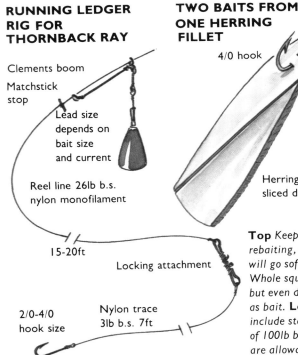

Top Keep mackerel slices ready to hand for rebaiting, but not too long in the sun or they will go soft and the skin will harden. **Above** Whole squid will also attract common skate, but even dogfish have been used successfully as bait. **Left** Common skate rigs must include stainless steel attachments and wire of 100lb b.s. For thornbacks less massive rigs are allowable.

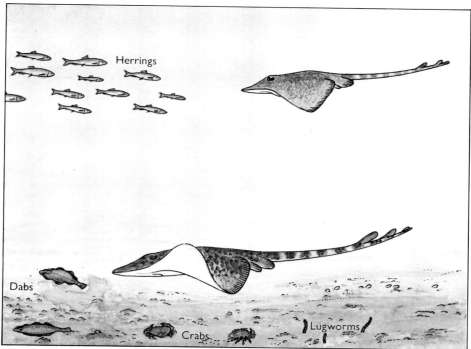

Herrings

Dabs

Crabs

Lugworms

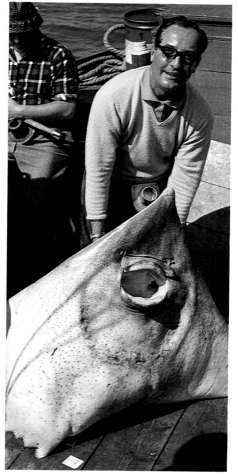

Above left *Although they are mainly bottom living fish, skates and rays will rise to attack passing schools of small fish.* **Left** *Note the strong jaws of this 136½lb common skate caught on a whole mackerel.*

depends on the speed of the local tide and the size of your bait. The larger the bait, the larger the lead needed to keep it on the bottom—where skate expect to find food.

The reel must be of top quality to withstand the lengthy playing of huge fish, for fights have been known to last an hour. The Tatler Mk IV and V, the Penn Senator 6/0 are reliable.

Anglers are recommended to wear full harness when using heavy multipliers for this saves bracing the back plate of the reel against the left forearm to prevent the rod twisting. When using a centrepin reel (which should be positioned under the rod) use only a butt socket as this cuts out any possibility of twisting. The butt pad is essential, to stop the rod-butt digging into the stomach or groin. Greater leverage can then be applied to the rod.

The hook
The weakest link in ray tackle is the hook. This must be very strong or the ray will grind it to powder. Thick wire, stainless steel hooks of the kind considered too rank for general fishing are ideal, as long as they are sharpened. Large hooks are seldom required because rays have relatively small jaws, and therefore swallow moderate baits more quickly than they could a bigger helping that needs to be crunched down to size. The smaller the hook, the sharper it is, and the easier to drive home. Hook sizes recommended for all the British rays are 1/0-4/0.

Bait needs careful attention, for it is the key to success. Rays feed on herrings and mackerel, crabs, sandeels, worms and small fishes like blennies and tiny dabs. The common denominator is absolute freshness. It cannot be overemphasized that the bait must be freshly killed or deep-frozen. All rays are extremely sensitive to smell and

taste, and ignore any bait that is less than perfect. It pays to collect your own baits or to obtain supplies directly from commercial fishermen.

Don't put your foot in it
Once aboard, the skate may appear lifeless, but do not become complacent. Keep away from its mouth at all times. If your foot were to get caught in those powerful jaws they could cripple you for life. Never try to extract the hook from a live skate—they can purse their lips and throw their jaws round fingers that seemed safe several inches away from the head.

Skate bait
The majority of skate are caught on fresh mackerel but small pollack, coalfish or almost any fish will do. Skate from Clew Bay, Ireland, have been caught on whole, small dogfish; others have been taken on large strips of cuttlefish. If using dogfish, split the gut open with a knife to give scent to the bait. Cut mackerel longways, from head to tail, and bait a full half, hooking the tail end. Skate have got such big mouths that they will not bite short but will consume the lot in one go. Unfortunately, if there are many dogfish in the area, the bait is often mutilated by these scavengers before the skates find it.

RAYS
Very closely related to skate are the rays. Although they do not reach such a size, they are very similar in appearance. The most common ray is the thornback, which can weigh over 30lb, although rarely exceeds 20lb. Fish of over 40lb are regarded as specimens (females are always longer than the males). Other rays encountered by the sea angler are the stingray, the blonde, the small-eyed or painted, the spotted or homelyn, the undulate and the cuckoo. Fish such as the eagle and electric ray are caught very rarely by the rod and line angler. Apart from the stingray and the thornback, rays have a localized distribution. The method is the same for catching all the species.

Much lighter tackle can be employed to gain the maximum sport. A lively, hollow-glass sea rod is quite adequate, except in deep water or in fast tides, where very heavy leads are necessary. If more than 1lb of lead is to be used, select a 30lb rod. For fishing from a dinghy, the rod should be 6-6¼ft, but a 6¼-7ft rod is generally better for charter boat use. Because relatively light rods are employed, it is pointless to add massive, weighty reels. If you like multipliers, choose the Mitchell 624 or the Penn Long Beach 60 or 65.

71

DOGFISH

There are three species of dogfish of interest to anglers fishing British waters —the lesser spotted, greater spotted (also called bull huss) and the spurdog.

As the dogfish is so widely distributed, every angler is bound to catch one sooner or later. The easiest way of extracting the hook without coming to harm is to either subdue the dogfish with a blow on the head or to hold the tail and fold it towards the fish's head, and so immobilizing the fish while the hook is extracted.

The greater spotted dogfish, also known as the nursehound or bull huss, differs from the lesser spotted kind in that, as the name suggests, it has bigger, but fewer, black spots on the reddish-brown upper half of the body.

Shore anglers often make large catches of the lesser spotted dogfish as it hunts in packs and can be caught in numbers. If three hooks are used, three fish at one time can sometimes be taken. The bait should not be too large for this fish as it has a smallish mouth. When hooking a fish strip—mackerel or herings are often used—a piece about 3in in length of 1in in width should be used with a 1/0 hook. On a strong tide a running trace of about 7ft is recommended, while on a slack tide the paternoster rig pays off.

The bite is slow and bouncy, and very distinctive. Do not strike until the fourth or fifth pull in order to ensure that bait and hook have been swallowed. The dogfish is slow-moving and sluggish, and indeed seems incapable of achieving any real speed. Once hooked, this fish's fight is unmistakable. There is a backward pull, followed by a move towards the boat, and this sequence is repeated all the way to the surface. Remember that very often the angler is convinced that he has hooked the fish only to find that it has merely been holding the bait, which it releases on being hauled up.

The greater spotted dogfish, by virtue of its greater size, puts up a much better fight than the smaller variety, although the bite is very similar. Once the strike is made, however, the similarity ends. On a strong tide this fish is capable of a short run, and takes full advantage of the flow for this. The jaws are lined with sharp teeth, which the fish often uses to chafe through the nylon hook length and so gain its freedom.

Dogfish baits

Reliable baits include whole small squid and large fish baits. A whole mackerel, intended for tope, presents

Right A small spurdog comes aboard off Coverack, Cornwall. **Below** *The main points of identification between greater spotted (A) and lesser spotted dogfish (B) are the nostril flaps which are quite distinctive.*

no problem to the huss. The strike should be delayed to give ample time for the bait to be swallowed, for, as with the smaller dogfish, the great spotted kind has the nasty habit of just hanging on and then letting go at the surface before it is within reach of the gaff. If this happens, lower the bait once more to the seabed for it is not uncommon for the same fish to attack the bait a second time.

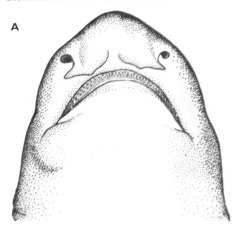

A   B

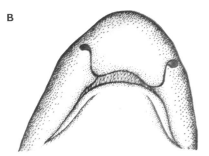

Right and below Dogfish will hunt small food fish in varied sea conditions. Their bite is quite gentle and they may hang on to a bait but let go when they reach the surface.

DEEP WATER

Molluscs   Squid   Dead fish   Hermit crabs

SHALLOW MURKY WATER

Fish fry

SPURDOG

There was a time when many anglers dreaded meeting a shoal of spurdog, as this meant that most other fish would leave the area. There are few fish in the sea that can strip an area of fishlife like a pack of spurdog. Voracious in appetite, they move inshore during the summer months to release their young and eat everything they find.

The spurdog is a small member of the extensive shark group, unique in having two extremely sharp, curved spines on the back, one in front of each dorsal fin. These spines can wound deeply if a fish turns on the angler when handled, wrapping its body around the wrist or arm.

The spurdog is not an exceptional fighter, but it can, nevertheless, cause havoc to the terminal tackle of sea anglers. Given a chance to show its ability on light gear, it can acquit itself well but, unfortunately, the spurdog is usually taken on tackle better suited to much larger fish. As a result it is hauled in, unable to put up much of a fight.

Challenge of light tackle

When the spurdog is sought deliberately on light tackle, it can really battle. Taken from the shore, as often happens when fishing a bass beach after dark, the fish will pull as hard as any bass.

The fierce attack methods of this predator and the continuous writhing of the hooked fish tend to tangle tackle. Unlike bottom-dwelling species, which suffer a decompression problem when being drawn to the surface, the spurdog has no swimbladder and will continue to thrash in its efforts to shed the hook —even after it has been brought abroad

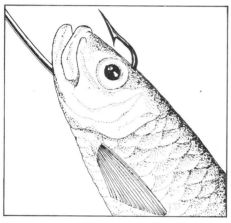

a boat. To avoid tangles, the tackle should be kept as simple as possible, with hook snoods only long enough to present the bait effectively. Long traces can only lead to massive tangles.

Importance of supple wire

The sharp teeth and rough skin of the species force the angler to use wire hook links or nylon of over-thick diameter. Wire traces need not be of over-strong breaking strain as the fish does not grow to the proportions of tope. But the wire must be as supple as possible. Stiff, single-strand wire kinks readily. If you catch even one fish it can reduce the breaking strain markedly by a twisting motion that quickly places a kink in the wire.

Spurdog are found close to the surface, near the bottom, and in midwater, so paternosters or ledger rigs with a single 6/0 hook on 20lb line and a light sea rod make adequate tackle. For boat fishing use rods in the 15-20lb class. From the shore, an 11ft light beachcaster suits most situations. This gives the fish a chance to move, and the angler obtains the best possible transmission of the vibrations from the hooked fish's movements.

Top *A smoothound, related to the spurdog, about to be put back in the sea.* **Above left** *The sharp dorsal spine of a spurdog can inflict a deep and painful wound.* **Above** *A single hooking method is all that is needed for fishing for hungry spurdog. No need for finesse here!*

Many baits can be used. Almost anything will be taken. Fish baits are best, however, as the predatory instinct is finely tuned to smell when a spurdog comes upon a lask of mackerel, herring or whole sprat. When a massive pack of spurdog arrives there are times when they can be caught with hardly any bait at all! They grab at anything—a flashing spoon attached to a cod paternoster rig has been known to take them continually for a whole afternoon.

Extracting the hook

Handling the boated fish can present a novice angler with a few difficulties. The best method of removing the hook involves first immobilizing the fish by standing on its tail. With the trace held out tight, the fish should be grasped just at the back of its head. The hook can then be extracted with a pair of long-nosed pliers.

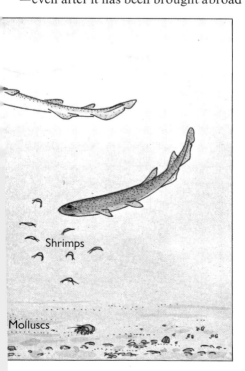

Shrimps

Molluscs

BASS

There are few sea fish that enjoy the reputation the bass has earned as a fighter. In the right environment the species gives first-rate sport on rod and line. Bass fishing is usually practised from the shore or small boats close-in, but the species can be caught wherever there are off-shore reefs or sandbanks.

The ideal rod

A medium casting rod with a small multiplier or fixed-spool reel, is ideal. The main criterion is lightness, because the tackle will be held all day. But it is well to remember that very light tackle —for instance, the 6lb class equipment recommended by some anglers—can be self-defeating. There is always the chance of a very big bass, a tope, a heavy ray; or that floating weeds and seabed rocks will snag the tackle.

Equipment of the 15lb class is ideal for surf bass, although there are occasions when 25lb line is necessary, for not all surf beaches are of clean sand. Some of the very best marks are strewn with rocks, pilings and break-waters and you need strong tackle to master a hooked fish before it can take

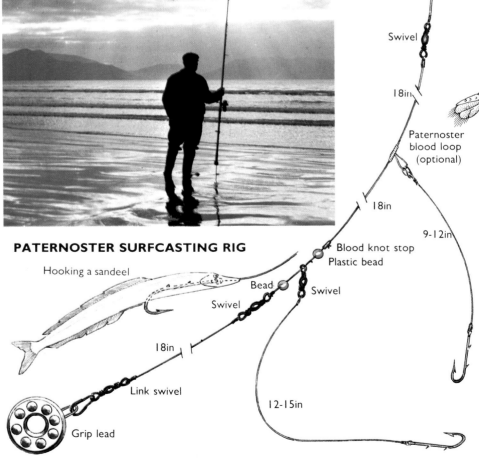

PATERNOSTER SURFCASTING RIG

Hooking a sandeel

18in

Link swivel

Grip lead

Reel line

Swivel

18in

Paternoster blood loop (optional)

18in

9-12in

Blood knot stop
Plastic bead

Bead

Swivel

Swivel

12-15in

HOOKING PRAWN AND SANDEEL BAITS

Sandeel

Prawn

the line around the nearest obstruction.

Another advantage of medium weight tackle is its ability to cast 3-4oz sinkers. A heavy sinker carries the baits more slowly so that they remain on the hook during the cast. Anchored firmly in the sand, a 3 or 4oz grip-wired or pyramid sinker helps drive home the hook by pulling the fish up short as it attempts to make off with the bait.

Terminal tackle

Single-hook traces should be used, as two hooks double your chances of getting caught up. Mostly, however, it is the sinker which fouls, so when using either a single-hook paternoster or a paternoster ledger, always attach your sinker with some rotten-bottom. If you

Above *The most effective means of using sand eel as bass bait. Keep the whole rig fairly light to ensure the best possible sport.*

Top *Bass fishing is done in all sea fishing venues. Rigs, baits, styles are varied to suit weather, sea and fishing conditions.*

must break a fouled line, only the sinker is lost. Sparking plugs, rusty nuts or bolts, or even suitable stones will serve as disposable sinkers.

Bass feeding over rough ground bite very delicately. A paternoster ledger allows them to take line without becoming alarmed. Give the fish time to get hold of the bait before striking the hook home. If the fish is played gently at first, it usually heads for deeper water over less snaggy ground, where it can be fought more safely.

Floatfishing over rocks

In areas of high rock and deep gullies, float fishing is effective and enjoyable. As the tide floods in over the rocks and fills the gullies and crevices, the bass move in, searching for food. They may be found close-in, often in very shallow water, so keep out of sight.

As the depth of water will vary considerably, your float will need frequent adjustment. Use just enough lead to take the bait down to the desired depth. In calm conditions a fine float is adequate, but in broken water it will not be seen, nor will it support the bait.

Allow the float to wander in the wash. The take is usually very positive, the float sinking down and away. Just tighten your line and lean back, and the fish will usually be hooked with ease.

Float fishing baits

Live prawns and peeler crab are the most effective baits for float fishing, but a string of mackerel, sandeels and other small fishes, and lugworms, are also useful. Crabs can be a nuisance to the angler fishing on the bottom; they quickly shred and strip soft baits. Peeler crab is the best bait as it takes them longer to demolish their own kind.

Spinning

Spinning for bass also embraces the use of a natural bait that is worked in similar fashion to an artificial one. A sprat or small herring that is fished 'sink-and-draw' style over known holding grounds can be extremely effective. Live sandeels are commonly used on the South West coast.

Shorecasters

Most of Britain's bass fishermen are shorecasters, using rods that have sufficient power to cast a 4oz weight, yet with enough suppleness to feel the movement of fish and current. They rely on the bass finding the paternostered or ledgered worms that are usually offered. Crabs in both the 'peeler' and 'softie' stage of shedding the hard carapace, are a bait that can be used to great effect from rocky shore platforms where there

is a mass of weed growth that bass recognize as cover for crabs.

Bass also frequent the shoreline close to rock faces and cliff edges. Float fishing takes the hookbait at the speed of the current to where bass will be picking morsels from both weeds and rocks.

TWO-HOOK PATERNOSTER RIG

Blood knot — Main line 12-15lb b.s.
Shock leader 20-25lb b.s.
Blood knot or swivel
1/0-4/0 hook (depending on size of bait)
4-6in snood
Blood loop
24-30in
Link swivel
12-18in
Surf bomb

ROUGH GROUND PATERNOSTER RIG

Main line 15lb b.s.
Blood knot
Shock leader 20-25lb b.s.
Blood knot or swivel
6in snood
Swivel
Rotten bottom 5lb b.s.
Rusty bolt or sparking plug

ARTIFICIAL LURES FOR BASS

Killer lure

Bar spinner

Toby spoon

Rubber eel

Sandeel

Top *Two rigs for bass. The bolt used as a weight prevents loss of expensive lead when fishing rough ground. Suitable stones or any expendable object can be used.* **Above** *A selection of popular bass lures. All these are intended to imitate small fish, bass being a predatory species.*

CHAPTER 6
TACKLE

BOAT RODS

The sea angler's boat fishing rod is simply an extension to his arm. The rod acts as a lever, converting the pulling power of a handline to lifting strength. What has happened, over half a century or so, is that anglers have applied sporting techniques to the business of deep sea fishing.

No standard boat rod

There is no standard boat rod, nor can there be, for fish vary tremendously in size and the conditions under which they are fished for alter constantly. A rod of the 20lb class is suitable for small species in sea areas with light tidal flow and allows the use of light leads of 2-8oz. This means that the rod blank is balanced for use with a 20lb line. It will have a test curve of around 4lb, which means that a pull at the rod tip of this weight will bend the rod at right angles. It does not mean that the rod is only capable of handling a fish that weighs or pulls to 4lb. In any case, a fish weighs only about one third of its true weight when in the water. The test curve given for a sea rod is multiplied by five to arrive at the correct b.s. of line to match it.

Selecting a boat rod

When selecting a boat rod it is very misleading to wave it about in the manner usually adopted with freshwater rods, which do have a flexibility that can be assessed, even if not accurately. A boat rod only proves its worth under the stress of a sizeable fish coupled with the dead weight of a pound lead in a moderate run of tide.

A 30lb class rod will cope with fish up to 50lb, leads up to 20oz and quite hard tides—anything up to four or five knots—when fishing from an anchored boat. The rod is intended to be used for tope and big shoal fish such as cod, pollack, ling, and rays, but would still handle the smaller species. A 50lb class rod will enable anybody to hook, fight, and land most of our larger species. Porbeagle shark, all but the largest of common skate, and the average deep sea conger, are all within the competence of a rod of this strength.

Boat rod lengths

Rods are becoming longer. At one time a 5 or 6ft rod was normal; now 7-8ft rods are commonplace. The longer rod gives better control of a fighting fish, especially when it comes close to the boat. At the same time it possesses more travel during compression, absorbing the wild lunges that can break a line when the angler is fishing with lightweight fishing tackle.

The rod's fittings

No glassfibre blank can perform as a rod without the right fittings. The quality of the glass and its design must be matched by a perfect winch fitting and rod rings. Ensure that the length of the handle is right for you, and remember that the winch fitting position is critical. Make sure too that you can reach the reel handle and control mechanisms. The choice of rings depends on the type of line that an angler prefers. Plain bridge rings are fine for use with monafilament nylon line but use at least a roller tip ring if the line is of braided Dacron or Terylene. There can be a lot of friction as these lines pass over the tip rings, and a roller will help to reduce this.

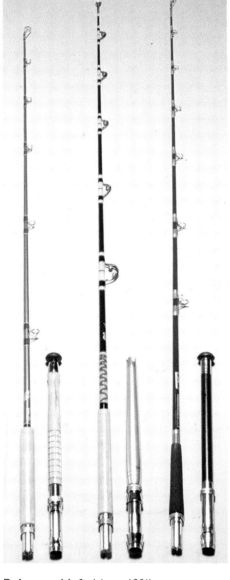

Below and left *A huge 192lb common skate being heaved aboard.* **Above** *A selection of boat rods.*

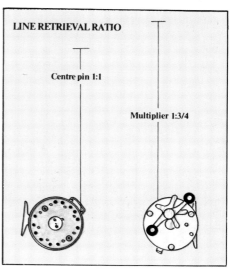

LINE RETRIEVAL RATIO

Centre pin 1:1

Multiplier 1:3/4

Above *Line retrieve ratios compared.*
Left *A multiplier sits on top of the rod handle, the thumb controlling line take. The centrepin has a 1:1 ratio compared with the multiplier's $1:3\frac{1}{2}$. An added factor is the amount of line on the spool.*

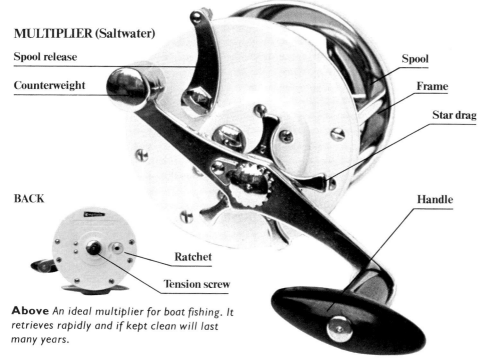

MULTIPLIER (Saltwater)

Spool release

Counterweight

Spool

Frame

Star drag

BACK

Handle

Ratchet

Tension screw

Above *An ideal multiplier for boat fishing. It retrieves rapidly and if kept clean will last many years.*

MULTIPLIERS

The multiplier is essentially a reel with a small-diameter drum geared to a ratio of 3 or 4:1 so that line is retrieved rapidly by winding. Models with automatic gears are available, but are far more expensive. These have ratios of about $2\frac{1}{4}$ and $4\frac{1}{4}$:1. As with the fixed-spool reel, there is a wide variety.

To the beginner the multiplier may appear complicated. But you should become familiar with its star-drag, brake and other parts before going fishing with it. Most multipliers are right-handed and are not adaptable.

The main problem with the multiplier reel is that of the line over-running and tangling into 'bird's nests'. To reduce the possibility of this, whether when lowering the bait over the side of a boat and down to the sea-bed or casting up to 100 yards from the shore, the thumb must rest gently on the line as it pays out. Various devices have been incor-porated by manufacturers in some of their models to overcome this difficulty. These include spool tensioners, centri-fugal governors, oil drag retarders and 'lift' and 'brake' gadgets, but bird's nests can be avoided by the angler if he learns how to use his reel properly.

The more expensive multipliers have ball bearings set in both endplates. Leading from one spindle is a governing mechanism, usually consisting of fibre blocks, which are thrown outwards by centrifugal force, thus acting as a brake when the bait hits the water. To stop the line from running with the weight while casting, a manual brake on the side of the reel can be employed. Another feature of superior reels is a 'line-spreader', which ensures the even dis-tribution of line on recovery.

The mechanism of smaller multipliers is extremely delicate, and sand, dust, and, worse still, saltwater, are to be avoided at all costs. The heavier salt-water models still need to be kept clean and oiled, but they are usually rust-proof. Unlike other reels, which are fixed to the underside of the rod handle, the multiplier is used with the rod reversed and the reel uppermost.

Maintenance

It is essential after each outing to rinse the reel thoroughly in freshwater and, after drying it, to apply a recommended lubricant, especially if the reel is not to be used again for some time.

Periodical inspection is also advis-able, for sand or grit in the gears can wreak havoc and a jammed reel while playing a strong fish is an event no angler wants to experience.

WIRE LINE

So far, fishing with wire line has still to be accepted by the average sea angler, although it is surely only a matter of time before this happens. Fishing with wire requires completely different techniques and equipment, but it is not difficult to learn. With a little practice, the average angler can become proficient in its use in a comparatively short time. Unfortunately, during its first introduction to Britain it received a bad reputation as many anglers, using it as just another fishing line, had poor results.

Used correctly, wire line can open up a new world to the sea angler. To hold bottom, you require a fraction of the lead compared with conventional monofilament or braided lines of Dacron or Terylene. In very strong tides, for example, and fairly deep water where you would require at least 2lb of lead on a monofilament line to hold bottom, you can achieve the same result using wire with less than $\frac{1}{4}$lb.

Bite indication

Bite indication with wire is a revelation in itself: bites from small fish are registered immediately and positively, where similar bites on monofilament would not be felt at all, due to its inherent stretch. So positive is the indication from wire line that an angler experienced in its use, can, even in deep water, tell you the composition of the bottom—whether it is rock, sand, shingle or soft mud—just from the feel of the bouncing lead.

The one disadvantage of wire line is that fishing from a crowded boat becomes inadvisable. When using wire you require plenty of room between you and the next angler, as it is absolutely essential to keep wire under tension at

all times, and should you become entangled with another fisherman's line this is not possible. Wire reverts to coil form when tension is relaxed, and most efforts to straighten it result in kinks, so that it then becomes so weak that it will snap under pressure.

This brings us to the first and most important aspect of its use, and the one that causes most problems to novices. Never, *never* lower weighted wire to the bottom from a free spool, as if you do you will not know when the lead hits the seabed. The result will be a pyramid of coiled wire on the bottom which will come back full of kinks. Lower it under slight tension, with your thumb on the spool of the reel and you will then feel the lead arrive.

Finally, one word of warning to

Right *A strong and single means of attachment to wire line.* **Below right** *How wire can cut a groove in an ordinary rod ring.* **Below** *Roller-type intermediate rod rings are a necessity when fishing with wire line.*

those fishing from an anchored boat, or more especially from a drifting boat. Never attempt to free wire with your hands should it become snagged on the bottom. It can cut through flesh like a hot knife through butter. Loop the line around a stanchion or stem post, and let the boat pull it out. It is also sound practice to use a trace of slightly lower breaking strain than the wire so that if you do have to break out, you will only

HAYWIRE TWIST FOR WIRE LINE

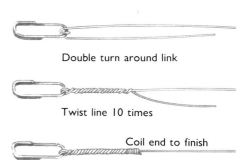

Double turn around link

Twist line 10 times

Coil end to finish

Break off free end by twisting with pliers

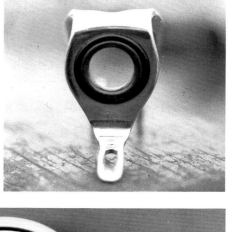

Right *Three popular brands of braided line. Terylene and Dacron are not suitable for boat fishing.* **Below** *An American stainless steel wire trolling line, slowly becoming popular in British waters.*

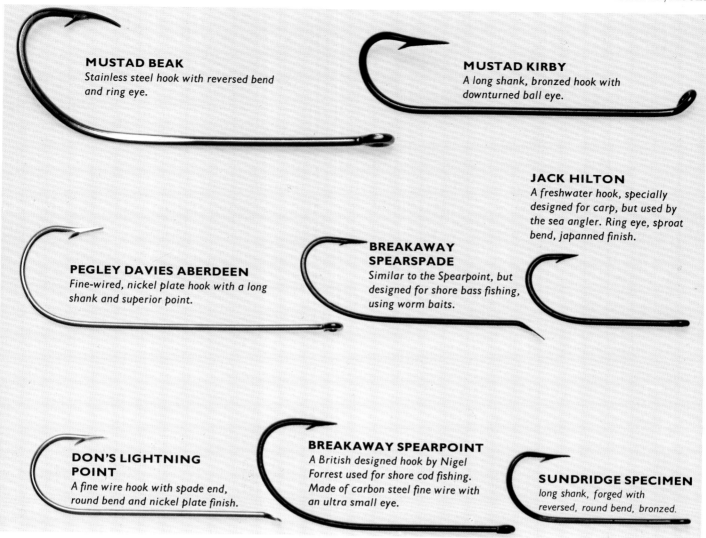

MUSTAD BEAK
Stainless steel hook with reversed bend and ring eye.

MUSTAD KIRBY
A long shank, bronzed hook with downturned ball eye.

JACK HILTON
A freshwater hook, specially designed for carp, but used by the sea angler. Ring eye, sproat bend, japanned finish.

PEGLEY DAVIES ABERDEEN
Fine-wired, nickel plate hook with a long shank and superior point.

BREAKAWAY SPEARSPADE
Similar to the Spearpoint, but designed for shore bass fishing, using worm baits.

DON'S LIGHTNING POINT
A fine wire hook with spade end, round bend and nickel plate finish.

BREAKAWAY SPEARPOINT
A British designed hook by Nigel Forrest used for shore cod fishing. Made of carbon steel fine wire with an ultra small eye.

SUNDRIDGE SPECIMEN
long shank, forged with reversed, round bend, bronzed.

lose a hook or part of the trace and not relatively expensive wire.

Braided line
Braided lines are soft, pliable, and can be purchased in continuous lengths of up to 1,000 yards. Unlike monofilament, however, the line is not translucent. Nor is it now manufactured in breaking strains of less than 10lb—a great loss to the angling world. In the sizes sold, its circumference is greater than that of monofilament, and it naturally follows that less line can be wound on to a normal reel which is, of course a severe disadvantage.

Braided line possesses numerous advantages, not least its complete lack of spring. This makes it easy to wind from the spool on to the reel, it knots easily, the knots pulling firmly together without slipping, making for greater security.

The almost complete lack of stretch is a great help in preventing line from jamming on the spool of your reel, where a direct pull with monofilament line can often force one strand under others below it and bring the whole reel to a halt.

Undoubtedly, it is the non-stretch factor that has endeared the braided line to anglers who need a strong and reliable line for really hard work.

While the initial outlay may cause many anglers to think twice before purchasing a braided line, there is a strong case for its use as a longterm money-saver.

HOOKS
No item of the sea angler's equipment is more important than the hook which, after all, is in direct contact with the fish and so has to withstand all kinds of strain.

For sea fishing hooks can be reduced conveniently to around half a dozen kinds. Among the most popular is the razor sharp, straight eyed Aberdeen hook which has a long shank made from light wire. Perfect temper prevents any straightening despite the extra leverage from the shank. This hook is used extensively for estuary fishing, particularly for bass, plaice and flounders. As it is so fine in the shank of wire the Aberdeen hook is most suitable for baiting live sandeel and prawn.

For general bottom fishing three kinds stand out—Limerick, Kirby and

Above All fishing hooks must be kept sharp. Sea hooks need particular care as salt water is corrosive. One wet sea hook put back in the tackle box will soon rust and corrode all the others not made of stainless steel.

O'Shaughnessy. The Limerick is well suited to use with a paternoster for bream, whiting, pouting, cod and ling, its pull being direct and its penetration excellent. For ledgering there is little to choose between the other varieties, which have a wide gape between the point and the shank, but the O'Shaughnessy is the strongest and particularly suitable for holding such heavy fish as the conger eel.

Care of hooks
No article on hooks would be complete without reference to the care of them. While most are sharp when they leave the factory, handling can easily dull them, and so it is essential to examine each one before it is used, and from time to time while fishing.

Lastly, never put wet hooks away with unused ones. The seawater will rapidly corrode any not made of stainless steel.

CHAPTER 7
BAIT

RAGWORM AND LUGWORM

The lugworm is the most popular of all baits used in sea angling, particularly with anglers fishing the East Anglian and Kent coasts. It is a smaller species than that other very popular worm, the King ragworm, but when used from beach or boat it can be one of the deadliest baits for cod.

Common lug can be threaded either singly or doubly, depending on size, when beach fishing for cod, but for boat fishing it is usually better to hang them from the bend of the hook, just passing the hook in and out of the body where the sandy tail section joins the fat part. The number of worms put on a hook depends, first, on the size of the worm and, second, on the size of the fish expected. When fishing for varieties of flatfish, a largish worm may be broken in half to provide bait for a small mouth.

A good percentage of the sea fish found around the coastline of the British Isles will usually take this bait readily and, besides being ideal for cod, it is useful for the small varieties of flatfish—plaice, dabs and flounders.

Lugworm vary in size from 3in–7in, although few reach the greater length. Being a non-wriggling worm, it is used almost exclusively for bottom fishing. As the body of the worm deflates the instant it is pierced, most anglers bait at least three worms at a time and quite often double the number on a hook.

Ragworm

The ragworm differs from the lugworm in that it tapers very gradually from head to tail and is much fleshier. Most ragworms are bright red and all varieties have hundreds of 'legs' down each side of the body. The head is armed with a pair of bony pincers which the worm can thrust out and retract at will and a large worm can inflict a painful bite on the unwary angler.

Mounting the bait

King ragworm can be an extremely effective bait, particularly for bass and pollack. For these fighting predators, worms up to 1ft long can be used whole. Secure just the head on the hook,

Below left *The popular lugworm, a standard winter and summer sea bait.*
Bottom left *Ragworm, not so well-liked but can be as effective as any sea bait.* **Below** *A 'cocktail' of lugworm and mussel offers a juicy meal for midwater fish.* **Bottom** *The barb of the hook must protrude from ragworm, the hook being pushed through the body.*

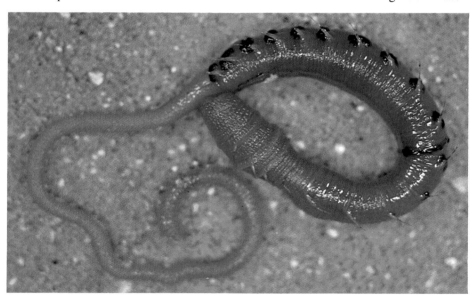

HOOKING A 'COCKTAIL' BAIT

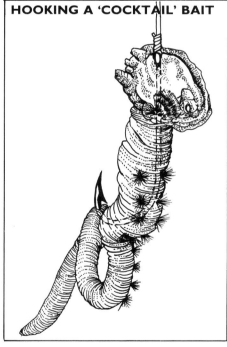

HOOKING A RAGWORM

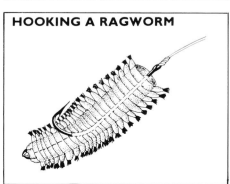

80

leaving the rest trailing. Mounted in this way it is very life-like and pollack and bass rarely bite short. They have insatiable appetites and take the whole worm into their mouth before making off with it. The largest worms can be cut in half and baited in a similar way. Other species that prefer ragworm to lugworm are flounder, thornback ray, and sharks such as dogfish and smoothhound.

MACKEREL AND FEATHERS

Hooks dressed with feathers are often used to catch mackerel for use as a bait, as well as for whiting, pollack, cod and coalfish. Less commonly, bass, ling, conger, haddock and garfish are taken by 'feathering'. The tackle is set among a shoal and jerked up and down to simulate the erratic movement of small fish. The use of several feathered hooks helps create the impression of plentiful food. Once a shoal has been located a greedy mackerel, whiting or codling can often be taken on each of the hooks.

The rig for feathering consists of up to six feathered hooks on traces or 'snoods' of about 5in, which are attached to the reel line. A line of 15-20lb b.s. should be used, for with a fish on every hook it will have to take a considerable load when being reeled in to a boat or a pier. The snoods should also be strong enough to avoid losing any fish when hauling in the catch and should be set 9-10in apart so that they do not tangle. The blood loop dropper is the strongest and most reliable knot to use to attach snoods to the reel line.

A fairly heavy lead should be used at the end of the reel line, for a smaller weight may take a long while to sink, by which time the shoal may have moved on, the feathers not having had a chance to attract them. For mackerel a size 1 or 1/0 hook is suitable; for cod a larger hook, a size 3 for example, is recommended together with plain white feathers.

When fishing for mackerel as bait (which is hard to beat for its appeal to many species) a six-hook rig will provide a plentiful supply. A group of boat anglers must remember though to be careful when swinging these multi-hook rigs in board, especially in a wind, for painful accidents and lost fishing time can result from lack of forethought.

Mackerel

Of all the fish species inhabiting Britain's coastal waters, there is none with a more mixed reputation than that enjoyed by the mackerel. Although some rate them highly for a variety of reasons, there are those who dismiss

TWO-HOOK TROLLING RIGS

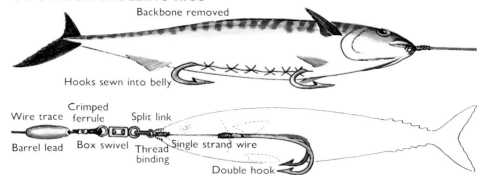

Backbone removed — *Hooks sewn into belly* — *Wire trace* — *Crimped ferrule* — *Split link* — *Barrel lead* — *Box swivel* — *Thread binding* — *Single strand wire* — *Double hook*

Above *Two trolling rigs using mackerel as bait. The lower rig shows how the combination of crimped ferrule is used.*

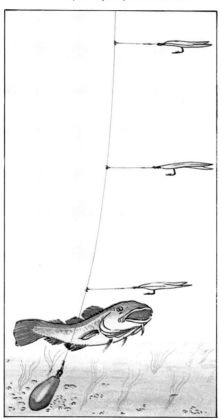

them as 'dirty eaters', or as being too easy to catch or not worth eating. But as bait, a fresh mackerel has no equal.

Mackerel as bait can be fished in a variety of ways, and methods of presentation attractive to most species can be found. Two important considerations must be borne in mind, whatever style of fishing is to be employed. First, the bait size and presentation should be appropriate to the quarry and its manner of feeding; secondly, the bait and hook should be matched in size.

Apart from its other advantages, the mackerel's shape and bone structure make it an ideal bait form. If can be cut in different ways according to requirements. The section adjoining the caudal or tail fin provides on each side a near-triangular patch—a 'lask' or 'last'.

Alternatively, a side or flank can be offered, either whole, halved or sliced

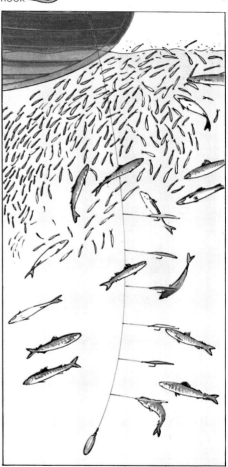

Above and above left *Fished near or in a shoal of small fry, mackerel feathers are taken avidly by many fish as well as mackerel. One of the more common species caught this way is the garfish which joins the mackerel shoal.*

into strips to resemble small fish. To hook a half-side or strip of mackerel, drive the hook right through the fish and then twist this to allow the hook to come through again in a different place. This ensures that maximum benefit is gained from the oily flesh.

A whole side of mackerel can be held in position and presented in an attractive manner by whipping a small hook on to the trace a couple of inches above the main hook. The top of the bait is then supported, the lower portion being free to move with the current to simulate the motion of a small live fish.

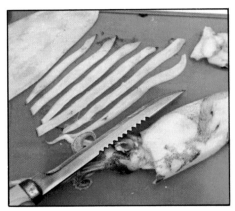

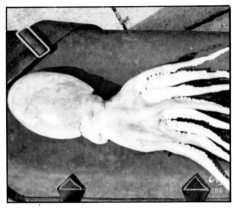

Left *Large bunches of squid tentacles are very attractive in the tide and make fine ray baits.* **Lower far left** *Squid can be cut into strips as cod bait.* **Lower left** *Put a whole squid on a large hook for conger. Do not cut the ink sac as it repels fish – as it is intended to do.*

A strip of squid about 10in long and 1in wide cut to resemble a fish, makes a fine trolling bait for bass. Mounted on a long-shanked hook and worked astern at about three knots, it will dart about in a realistic manner and soon find a taker.

The ideal bait

For shore fishing on storm beaches, squid is ideal bait as it stands up to long casting and can take any amount of battering from heavy surf. Many flat-fish enthusiasts use it extensively as a bottom bait for turbot, plaice and dabs, although it has never been much good for flounder.

During the winter months, monster mackerel have a definite liking for a thin strip of squid, and give great sport on light tackle.

Squid caught on rod and line

Although most squid are obtained from commercial sources, they can be caught fairly easily on rod and line during the winter months when they shoal in vast numbers particularly at the western end of the English Channel. Between October and March they can be a problem in deep water as they snatch at baits put out for pollack and coalfish with a 'take' that is similar to those of both species. The similarity ends after the take however, as they let the bait go a few feet from the boat, even after making a number of powerful dives giving the impression that they are securely hooked. So back they go down to the depths.

SQUID

The squid is commonly used as bait, as its distribution in the Atlantic, English Channel and North Sea means that it is plentifully available all round the coast. Cuttlefish are sometimes available but in nothing like the numbers of squid.

Advantages of squid bait

Squid is the cleanest bait to use in sea fishing as the flesh is firm, cuts cleanly and easily, and can be presented attractively in a variety of ways. Above all it keeps well, and a supply laid down in a freezer can stay perfectly fresh for two years. This applies if you follow simple rules. The squid must be thoroughly cleaned by severing the head and cutting evenly down through the centre of the body to the tail. It should then be opened and laid out flat, and the stomach removed in one easy movement. With care you can do this without bursting the ink sac which has an acid content that is irritating to human skin. Squid wings are useless as bait and can be thrown away. Finally, it needs thorough washing using two changes of fresh water, and then the bait is ready for freezing.

Squid heads make a great bait for conger, ling or any other large species, and should be frozen separately. If they are mixed in with the bodies of the squid and taken out on shore trips when small fry are the quarry, it is likely that the heads will be wasted.

All fish will take squid, and some species particularly relish it. Heading the list are red and black bream, which are caught in their thousands on very thin strips about 3in long offered on fine hooks to paternosters, or a single hook on a flowing trace.

Change a frayed bait

As the squid is so tough, it is possible to catch several bream on the same strip of bait. As soon as the edges show signs of fraying, however, it must be changed. Large numbers of conger eels to 100lb are also taken on squid head, or a whole squid hooked through the body and ledgered close to a wreck or on rough ground. Similarly it is a great favourite with the ravenous ling.

Top right *Many colourful artificial squid lures are marketed.* **Right** *This squid catcher is called the 'Murderer' because it catches squid by ripping into them as they are drawn up.*

'MURDERER'

SANDEEL

The sandeel is not only one of the best baits for sea angling, but a very important part of the food chain for most species of fish. Three varieties are found in British waters: the greater sandeel, which can be easily identified by the black spot on the sides of the snout, the sandeel and the smooth sandeel.

They all have elongated bodies and no spiny rays in the fins. The upper jaw is extensible and shorter than the lower; the tail forked and separate from the dorsal and anal.

Sandeels are generally caught by towing a fine-mesh seine net from a small rowing boat off sandy beaches, or by digging and raking in the sand on the beach. The latter is best done at low tide right at the water's edge, as the eels like to hide in very wet sand. If there is a freshwater stream running down the beach this is a good place to search.

Shop-bought sandeel

The undoubted effectiveness of live sandeel has made them a familiar sight in tackle shops alongside more traditional baits like lug and ragworm. In areas where the fish is common, an average size eel sells for about 10p or so, but you should be prepared to pay considerably more if they have to be transported long distances. Tidal conditions affect the commercial catching of eels, so it is always best to reserve a supply far in advance of your trip.

Keeping sandeels alive while boat fishing can be done by the use of a wooden box with a pointed end and many holes to admit the passage of water. It can be towed behind a slow craft without damaging the eels, but is usually placed in the water on a tether, when the boat is either drifting or at anchor over a mark.

Keep sandeel fresh

During the journey out, the eels are kept fresh in a plastic drum to which buckets of seawater are constantly added. Some boats with glassfibre hulls have livebait tanks built in at the waterline. A constant change of water can be obtained by simply opening a sea-cock. With this refinement, both eels and other fish can be kept alive indefinitely.

To bait up with a sandeel, hold it firmly but lightly between the fingers and thumb, throat outwards. Put the point of the hook through the bottom lip and nick it into the soft skin of the belly just behind the head—this is the normal way of offering it in a fair run of tide. When fishing in slack water, however, it is often better to simply hook the eel through the top of its body, in front of the dorsal.

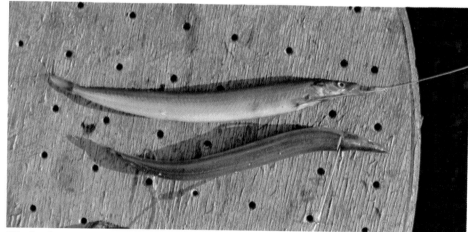

Hooks for sandeels

Hooks must be long in the shank, needle-sharp, and fine in the wire—a description that fits the Aberdeen perfectly. Live eels must be offered on a very long trace, which allows them to swim around in a natural manner. The movement is enhanced if mylon monofilament with a b.s. of no more than 12lb is used.

Top A catch of bright sandeels compared with coloured artificial lures intended to imitate them. **Centre** The wicker courge keeps sandeels alive by allowing water to pass through while it is hung over the side. Sandeels die quickly when not kept in fresh sea water. **Above** Two methods of hooking sandeel for bait. It is important that the small fish remain lively if they are to attract the attentions of a hungry bass.

LURES AND RUBBER EELS

Plastic lures are available in a wide range of colours, but it is known that below 30ft, even in clear water conditions, colour (as we know it) begins to disappear. At 100ft it has gone altogether. So what is the point in painting artificials so attractively when most are used in depths of 40 fathoms (240ft) to which no light penetrates? The clue is surely in the phrase 'colour as we know it'. The human eye may perceive quite differently from the fish's eye.

Recent studies have shown that lures coloured deep purple with a blue head, and dark red with a gold belly catch extremely well even at depths where light does not penetrate.

Profusion of metal lures

As well as plastic lures there are a great many manufactured in metal. This type is used extensively for shore spinning, and, to a lesser extent, trolling from small craft over inshore grounds. The range of shape and colour is bewildering. The newcomer to sea angling is easily confused by the profusion of different types, all of which profess to catch fish when, regrettably, most are designed to catch anglers.

Pirks

In recent years pirking or jigging for free swimming fish such as pollack, coalfish and cod, has gained ground with deepwater boat anglers, and the method is now in wide use. It entails fishing with a weighted lure, invariably fitted with a treble hook. Pirks take many forms and range from lead-filled pipes, already chromed or painted in a variety of colours, to old plated car door handles or to sophisticated stainless steel and chrome-finished models from Scandinavia.

Anglers fishing pirks from conventional positions in a boat adopt a quite different approach to the quick retrieve method of the boatman in the bow, and instead work the rod with a pumping action, as one would with feathers. While it is effective if not more than six anglers fish at a time from just one side of the boat as it moves across the wreck, this method does not match the fast-retrieve system.

Jigs

Jigs are generally smaller lures, often with coloured feathers set in a metal head rather than the all-metal body of a pirk. They are used in a similar way to pirks and range from 4oz–26oz, the weight varying with the depth of water and the strength of tide. In general terms, few of less than 12oz are used in more than 20 fathoms of water.

Below *A selection of colourful deepwater pirks. Large metal pirks such as these can weigh between 1½ and 26 oz, for they have to go deep down alongside reefs.*

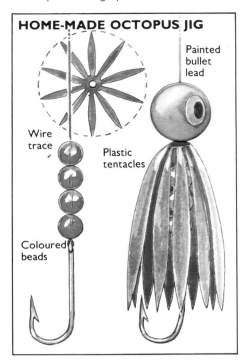

Below *An interesting homemade octopus jig is used for catching squid as bait.*

HOME-MADE OCTOPUS JIG

Painted bullet lead
Wire trace
Plastic tentacles
Coloured beads

Right *Trolling lures come in many shapes and sizes. The squid are on double hooks to make the 'wings' stand out. Below them is a plastic squid/dead herring combination, and to the right is a Jardine lead to keep the Red Gill lure well down. Red Gills come in yellow, green, red and silver and each colour is one that, according to different anglers, is the only one that works. A four-turn blood knot is illustrated which is used to attach the lure to the reel line. The range of present-day artificial lures for sea angling increases steadily. Most new patterns come from the US, where such lures are very popular but it takes time before British anglers accept them.*

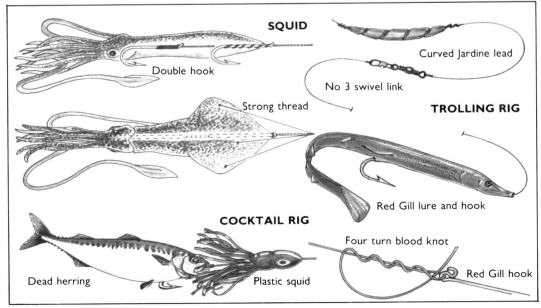

SQUID
Double hook
Curved Jardine lead
No 3 swivel link
TROLLING RIG
Strong thread
Red Gill lure and hook
COCKTAIL RIG
Four turn blood knot
Dead herring
Plastic squid
Red Gill hook

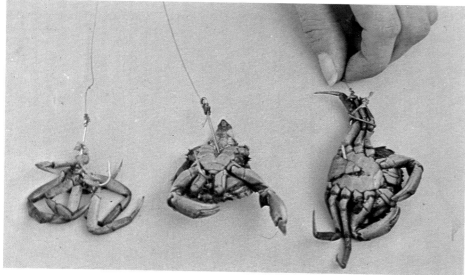

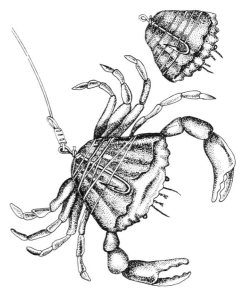

Above *A crab can be tied to the hook with elasticated wire or thread. It prevents the flesh being stripped off by other crabs and small fish. It also avoids the bait flying off the hook during a long beach cast.* **Above left** *A rocky shoreline carries an endless supply of bait, especially crabs, which are only effective in the peeler stage.* **Left** *Crabs can be hooked in a variety of ways or bound on as shown top right.*

PEELER CRAB

Crabs have their skeletons on the outside of their body and their muscles and organs inside. Growth is only possible by changing shells, and this is done by growing a new, larger shell, which has at first to be soft in order to fit beneath the existing hard shell. When the new, soft shell is fully formed, just before the old one is discarded, the crab is known as a 'peeler'.

Vulnerable peeler

A short time before shedding takes place the new shell beneath has so cramped the crab's muscles that much of the power leaves its legs and claws. This is when the angler will find the vulnerable creature hiding under seaweed, around rock ledges, in soft sand and mud around rocks, harbour walls and breakwaters—anywhere which provides protection from tide and enemy.

Of the many varieties of crab found around our coasts, the best, and most widely used, for bait is the common shore crab. The young crab starts life from an egg which hatches in the upper layers of the sea. At this stage the larva bears no resemblance to the adult, but in a few weeks it undergoes five moults, after which it sinks to the seabed and takes on the characteristic form of a crab.

Immediately after casting off its shell the crab becomes what is known as a soft-back or soft crab. It is defenceless and so hides itself, but a new shell begins to form straight away. After a few hours the shell is like parchment but the crab is still not at its best as a bait.

A deadly bait

Peeler crabs are highly attractive to all sea fish but are especially deadly with bass and cod. Inshore boat fishing and beachcasting will both produce good results with this irresistible bait. The cod is greedy and is relatively easy to hook, but the bass will often suck the bait from the hook and so demands the angler's full attention.

Many anglers hold that the peeler crab is the supreme sea fishing bait, while others criticize it because of the preparation needed. With care, however, several fine pieces of bait can be obtained from one crab. First remove the eight legs and two claws from the body and then, using the thumbnail, remove the carapace. With the aid of the thumbnail, or a knife, remove as much of the shell from the underside as possible.

Small baits

The crab can be used whole, depending on the size but, more often, the body is cut crossways in two or quartered to provide four small baits. Anglers often discard the legs and claws but these, hooked in a bunch like worms, can prove a deadly bait. By carefully removing the four segments one at a time from the legs with a gentle twist and a pull they can be peeled off. The claws can be dealt with in the same way.

When starting a day's fishing it is advisable to leave the peeler crabs in a bucket of sea water for a while as this makes them softer and easier to peel. Beachcasting crab puts considerable strain on this soft bait and so the whole body or segments should be tied to the hook with elastic thread or wool.

SHELLFISH

In the sea, molluscs are a very important link in the food chain. Most important to the angler for bait are mussels, cockles, limpets, winkles and whelks. Many fish—the plaice is a typical example—will feed almost exclusively on baby molluscs, preferring 'seed' cockles and mussels. It is not surprising, then, that many species of shellfish have been used as a bait by the sea angler for many years.

Mussels as bait

The mussel, which is a bivalve, or two-shelled creature, has been a very popular bait for years, particularly on the East Coast. It is very easy to gather but it does require some preparation as it is virtually impossible to bait with the seed mussel which the fish feed on.

For beach fishing, a good method is to put three or four of the prepared mussels in a very fine-mesh hair-net, which is attached to the hook and enables the bait to be cast a greater distance without flying off. Used this way, the mussel can be a deadly bait for cod.

Cockles as bait

Cockles are another variety of bivalve which will take many different species of sea fish. They are used extensively in Scotland, particularly on the Clyde. Cockles may take longer to gather as they have to be raked out of the sand in their preferred habitat of sheltered bays without strong tides or heavy surf. This bait requires no preparation other than the opening of the shell and the removal of its contents.

Limpets

The limpet is another mollusc, cone-shaped and dark brown in colour, which the angler can gather himself. They can be detached by prising them off with a knife or similar implement. The animal is then exposed and removed from the shell with the thumbnail, to reveal orange disc-shaped flesh and a blackish patch. Used singly on a small hook it is a good bait for flatfish, particularly dabs, while several on a large hook will attract most other species. Unfortunately, its soft texture means that it cannot withstand forceful casting and is likely to be mutilated very rapidly by any crabs in the vicinity.

Whelks

Whelks are not really sought after as a bait by anglers, although commercial fishermen often bait their longlines with them very effectively. Their success, however, can probably be attributed to the fact that a longline is left for several hours undisturbed and that the whelk is

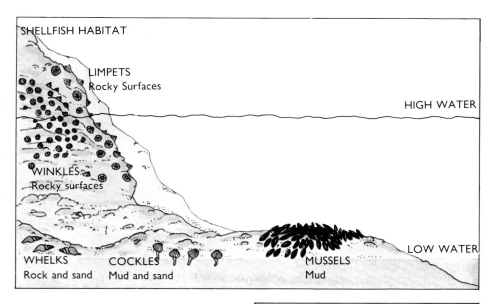

Above *There is an abundance of marine life among the weed-covered pools on a rocky shore. Almost all can be used as bait.* Right *Razorshells, or the creature inside, make very good baits but collecting them is not very easy. A special razorshell 'spear' is used to collect them.*

so tough that it will remain on the hook until eaten by a fish. For the rod and line angler it is best as a bait for cod and pouting as these two species are not particularly fussy.

Gathering limpets for bait presents few problems for the angler. They are common on the East Coast, the South East and the Channel coasts. Beds are usually found near the low water mark on average spring tides, with the most likely areas being sheltered, sandy bays and estuaries.

Razorshell

The traditional method of gathering razorshells for bait is by the use of a tool about 3ft long with an arrowhead point. One must approach the area so as not to create the vibrations which will send the animal burrowing downwards. The 'spear' must be thrust down the hole into the shell's two halves and twisted so that the point grips the sides of the shell to prevent further burrowing. The razorshell can then be withdrawn quickly.

To extract the animal from its two hinged shells, carefully cut through the hinge with a sharp knife. Do not prise open the two shells along the unhinged side as this will damage the creature. The attractiveness of the razorshell as a bait lies in its meaty foot, but the whole animal is hooked by the foot.

The whelk's muscular foot holds it securely to the hook where it provides an excellent bait for cod, ling and bottom-feeding fish of all cod-type species.

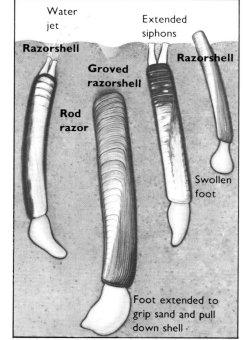

CHAPTER 8
SKILLS

HARBOURS AND PIERS

Seaside piers have long been the favourite fishing stations for elderly, comfort-loving sea anglers, small boys and beginners who initially require the moral support and companionship of other fishermen as they make their first unsure casts.

One great advantage for young anglers fishing from above-water structures is that they can learn to operate their tackle by lowering it rather than casting. This eliminates the 'crack-offs' and tangles associated with multiplier reels.

Pier rods should be powerful enough to cope with the conditions—such as the strength and height of the tide—as well as being strong enough to land the fish when caught. When float fishing for bass, for example, on the lower deck of a pier, it would be inadvisable to fish with 'open-water' tackle—a light spinning rod, a fixed-spool reel and 5 or 6lb line. The first good bass hooked would immediately dive for cover among the old barnacle-covered iron girders and smash such tackle. For such a snaggy angling condition, a stout beachcasting rod, a powerful multiplier or centrepin

Right *For those to whom sea fishing from boats means seasickness, pier fishing supplies the answer. Some piers demand payment from sea anglers.* **Below** *The South African beach-casting action. Timing is all-important in order to avoid the dreaded bird's nest when the spool overruns the rate of line pulling off and jams into a fearsome, knotted mess. Such a tangle takes hours to unravel.*

reel and 15–20lb b.s. line is effective.

Winter fishing from piers, harbour walls, groynes and jetties may necessitate the use of stout rods and strong line to combat rough weather as well as the energies of the fish. In the warmer spring, summer and autumn months, however, a great deal of fine sport can be had by employing light, fine tackle and the appropriate techniques.

To avoid accidents and loss of life it is important that all shore anglers, particularly those fishing from angling stations above deep water, observe certain safety rules. Always respect the rules of the pier or harbour wall as far as overhead casting, line strength and sinker weights are concerned. In rough weather, when waves are apt to break over the fishing station, leave the place well alone. On some piers, Tilley

lamps and lanterns are banned because they constitute a navigational hazard when shone seawards.

Be careful when using a dropnet from piers or harbour walls with no guard rails and when climbing down perpendicular iron ladders or negotiating steep, weed-covered stone steps.

BEACHCASTING

Learning to cast is not easy. although there is no magic involved, no superhuman strength required and no demand for enormous talent. What you need is a basic understanding of the principles, well-matched tackle and sensible practice. Beachcasting 100 yards or more is demanding of time and effort, but anyone can do it.

The best casts

The best introductory casts for general beachcasting are the 'South African' and 'Layback' styles.

The South African cast, where the sinker is laid on the beach then swept over the shoulder with a twist of the shoulders and push-pull of the arms is an excellent teaching style and the foundation for all other casts, except the Norfolk methods. With properly matched tackle and sensible practice, the newcomer to shorefishing can learn to cast over 100 yards in less than three hours if he is instructed by a competent coach.

Teaching oneself to cast takes longer, but a couple of weeks are enough to work out the details and to form the basis of a good style.

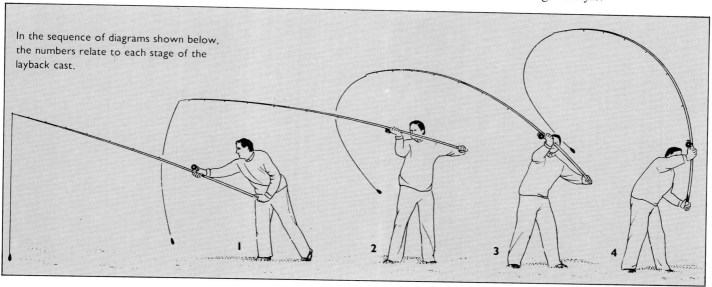

In the sequence of diagrams shown below. the numbers relate to each stage of the layback cast.

1   2   3   4

OFFSHORE FISHING

The off-shore fishing grounds round the British Isles have something for everyone. There are large skate, halibut, shark and conger, as well as cod, tope, ling, and a wide variety of lesser fish, all of which provide good sport on rod and line.

The secret of off-shore fishing is to know and understand the various species and their favourite habitats. For example, it will be a waste of time fishing over rocky pinnacles for tope. This small shark lives mainly by hunting flatfish and pouting, and usually confines its activities to flat, sandy or shingly ground. But pinnacle rocks are a good place to bottom-fish for conger, ling and cod. In mid-water around the pinnacles you will find the free-swimming fish such as pollack and coalfish.

As basic equipment, the off-shore angler will need a 6ft boat-rod. Longer rods are becoming popular, but as the hook is dropped straight down over the side and there is virtually no casting to be done, length is not necessary to provide leverage for distance casting. Most boat anglers use the very effective multiplier reel which has a fast rate of line retrieve (useful when winding in from deep water), good braking and a ratchet which enables the angler to prop his rod securely and adjust the brake to a correct tension so that a bite will be registered by the 'clack' of the ratchet. For off-shore fishing, line breaking strain should be about 30lb, although a stronger line should be used if you are fishing specifically for conger. In shallow water, when fishing for flatties, or out deeper for black bream, a lighter line will be adequate, but the 30lb b.s.

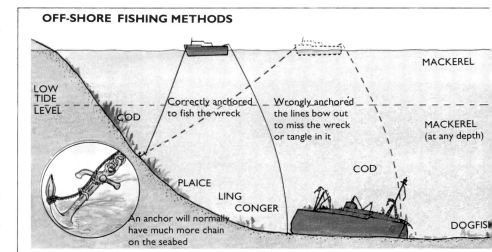

OFF-SHORE FISHING METHODS

LOW TIDE LEVEL

COD

Correctly anchored to fish the wreck

Wrongly anchored the lines bow out to miss the wreck or tangle in it

MACKEREL

MACKEREL (at any depth)

COD

PLAICE

LING

CONGER

An anchor will normally have much more chain on the seabed

DOGFISH

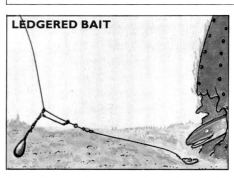

LEDGERED BAIT

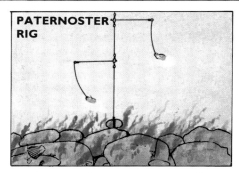

PATERNOSTER RIG

line will stand a great deal of punishment if a sizeable conger is hooked.

Terminal tackle

One of the most effective terminal tackles is the running ledger, with the sliding boom holding a lead of sufficient weight to hold the bottom. This will depend on the strength of the tide. Leads come in all the standard shapes—grip, torpedo, and bomb—and all do their job well when used at the right time and place. The running-ledger rig

Above left *A ledgered bait should be placed close enough to a known mark to lure fish to it.* **Above** *The two-boom paternoster presents baits just above the seabed where the broken ground may snag hooks.*

with boom, swivels, a two-yard leader and end hook, will work well on practically all types of seabed, except rocks. Here, some form of paternoster is necessary. With this rig, the angler will feel the weight hit bottom but know his hooks are placed above this. If care is taken to keep the sensitivity to a fine degree, with the lead just in touch with the bottom, the hooks will not snag.

Tackling-up is the first job, while the boat is heading out to the mark. First make sure that any items of gear not needed immediately—extra clothing in case of a squall, spare rods, food and drink—are all stowed away in the cabin, or somewhere out of sight. When fish are coming aboard there must be no gear to get in the way, especially if a conger is thrashing about in the boat.

Boat owners do not look kindly on anglers using seatboards or the gunnel for cutting up bait strips from mackerel or squid. Use a board and sharp knife.

Wait before dropping down

When the boat anchors, wait until the craft is steady before dropping down

Left *Boat fishing off Lowestoft in an unusual flat calm. But sea conditions can change quickly so have suitable clothing handy.*

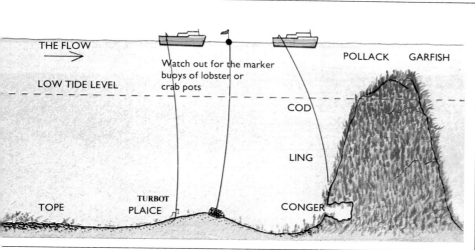

THE FLOW

LOW TIDE LEVEL

Watch out for the marker buoys of lobster or crab pots

POLLACK   GARFISH

COD

LING

TOPE   TURBOT PLAICE   CONGER

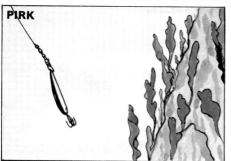

PIRK

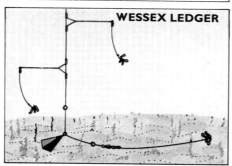

WESSEX LEDGER

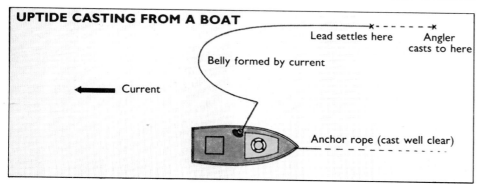

UPTIDE CASTING FROM A BOAT

Lead settles here   Angler casts to here

Belly formed by current

Current

Anchor rope (cast well clear)

Left In one diagram, all off-shore fishing methods are shown. Wrecks, reefs, sandbanks, open seabed all offer the sea angler a challenge. **Below left** The pirk is fished on the drift close to rocky pinnacles to tempt pollack. **Below** The Wessex ledger is drifted over sandbanks.

especially if the day's fishing is good.

Remember not to anchor in a busy sea lane; watch for the onset of a sea-mist; keep and eye on the sky. Squalls can blow up in minutes and the time taken to up-anchor may be just enough for real trouble to develop as the wind rises and turns a calm sea into a heaving and dangerous place for a small boat.

UPTIDE FISHING

A fish taking the bait in a tide-run normally backs off downtide with it, unseating the lead from its grip on the bottom. If the cast has been uptide, the line is suddenly swept downcurrent in an unmistakable manner, looking as if the lead has suddenly lost its grip for no reason. Unfortunately, floating weed causes the same thing to happen, but if a fish has taken the bait, tighten up and strike—a high proportion of hooked fish will result, with few bites missed.

Many boat anglers are now also casting uptide, most of them using boatcasting rods and reels, flowing traces, and wired leads of between 4oz and 8oz. Compared with more conventional boat tackle, these hold the bottom remarkably well, partly due to the position they are cast to, partly due to the fact that the main line is normal beachcasting nylon—thinner than the usual lines that boat anglers use.

To ensure that the lead stays put, the amount of line between rod and lead should be at least twice the depth of the water, and preferably more. The longer the line the more the current will tend to pull the lead *into* the bottom rather than out of it. Remember though, that a lead cast 50 yards uptide in a strong current may be swept back halfway to the boat before the lead reaches the bottom.

Fast taper for best action

The strike is vital in uptide fishing, and to match the rod length and obtain as much action as possible a fast taper is generally favoured. An ideal length is 8ft 6in, comprising a 6ft 6in tip with a 2ft handle. Beachcasting rings should be used for rods with very fast tapers.

The uptide outfit is completed with a beachcasting reel; the heavy metal spools of the larger boat multiplier reels make them unsuitable. But if a plastic spool is used, it is a good idea to use some string as a backing to lessen the chance of the spool breaking.

the lines. It may take a few minutes for the boat to sit right in the tide. Sometimes a small sail may have to be hoisted to hold the craft steady in the tide if the wind is coming from the side. The stern corners are the ideal places from which to fish. From these places the lead can be of just enough weight to get the bait down, and then allowed to work out with the tide, but always being kept in contact with the seabed. The anglers behind them must have heavier weights to avoid tangling.

The successful off-shore angler will adjust his tackle so that he is in constant touch with the bottom. He will not allow his lead to bounce up and down in the sand or mud because this will set up vibrations and echoes in the water that may well keep fish away. The ideal method is to be able to 'feel' the seabed all the time, and be able to differentiate between the small tugs and pulls of the tide and anchor rope, and similar sensations from fish.

Above When uptide casting, watch for the line to suddenly droop. This is the sign of a taking fish, so tighten up and strike.

Don't snatch!

Different species of fish have different 'bites'. But as with other forms of fishing, it is not necessarily the biggest fish which give the strongest bites. Some large cod will give tentative pulls at first, but this fish has a very large mouth, so a hurried snatch by the angler may well pull the bait out of its mouth. Wait. Let the take develop, and strike when the cod has taken the bait, turned, and is swimming away. The hook will then be set properly and the fish can be played to the boat.

Before setting out, whether in your own boat or not, be sure to have enough food and drink for the trip, a thick pull-over and some weatherproof clothing. The day may be fine and the forecast good, but things can change in the long periods that sea anglers stay out—

WRECK FISHING

Wreck fishing is the most spectacular branch of sea fishing and it provides anglers with the opportunity to consistently catch specimen fish. Reasonable catches are occasionally made from wrecks lying close to shore, but their accessibility can lead to overfishing and the numbers of fish living in them is drastically reduced. The best action is now found on sunken hulks lying more than 30 miles out, a distance which can only be reached in good weather conditions by skippers operating large, licensed charter-boats.

Dominant wreck species

While many different species are found on wrecks, the sport is dominated by conger, ling, pollack, coalfish and bream, all of which fall into three distinct categories. Conger and ling are taken on heavy-duty tackle and big baits are ledgered on the bottom. The pollack and coalfish fall to medium-weight gear, artificial and natural baits, between the wreckage and the surface, although the bottom 10 fathoms is usually the productive zone. Black and red bream are caught by using more sensitive tackle on baits dropped right into the wreckage.

Secret wreck marks

All charter skippers keep a record of the position of wrecks and jealously guard their whereabouts. Every year new wrecks are discovered by accident and as each is likely to be sheltering hundreds of fish, it is understandable that skippers prefer to keep such information to themselves. Some skippers go to great lengths to preserve the secrets of such a mark only visiting the place when no other vessel is in sight. They then keep a vigilant look-out during the time the boat is anchored over it, and should another charter boat be spotted they leave the area quickly.

Pollack and coalfish

Wrecking for pollack and coal fish is tremendous fun. Both species are grand fighters and the line-stripping plunge of even a 15lb pollack is one of the most thrilling experiences in sea fishing. During the summer, most are caught on medium-weight tackle from anchored boats. The usual rig is a single 4/0 hook to a 20ft trace, worked from an 8in wire boom, or the recently introduced plastic variety. The boom effectively keeps the trace from tangling with the reel line during its long journey to the bottom. It

Right *Some of the tackle rigs for fishing over wreck marks. Rotten bottom links and odd weight items avoid loss of expensive lead.*

is then steadily retrieved until the bait or artificial eel is taken. At this point the fish will make its characteristic plunge, and line must be given out again or it will certainly break.

Tough on man and tackle

To cope with winter wreck fishing, tackle must be heavy, and it is customary for 50lb class hollow glass rods and 6/0 multipliers to be used. It is tough on equipment, too, as many would-be record breakers have found to their cost, when a rod has cracked under the strain, or a multiplier has jammed. Anglers also suffer: after the first dozen drifts and perhaps 20 big fish, stomach, arm and back muscles start protesting. More than a few men have been exhausted to the point of giving up fishing, although down below it seemed as if fish were almost queueing up to get on to a hook.

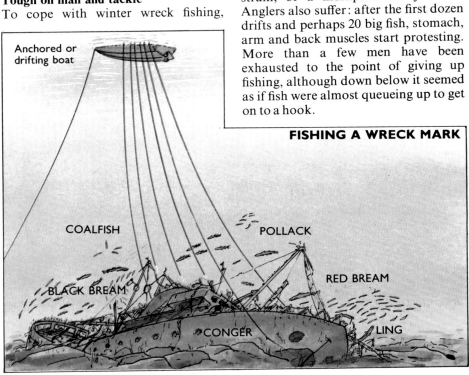

FISHING A WRECK MARK

Anchored or drifting boat

COALFISH

POLLACK

RED BREAM

BLACK BREAM

CONGER

LING

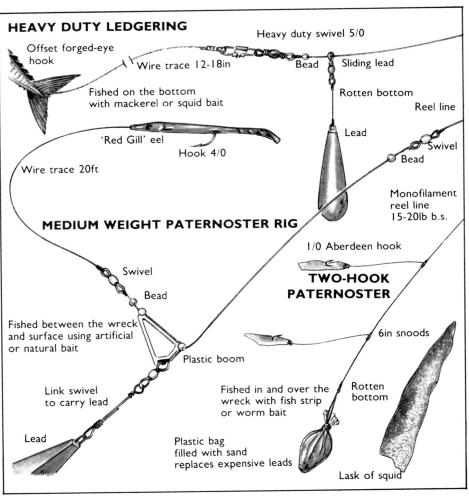

HEAVY DUTY LEDGERING

Offset forged-eye hook

Heavy duty swivel 5/0

Wire trace 12-18in

Bead

Sliding lead

Fished on the bottom with mackerel or squid bait

Rotten bottom

Reel line

'Red Gill' eel

Lead

Hook 4/0

Swivel

Bead

Wire trace 20ft

Monofilament reel line 15-20lb b.s.

MEDIUM WEIGHT PATERNOSTER RIG

1/0 Aberdeen hook

Swivel

Bead

TWO-HOOK PATERNOSTER

Fished between the wreck and surface using artificial or natural bait

Plastic boom

6in snoods

Link swivel to carry lead

Fished in and over the wreck with fish strip or worm bait

Rotten bottom

Lead

Plastic bag filled with sand replaces expensive leads

Lask of squid

REEF FISHING

Boat fishing over rocky ground can be one of the most rewarding methods in sea angling. Even a small patch of reef provides shelter for many fish, and several species can be caught throughout the year. Inshore reefs are generally accepted to be those lying in shallow water within three miles of land. Beyond, in depths of 50 fathoms or more, reefs are classed as offshore.

Around the British Isles there are many places where excellent catches are made by rod and line fishermen, but it is the great reefs of the western English Channel that provide spectacular sport.

Light tackle a key to success

Light tackle is one of the secrets of good pollacking over reefs. Most experts use a hollow-glass, two-handed spinning rod, 9-10ft long, matched with a small multiplier and 12-15lb b.s. monofilament. A trace 15-20ft in length gives both natural and artificial baits an attractive movement. It is vital to keep them moving at all times as pollack rarely go for a stationary offering. In the West Country the long trace is called a 'flying collar' and it surpasses any other method. It comprises a single wire boom about 8in long with a split ring swivel at either end and one where the weight is attached. On this tackle, hooked fish are able to work up great speed, which raises the quality of the sport to a magnificent level.

Pollack keep close to the bottom during daylight, but at last light they rise much higher in the water, and hectic action can be expected. This is also a good time to troll an artificial sandeel 6ft beneath the surface. It is often the large fish that are caught by this method. From June, red bream swarm over the reef and tackle should be scaled right down for this species.

Reef conger

Reef conger fishing during daylight, in water of less than 25 fathoms, is usually on the slow side. Few bites come in the first hour of a session, but things do improve after the eels get the scent of food. Seldom is a bait attacked with gusto, so it is important to allow ample time for it to be taken down. The usual way of detecting bites is to hold the reel line between the thumb and forefinger, with the rod resting against the boat's gunwale, and the reel in check. When the line jerks strongly, the rod is picked up and any slack line wound in until the weight of the fish can be felt. A firm sweep of the rod will set the hook.

The best bream fishing is found in deep water, and tackle must be suited

to the prevailing conditions. If the strength of tide is not great, a 9ft spinning rod will do nicely, as lead can be kept to a minimum. The normal method of fishing is with a two hook paternoster trace made up from 15lb line. This should be about 3ft in length with 6in snoods and 1/0 fine-wire hooks. Bream accept all fish-baits, crabs and marine worms. All bites must be struck very quickly as the bream has a knack of ejecting in a flash anything suspicious.

Drift fishing over many reefs in the western English Channel produces

Top *A very large ling of the kind taken during wreck fishing.* **Above** *This is the record wreckfish of 10lb 10oz. Strangely, the wreckfish is usually caught when the boat is at anchor or drift fishing over a reef.*

whiting, pouting and, unfortunately, loads of dogfish, which are a bait-robbing menace.

Fishing deepwater wrecks is a sport full of surprises, for large and powerful fish live in those shattered hulks. Therefore tackle must be of the highest quality.

GAME FISHING

Every year, among the millions of anglers in Britain, there are those who, never having cast a fly in their life, turn to trout fishing and thus add yet another facet of sportfishing to their list. Why is the number of trout fishermen increasing so dramatically? The reason is that there has been a steady build-up of every kind of coarse fishing in the past decade.

There are basically two kinds of trout fishing waters, the river and the reservoir. Britain's trout rivers are renowned throughout the world both for the quality of their trout and the stunning beauty of their scenery. The chalkstreams of Hampshire, to name only the Test, are hallowed places where fishing is conducted with a quiet dignity and much grace; the becks and streams of Northern England and Scotland do not hold many very large trout, but their attraction lies equally in the splendour of the fells and dales through which they run.

It is through reservoir fishing that the new fly fisherman will first experience the thrill of hooking a trout on the artificial fly. One of the first things the beginner must learn is never to strike in the manner usually adopted when coarse fishing. Such a strike can pull the fly from the trout's jaws. The correct action to take is simply to tighten the connection between angler and fish and never allow it to slacken.

The explosion in the number of reservoir trout anglers has led to many improvements in equipment and in the techniques of breeding both brown and rainbow trout to be released prior to the opening of the trout season. The rainbow has come in for special treatment now, especially at Avington, a water in Hampshire. This trout has been released after having been reared to the huge weight of 20lb. The reply to an angler who asked what one should do when such a huge fish was hooked was, 'Just hang on for the rest of the day!' These giant rainbows may be artificially reared, but power they have in plenty.

The costs involved in game fishing can vary from astronomically high prices for fishing Scotland's famous salmon rivers such as the Tay, the Dee, the Spey and so on, to virtually nothing for worming for trout in a tinkling burn among the Highlands. English reservoirs, they include vast, man-made lakes such as Rutland and Chew Valley, offer bank and boat fishing for quite reasonable prices. As with coarse fishing, the angler must be aware that not only is the cost of the day's fishing to be considered, but the River Authority licence for game fish.

Once the angler has fallen to the spell of casting that tiny knot of feather, fur and hook towards a feeding trout chomping happily on dead and dying mayflies littering the surface of a rippling stream, he will soon explore the greater delight, if that is possible. These delights are twitching an imitation nymph deep down near the bottom of a rainbow-stocked reservoir, waiting for that giant fish to take in a crashing lurch on the rod; or perhaps he will find the time—and money— to seek a fresh-run salmon from a Highland river using a spinning rod to fish the prawn or lure.

Artificial flies, spinners, prawn and shrimp, of course, are not the only means of catching trout and salmon. While the dry fly purist's heart will miss a beat or two at the mention of the dreaded worm, freelining a large wriggling lob upstream to wary trout can be very rewarding. It was once said that fly fishing was invented because game fish were so easy to catch by other means, so a way had to be devised to make fishing for them difficult. But since fly casting is not difficult, and trout are just not easy to catch by 'other means'—and bearing in mind that trout have never heard of the man-made fly-only rule—worming for them must be just as legitimate, if the rules of the water allow it.

The trout fisherman's accessories are not as profuse as those of the coarse angler, but there are a few which no well-appointed game angler should travel without. One is the item which, when quickly and properly used, kills the fish decently. It is known as the priest, perhaps because it gives the fish the last rites. But a smart rap on the head with a priest will kill without unpleasantness. For fishing the floating line, specially prepared floatants are available that keep the line on the surface, while a dab of washing-up liquid on the leader will ensure its sinking properly. For landing nets, most game fishermen prefer the collapsible type that is worn attached to the belt. On release, a quick flip of the wrist opens it out ready for instant use.

As for the game fisherman's clothing, it does the ego good to look the part, although the only necessities are good waders, thigh or chest high, high quality rainproof wear (it has been known to rain in Scotland) and a fisherman's hat that comes down near the ears. Why? Because a large artificial fly, on the end of line cast badly during the forward stroke, travels very fast and should it connect with the head or an ear the angler will not only look bloody *and* silly, but his fishing could well be over for a day or two while the wound heals.

Every trout angler should learn the simple art of fly tying. The ultimate satisfaction comes on the day when you net a good-sized trout that has been deceived by a home-made fly.

Coarse anglers must forget the outdated image of the lofty game fisherman exercising his fly-fishing skills and looking disdainfully at the man fishing the carp lake with ledgered bread. Both kinds of fishing demand the acquisition of angling skills and a high degree of expertise.

CHAPTER 9

THE FISH

SALMON

The Atlantic salmon is one of the most mysterious fish in the world. Considered by many to be the king of fish, its reputation as a fighter, its great stamina and unusual life-cycle is still fascinating despite our increased knowledge.

Tackles and techniques for salmon fishing depend on three main elements —the time of the year, location of the beat (particularly to its distance from the sea) and weather and water.

Salmon fishing in Britain and Ireland begins in the early days of the new year, and on some rivers closes as late as the end of November. There are four main periods—early spring, late spring, summer and late summer/autumn.

From January to mid-April, you not only have to catch your fish, but also identify whether or not it is 'clean'. In the early months, many salmon will be fish which entered freshwater the previous year, spawned in November and December, and are now dropping back to the sea as kelts. These fish are protected by law, and should be returned carefully to the water. They do not provide rod and line sport.

Big autumn fish require heavy tackle and strong lines. Flies too should be bigger. As the water cools, return to sinking-tip or fast-sink lines and bigger tube flies. By November, 2-3in tube flies are common.

Other methods

Although spinning and fly fishing form the basis of most salmon fishing techniques there are several other legitimate methods which the angler may resort to when the going gets tough. It is possible to limit all salmon fishing to small flies and floating lines in late spring and summer and big flies and sinking lines for early spring or late autumn. However, worm, prawn or shrimp have many a time saved an otherwise blank day or week. At certain times and seasons the use of these natural baits can be very effective, but there are still too many anglers who will resort to them without trying other more sporting methods.

It should not be implied that fishing with any of these natural baits is easy. There is a sense in which successful fishing with a worm or prawn is more difficult than fly fishing, but there are times, conditions and situations when they might prove too effective and spoil the sport for others.

BROWN TROUT

The brown trout is indigenous to Europe, North West Asia, and North Africa. It shows a remarkable diversity of shape and coloration, often according to locality. It can be categorized into two distinct forms which differ chiefly in life style but also in size and colour. The

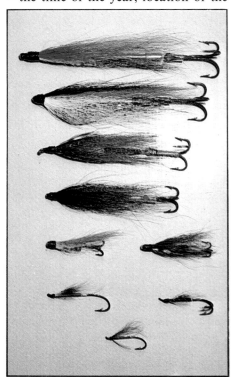

LEAD WIRE RIG

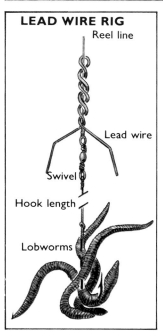

Reel line

Lead wire

Swivel

Hook length

Lobworms

Top left *An assortment of salmon flies used at various times of the season.* **Above** *The proud captor of a beautiful 19lb summer salmon from Scotland.* **Far left** *A spiral of lead wire put above the swivel can stop hooks from snagging the bottom.* **Left** *The complete salmon spinner's outfit: two reels, with spoons and Devon minnows.*

THREE FLY TEAM

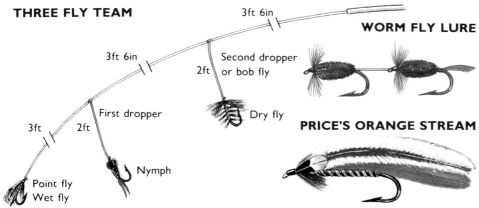

3ft 6in

3ft 6in

2ft — Second dropper or bob fly

First dropper

3ft — 2ft

Dry fly

Nymph

Point fly
Wet fly

WORM FLY LURE

PRICE'S ORANGE STREAM

Top left *A handsome 7½lb brown trout from a famous trout river, the Test.* **Left** *A three-fly team of dry fly, nymph and wet fly. The dry fly will bob on the surface as the line is being lifted and often attracts an otherwise suspicious trout.* **Above** *Fishing a bay in the beautiful Blagdon Reservoir, Somerset.*

sea trout is the migratory form.

The brown trout is the non-migratory form which lives in rivers and lakes. The steeper gradients of the rivers where brown trout survive best are often a long way from the sea, and in many rivers they are separated from the sea by the slower sluggish zones which trout tend to avoid. Often mild pollution also bars the way to the sea. In any event the brown trout has been separated from the sea for many generations and has adopted an entirely freshwater mode of life.

Although trout can be taken on many baits, including the lowly maggot, worm, spinners and lures, the artificial fly is the offering most used to attract this game fish.

Wet and dry flies

Trout are taken on wet and dry flies. The basic difference between these is that the hackles on the dry fly stand out, making it float, while the wet fly's 'wings' run back along the body.

Boats have both advantages and disadvantages for the trout angler. Although a boat gives access to the whole of a large water, unless you are anchored or in a flat calm, it also makes

it difficult to fish a fly below 2-3ft.

Methods and/or flies are restricted on some waters, although the rules may be eased as the season progresses. But do not worry if the rule is nymph-only. Records show that more heavier fish are caught on imitation flies than on lures in these waters. The reason is probably that the newly stocked fish either get wise to lures quickly or get caught.

Most small fisheries are shallow, so there is no need to plumb vast depths for big fish. Typical tackle for nymphing is an 8¼ft glassfibre rod with matching floating line and an 8ft leader of 8lb b.s. line, with perhaps one dropper. Popular flies are black, brown and green midge pupae, orange and brown sedge pupae, leaded and unleaded Pheasant Tail nymphs, Shrimp, Corixa and Black and Peacock spider.

RAINBOW TROUT

Though deplored by some trout purists, the introduction of rainbows has made fly fishing available to many more anglers, and most reservoir anglers welcome the rainbow and the exciting sport it offers in a hundred subtly different ways in different conditions.

Generally a far hardier fish than the

brown trout, the rainbow can withstand high temperatures, low oxygen levels, and murky waters. It is also a far more active fish, being a free riser to the fly and living and moving in loose shoals, with a strong urge to migrate upstream for spawning, falling back into lakes or lower reaches for the rest of the season. At the extreme it is anadromous, like sea trout, migrating from dense to less dense water to breed.

When to use the dry fly

Rainbows often rise freely in boisterous weather, feeding well on the surface during high winds, following the wind lanes in large groups and fearlessly rising under the bows of the angler's boat. They will often cruise upwind in such conditions, dropping into the depths when they come to the far shores, and then feed earnestly either in mid-water, or on the bottom.

In calmer water, when the angler despairs of getting his wet flies to work without creating a heavy wake, the rainbows will often rise maddening at midges and other small flies on the surface, ignoring the wet flies offered by the fisherman. Then the dry fly is often useful. Takes are sudden, and the rainbow is usually moving fast when it hits the fly. Smash-takes occur in these conditions, even when the cast is realistically heavy. The angler should not let his rod be pointing at the fly, for the shock must be absorbed by the rod when the fish takes.

FISHING A WORM THROUGH SEA TROUT LIES

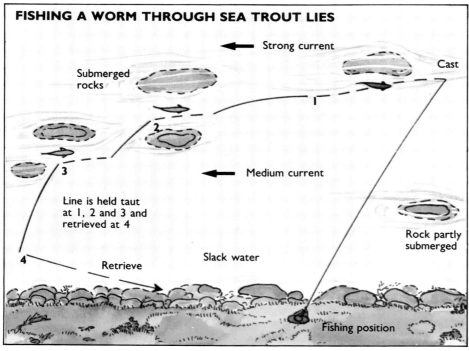

Strong current

Submerged rocks

Cast

Medium current

Line is held taut at 1, 2 and 3 and retrieved at 4

Slack water

Rock partly submerged

Retrieve

Fishing position

SURFACE LURE FOR SEA TROUT

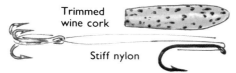

Trimmed wine cork

Stiff nylon

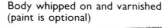

Body whipped on and varnished (paint is optional)

Top *How to work a worm through a sea trout lie.* **Above** *During the cast this lure whistles past your ear like a hornet. But it takes sea trout.* **Below** *Two fine sea trout from Wales.*

Above *The home-made sea trout lure is made from a wine cork, a treble and a single hook, stiff nylon and some whipping. After being varnished it can be painted. It looks crude —but it works.*

SEA TROUT

Until recent times it was thought that the sea trout was a separate species and different from the brown trout. Scientific opinion now is that they are both of the species *Salmo trutta*. Unless further evidence comes to light we must accept that the sea trout is nothing more than a migratory brown trout.

There is little doubt that most sea trout spend some part of their year running up from the sea into freshwater.

A good motto for the angler seeking sea trout today would be, 'First find a sea trout river!' The sea trout's environment, like that of the salmon, is slowly being eroded; and where it abounds its runs and migrations tend to be more fickle and unpredictable than previously. So the angler must do some intensive homework: to find an adequate sea trout river and then, miraculously, contrive to be there when the sea trout is in the pools of his own beat.

Many dedicated sea trout anglers feel that fly fishing for sea trout with a floating line presents the ultimate angling challenge in Britain today. This must be a matter of opinion and opportunity, but undoubtedly the sea trout is one of the shyest fish to inhabit our waters. For this reason, most sea trout fishing, in normal to low water, is done under cover of darkness.

Basic tackle
The ideal sea-trout rod is single-handed and about 10ft long. It should be rigged with a No. 7 double or forward taper line, attached to a 9ft monofilament leader of not less than 6lb b.s. To this tie on a No 10 single or double-hooked fly. Add waders and net and the sea trout angler is ready for the fray.

Patterns of sea trout fly are legion. Most anglers have their favourites, but there is little doubt that the angler is much more fussy in this respect than the fish. In the dark it sees the fly as only a vague silhouette, so it is size and not colour which is more important.

Freelining a lobworm calls for a ledger or spinning rod of about 10ft and a fixed-spool reel bearing a main line of 6-8lb and a slightly weaker leader ahead of that.

A great deal of sea trout fishing is done with spinning gear and Devon minnow lures and other colourful, attractive lures.

Once the angler has come under the spell of sea trout fishing he is usually lost to all other parts of the sport. For him the only existence worthy of the description comes when he is wading thigh deep in barely moonlit water and casting to those speckled giants he knows are there!

CHAPTER 10
TACKLE

SALMON RODS

Salmon rods may be divided into two main types—spinning rods (sometimes known as bait casting rods) and fly rods.

Spinning rods

Spinning rods, the kind more widely used for salmon fishing, are usually 8-10ft in length. For rivers requiring the use of heavy baits and lines with high b.s., that is, over 15lb, a double-handed rod of 9¼-10ft, used with a multiplier reel, is the best type. This combination gives good control of the bait and will handle big fish in the larger, stronger rivers such as the Hampshire Avon and the Wye. It is also suitable for fishing with a prawn bait. Smaller rivers, where lighter lines and bait may be used, call for a shorter rod, 8¼-9ft long, used with a fixed-spool or multiplier style reel. Line

of 10-15lb and casting weight of up to 1oz are suited to use with this combination. This outfit can be used for worming for salmon, although a longer rod is probably preferable with this technique.

Ideally, a salmon spinning rod is strong, with a medium-to-stiff action. The through action favoured in the past to assist in avoiding casting problems, such as overruns by the multiplier reel, is no longer essential as reel design has improved. The newer kind of action is preferable, even for use with the multiplier.

Two-piece construction, with glass spigot joints in the case of carbonfibre and tubular glass, is standard in salmon spinning rods. Handles are usually of cork, with either sliding fittings or a fixed screw winch fitting to hold the reel. Stainless steel rod rings are the most commonly used. These have a hard chrome finish to withstand wear from the line. The rod should have enough rings to ensure that the strain on the line is evenly distributed along the rod's length. On rods used with the multiplier style of reel, which sits on top, the rings need to be carefully positioned so as to avoid any contact between the line and rod.

Fly rods

Salmon fly rods are designed for use by one or two hands, according to the style of casting employed. The double-handed variety are usually 12-14ft long, certainly over 11ft. The ideal length for an all-round rod is 12¼-13ft, and this, coupled with a double tapered size 9 line, is suitable for fishing most of the salmon waters in this country.

The modern carbonfibre fly rods, although still expensive, have several advantages and are increasingly popular. Apart from casting as well as a top quality built cane model, they have the valuable assets of lightness and strength, and so may be used, where necessary, in greater lengths without any strain on the angler. Their small diameter is a great advantage in windy conditions, where built cane would offer more wind resistance.

Rod materials

However, the most common material for salmon rods is tubular glass for, apart from giving a serviceable rod, it is much cheaper than either carbonfibre or built cane. Although heavier than carbonfibre, the tubular glass rod has the advantage of lightness over the built cane variety. A 12¼-13ft model makes a good all-round rod for most types of salmon fly fishing and will control the largest fish.

Single-handed fly rods of 9¼ft or longer are suited to fishing for salmon in small to medium sized rivers, where smaller flies are used. They should not be used, though, to lift long lines, as this subjects them, and the angler's arm, to considerable strain. Fishing in these conditions requires a light, 10ft rod of carbonfibre, tubular glass or built cane, equipped with a double tapered line, size 7, on a reel large enough to take 100 yards of 15lb b.s. backing line. This outfit should prove adequate for the salmon encountered in the smaller waters.

Action

Most salmon fly rods today have an action that may be felt right through from the heavy tip to the butt. A tip with this fairly rigid action is required because of the need to 'mend' the line or straighten it out. This need arises when the strength of the current varies at different points across the stream and the line is pulled into a bow shape as it is carried downstream. This in turn carries the fly back across the flow at an unnatural angle, making it unacceptable to the salmon.

Top left *How to use the correct tailing grip to pick up a salmon.* **Left** *A prime Irish salmon and the double-handed rod with which it was caught.*

RESERVOIR RODS

Reservoir fishing has become an important part of game fishing. Large numbers of anglers fish these waters from the banks and from boats. This type of fishing demands distance casting and continual retrieval of the line. This means the rod will be in constant use, so the angler must choose a rod which will enable him to cast efficiently into the high winds often present on reservoirs, without becoming too tired.

Purpose of the rod

The purpose of a rod in any type of fishing is to act as a guide for the line and as a spring to absorb the effects of hard-fighting fish. But in fly fishing the rod must also be supple enough throughout all, or part, of its length to cast a fly which is virtually weightless. The line is weighted according to the type of fishing it is designed for and so rods will differ according to the weight of line they can carry. Rods also have different actions, and there is variation of construction as well.

Wood has always been considered the best material for fly rod construction. The peak of wooden fishing rod construction is split cane, which tends to have an 'all-through' action which means that the full length of the rod will be involved when playing a fish or casting. But split cane has drawbacks in its maintenance and in its casting ability. Split cane cannot be stored even slightly wet because it will quickly warp and rot. The problem with its action is that when used for casting long distances it can take on a permanent curve, called a 'set'. But its greatest drawback is its weight when compared with today's man-made materials.

Glassfibre

During the 20-odd years since it was introduced, glassfibre has progressed from the solid section to 'hollow glass'. The great advantage of hollow glassfibre rods is that they can be tailored to give any kind of action to suit individual preference. Some anglers prefer to use nymphs to tempt fish rising to the surface and would probably choose a double-taper line. Consequently a rod with a through action will be preferred. For reservoir fishing, involving huge areas of water, long casting is essential and so, coupled with a heavy line, a fast taper rod with a tip-action will be the choice. Some reservoir anglers prefer through-action rods, but a rod with the action in its top part tends to be more powerful propelling the line farther.

Carbonfibre

Carbonfibre has all the advantages of glassfibre but is much lighter, and has a smaller diameter for the same power. There is one big difference—carbonfibre rods are much more expensive than all the others. Carbonfibre was originally seen as a short, very light fishing rod. Now a number of tackle manufacturers are offering their brands of carbonfibre rods in lengths between 7ft

Below left Reservoir rods must have an action that can cope with large rainbows such as this 14½lb fish. Below A comparison between fly rods for reservoir fishing and streams. Cutaways show the materials from which modern fly rods are made.

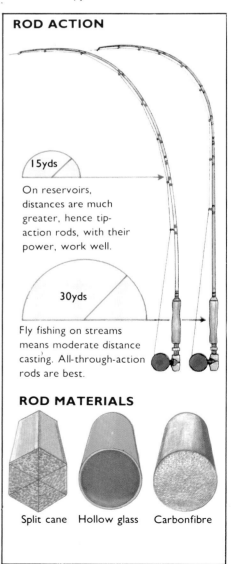

ROD ACTION

15yds

On reservoirs, distances are much greater, hence tip-action rods, with their power, work well.

30yds

Fly fishing on streams means moderate distance casting. All-through-action rods are best.

ROD MATERIALS

Split cane   Hollow glass   Carbonfibre

and 10ft 6in for fly fishing for trout.

The selection of a rod must take into account the use to which it will be put, and the type of water to be fished. One can then choose between split cane, glassfibre or carbonfibre. The advantage of this material is that less effort is needed in casting, partly because there is more 'power' in the carbonfibre sections from which the rod was made, and partly because the smaller diameter of the rod creates less air resistance.

Cost is a factor we all have to bear in mind. At present carbonfibre rods are expensive, but because inferior carbonfibre is worse than inferior glassfibre, selection must not be based purely on cheapness. Your selection of a reservoir rod must be based on sound advice from the dealer, your experience and judgement of the rods you are offered, and the style of fishing which you intend to do with it.

FLY REELS

While all anglers agree that a casting reel must be properly designed if it is to work efficiently, many feel that the fly reel is a very unimportant tackle item. This may be because in fly fishing the reel has no influence on the cast, whereas in other modes of fishing the reel has a dominant effect on distance. But the fly reel is an item which warrants careful

thought, because a fly reel often does more than a fixed-spool when playing a fish.

There are several reasons for this, and one is the faster runs made by game fish when compared with most coarse and saltwater species. Fly lines are thicker than monofilament so a fly reel empties quickly and as the line pile gets smaller so the spool turns faster. Under these circumstances, if the spool is a poor fit within the reel frame it will jam and the fish will be be lost.

Three basic types of fly reel

Fly reels fall into three basic categories: the single-action type where the drum moves one revolution for every turn of the handle (on a well-filled trout reel this recovers approximately 8in of line); the multiplier type where the drum performs perhaps two revolutions (thereby recovering approximately 16in of line) for every turn of the handle, and the clockwork or automatic type where the spool is driven by a spring. This spring winds itself up when you take line from the reel.

The basic function of any reel is to hold a sufficient quantity of line for the type of fishing being practised. Once that condition has been satisfied, reels become increasingly sophisticated. There are different methods of fly

The basic fly reel needs to be no more than a reservoir for the fly line. Such reels today have varying degrees of sophistication, but the reel top right is a Hardy model which has remained practically unchanged since 1891. **Above left** *These three fat trout were caught by angling skill, but the Intrepid reel did its part, too.*

fishing and reel requirements will be different for each.

A simple, single-action model will do all that is needed, for the reel does little beyond serving as a convenient line store. The multiplier and the automatic would also be suitable but in the situation described their more sophisticated features would not be used to full advantage and may be altogether unnecessary in this setting.

Maintenance

There are so few moving parts in a fly reel that maintenance is hardly worth mentioning. An occasional spot of oil on the spool spindle takes care of the revolving parts and a liberal smear of grease on the check pawl is all that is needed. With the automatic reel, follow the maker's instructions regarding oiling.

As with all reels, clean them after every outing to keep deterioration to the minimum.

FLY LINES

The oil-dressed silk line was in universal use for three-quarters of a century, until it was replaced by the modern plastic-coated fly lines which consist of a plaited Dacron core with a coating of polyvinyl chloride (PVC). For sinking fly lines, the PVC is impregnated with powdered metal, the quantity used determining the rate at which the line sinks through the water.

A wide variety of line is now available, identified by a code known as the AFTM (Association of Fishing Tackle Manufacturers) system. This code tells you the kind of taper the line has, the weight of the first 30ft of the line, and whether the line is a floating or a sinking one.

So-called 'level lines' are of the same thickness all along their length; they are little used and their only merit is that they are cheap. They are designated by the letter L.

Double taper lines

'Double taper lines', designated DT, have both their ends tapered for more than 10ft, giving a fine end which falls more lightly on the water. The idea of a double taper is that when one end is worn, you can reverse the line on your reel and use the other. These lines usually come in lengths of 90ft.

'Forward taper lines', otherwise known as 'weight-forward' (WF) resemble the first 30ft or so of a double taper with 40ft of very fine fly line attached. (In fact there is no actual attachment, both core and coating are continuous.) This allows more line to be 'shot' through the rings when casting. Lines are now available with the first, heavier part longer than 30ft. These are called 'long belly lines'.

'Shooting heads' are similar in principle to 'forward taper lines', but instead of the fine shooting line being a continuation of the PVC-coated fly line, it consists of nylon monofilament attached to the fly line by a special knot. This allows even more line to be 'shot' in casting, and as the fly line is usually cut from a double taper, shooting heads are much cheaper than either double or forward taper lines.

Shooting heads

Good tackle shops will usually sell halves or 'double tapers' for making shooting heads, which will need a further reduction in length, usually to 30-36ft.

All these lines can be of different floating or sinking qualities. There are

*When to use the three different fly line profiles **A**, **B** and **C** and the relative rates of fast, medium and slow sinking lines.*

floaters, slow sinkers, medium sinkers and fast sinkers, as well as floating lines with sinking tips. They are all available in a range of weights, numbered 3 to 12. The more powerful your rod, the heavier the line it will need.

When you buy a rod you will find that its maker has specified what size line it will carry. Remember that this refers to 30ft of line in the air. If your rod has a recommendation of No 7 line, that means it will work nicely when you are switching 30ft of line in the air.

For dry fly and nymph fishing, floating lines are used: the sinking lines are mainly for lake and reservoir fishing when wet flies and lures of various kinds are needed. Slow sinkers sink at a

rate of about 1ft in 7 seconds: medium sinkers 1ft in 5 seconds: fast sinkers, or as they are sometimes called, 'Hi-D' lines sink about 1ft in 3 seconds. By counting the seconds after casting, you can decide how deep you allow your line to sink before starting the retrieve.

Backing line

For most kinds of fly fishing, your fly line needs backing: that is, some monofilament or braided, uncoated line is wound on to the reel first, and then the coated fly line is attached to it. Flattened monofilament of about 25lb b.s., or special nylon sold for backing purposes, is cheaper than braided backing, and easier to connect to fly lines.

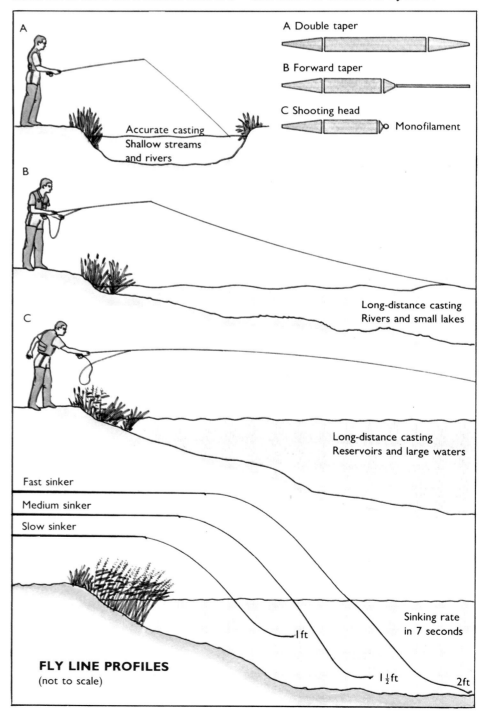

A Double taper

B Forward taper

C Shooting head — Monofilament

A — Accurate casting. Shallow streams and rivers

B — Long-distance casting. Rivers and small lakes

C — Long-distance casting. Reservoirs and large waters

Fast sinker

Medium sinker

Slow sinker

1ft

1½ft

2ft

Sinking rate in 7 seconds

FLY LINE PROFILES (not to scale)

ANATOMY OF THE DRY FLY

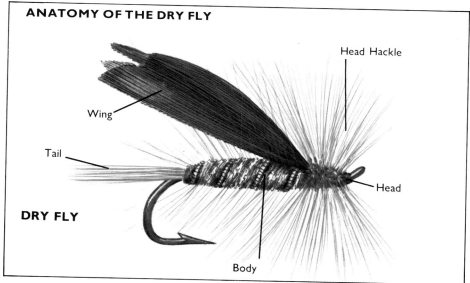

Wing

Tail

Head Hackle

DRY FLY

Head

Body

Left Dry fly hackles stand out to ensure the artificial floats on the surface. Floatants can be applied when the hackles become wet.

flies start to hatch in July and August and are present throughout the day, and in vast numbers at nightfall. If weather conditions are good and flies are hatching, a pattern representing a sedge can be very effective, for the 'spent' sedge falling back upon the water is the fly most likely to attract the attention of the trout. But they are by no means the only ones. Throughout the year there are hatches of buzzers, the dreaded caenis, which is too small to be imitated, and a number of Ephemerids such as the olives. These insects all hatch from the water and return there to lay their eggs, and this is when the trout will rise.

Patterns of dry fly

In almost all instances where trout feed on land-borne insects, the rule is not to move the fly. It is not possible to simulate the vibrating motion of their legs and in any case they are soon dead or exhausted and then lay still. An imitation is far more likely to succeed if it is cast out and then left. Regarding the patterns of dry fly that are needed, every angler should include in his collection the following: Tupp's Indispensable, Mayfly, Sedge, Black Gnat, Grey Duster, Iron Blue, Daddy Long Legs, Sherry Spinner, Pond Olive, Lunn's Particular, Flying Ant, Drone Fly, Greenwell's Glory, Royal Coachman, Wickham's Fancy, Silver Sedge, Kite's Imperial, Grey Wulff, Grey Duster, Lake Olive and perhaps appropriately Last Hope, which was originated by John Goodard to represent the Pale Watery dun or similar, light coloured river insects.

These are only a few of the many hundreds of dry flies available. The tremendous growth of fly fishing, and the advent of the relatively cheap package holidays abroad, has led to English fly fishing enthusiasts travelling all over the world, notably the United States, Canada, Alaska and even New Zealand. This has resulted in many flies with origins far from our waters.

Unless treated with a floatant, dry flies will quickly become waterlogged and need frequent changing. This is especially true of the wool bodied types. But the invention of Permaflote by Dick Walker and Arnold Neave means that you can fish the same fly all day without a change, unless, of course, a fish has taken it, when it will need a change. One word of warning—it's best to treat the flies and leave them to dry thoroughly before use if you want the best results from them.

Blue-winged olive dun
Ephemerella ignita

Mayfly
Ephemera danica

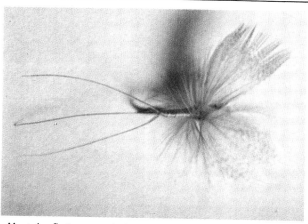

Most dry fly patterns imitate the natural insect. The Mayfly **(left)** is imitated by the fluffy Green Drake **(above)**. Crawling up the stem above the Mayfly is the blue-winged olive dun, seen **(right)** in the artificial Orange Quill, an evening fly. Some dry fly patterns bear little resemblance so far as the human eye is concerned to natural insects, but neverthéles prove very attractive to trout.

DRY FLIES

Dry fly fishing has always been regarded as the supreme art in fly fishing circles. This is particularly so on rivers and chalkstreams where matching the hatch is only the beginning of the problem and where presentation has to be considered as well. But dry flies also play an important part in reservoir and lake fishing where trout are attracted by insects on the surface.

Favourite season

Of all the periods during the season when trout rise to a dry fly, the favourite is the time that the mayfly hatch. The huge flies energe from the water in such large numbers that the trout literally gorge themselves to capacity, and the better fish rise freely. On these occasions almost any artificial pattern representing a mayfly will take fish.

Early in the season the hawthorn fly hatches in large numbers and very good catches can be made with the aid of a Black Gnat. Again this mostly applies to running waters, but vast numbers of hawthorn flies were noticed at one huge Midlands reservoir. Although the fish were not rising to them at that time, they will probably do so in the future.

In late summer, one of the most popular flies that hatches on every water is the sedge. These medium sized

WET FLIES

In contrast to the dry fly which is intended to simulate an insect floating or alighting on the water, the wet fly represents some small insect or creature living and moving actively below the surface.

The dry fly usually represents the winged fly only, but a wet fly may represent the insect at any stage of development except the egg. It *may* imitate a half-drowned winged fly or even the critical transition stage when the pupal nymph is struggling to hatch into the adult stage and break through to the surface. It can also represent the free swimming or crawling larva, or the partially developed nymph darting among the lower layers or ascending towards the surface. Other creatures simulated by many wet fly dressings include water spiders, shrimps, snails, beetles, and fish fry.

Difference between wet and dry fly

The fundamental difference of function between wet and dryflies is in the manner of tying and in the softer, more absorbent, materials used for wet flies. Wet flies must sink, and generally fairly quickly. Soft, easily wetted hen hackles or the larger, softer, cock hackles are used, both to provide a clean entry and to give a semblance of limb movement when the fly responds to the vagaries of the current, or when it is retrieved. If the fly is winged, the wings are tied sloping rearwards, almost horizontally over the hook shank. This also assists entry and streamlines the fly in the water.

Swift sinking is essential for those flies intended for deep fishing. In this event the body is weighted with lead or copper wire to get the fly down quickly to the right depth.

Traditional wet flies

Traditional wet flies very often tend to fall into the 'attractor' category, bearing no close resemblance to anything in nature. Nevertheless, there are others that imitate, either in colour or shape, living creatures such as small fry or the pupal or lorval forms of insects.

Of the vast range of lures now available, some are designed to resemble small fry of all manner of species, while others merely suggest small fish by their outline and the way that they move in the water when retrieved correctly. It is probable, however, that the majority are neither shaped nor coloured like small fish or fry, and succeed in catching trout by the attractor principle.

'Point' and 'dropper' flies

The traditional version of wet fly fishing involves the use of a team of three flies, although in times past there are records of anglers using a dozen or more patterns at the same time. A modern wet fly leader has one fly attached to the end of the leader: this is the 'point' fly, and more often than not is a dressing tied to simulate a nymph or bug. Perhaps a yard above the point fly there is a 'dropper', a loose length of nylon projecting from the leader to which the second fly, also called a dropper, is attached. This often tends to be an attractor pattern, like a Bloody Butcher, which some anglers believe to be recognized by the trout as a tiny minnow or stickleback.

The bobber

A yard or so above the dropper is another dropper, to which the 'bob' fly is tied. This usually tends to be a biggish, bushy dressing, such as a Zulu or a Palmer, which bounces across the surface of the water when retrieved and is often snapped up by a roving trout.

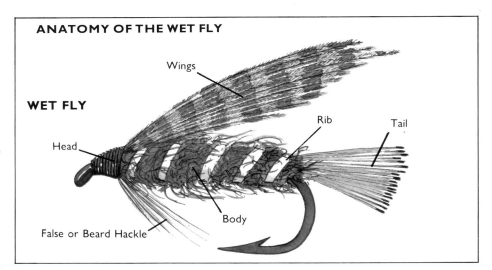

ANATOMY OF THE WET FLY

WET FLY

Wings · Rib · Tail · Head · Body · False or Beard Hackle

Top *Parts of the wet fly.* **Above** *All wet flies have wings or hackles that run back from the head. In water they simulate small fish or the larval form of insects.* **Below** *Some of the well-established, commercial wet fly patterns.*

Peter Ross · Mallard & Claret

Dunkeld

Alexandra

Blue Zulu · Black Zulu

CHAPTER 11

SKILLS

FLY CASTING

The action of fly casting, simply described, is that the line is lifted from the water by the rod and briskly thrown back behind the caster. This is called the 'back cast'. There is a pause while the line streams out and straightens behind the caster, who prevents the rod from straying back beyond the vertical by thumb pressure on the top of the handle. In that essential pause, the line, while streaming out behind the caster, is also pulling back the rod tip, making the whole rod flex. The rod and line are then driven forward again on the 'forward cast'. This action is the equivalent of a spring being wound up.

The base of the spring, in this case, is the butt of the rod. As with all springs, the base has to be locked firmly, or its energy will leak away. The locking action is achieved by the 'stopping' of the wrist at the point when the rod butt is roughly level with the ear during the back cast. The wrist is locked and as it is dragged back by the power applied to the back cast and the weight of the pulling line, the rod is forced to flex.

Correctly done, fly casting will seem to require little effort or have little power behind it but will have maximum results, that is, the angler will be able to cast a long way without feeling tired. It is correct to say that if the casting arm is tired after half an hour, then there is something wrong with the angler's casting technique.

Use the spring—not force

Really good fly line casters are extremely rare, and the gap between the standard of their performance and that of the average fly fisherman is enormous. Many fly fishermen with years of experience do not use their fly rod as a spring. They use force instead, but nevertheless believe that they are casting correctly because they can send the line some distance.

The technique of fly casting has been shown many times as a series of frozen poses, each one illustrating where the angler's arm, wrist, or the line, should be at a given moment. But it must be stressed that the action of the fly rod and line is a fluid motion which should comprise one graceful arm movement. Any errors picked up and not corrected immediately by a teacher could easily become a habit. If you practise the wrong technique several times and become used to it, it will be very hard to correct later.

Right *Fly casting has to be learnt, but it is not difficult to master. It is merely a means of using the spring inherent in the rod and the weight of the fly line to cast the very light fly.* **Below** *A fly line seen clearly against a dark background. The angler is casting upstream to a likely trout lie.*

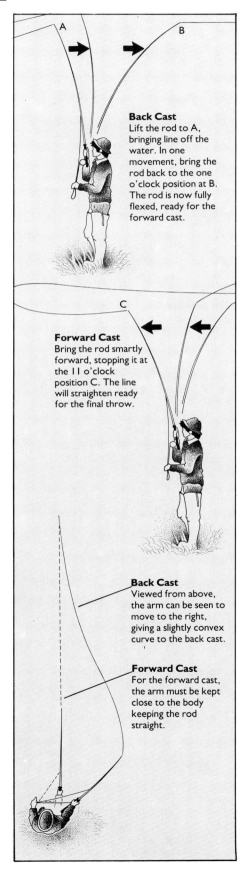

Back Cast
Lift the rod to A, bringing line off the water. In one movement, bring the rod back to the one o'clock position at B. The rod is now fully flexed, ready for the forward cast.

Forward Cast
Bring the rod smartly forward, stopping it at the 11 o'clock position C. The line will straighten ready for the final throw.

Back Cast
Viewed from above, the arm can be seen to move to the right, giving a slightly convex curve to the back cast.

Forward Cast
For the forward cast, the arm must be kept close to the body keeping the rod straight.

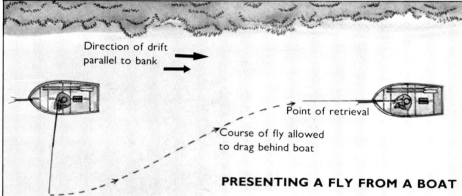

Direction of drift parallel to bank

Point of retrieval

Course of fly allowed to drag behind boat

PRESENTING A FLY FROM A BOAT

The most popular kind of fly fishing is done today on reservoirs, where long-distance casting is required. Some really splendid brown and rainbow trout can be caught from man-made reservoirs all over the country. **Above** *Two fine trout from Graffham Water.* **Top left** *Still in its jaws is the Whisky Muddler fly that tempted this rainbow trout.* **Below left** *Drifting over the waters of a reservoir can bring good trout fishing. Cast the fly at right angles so that it finishes up astern.*

RESERVOIR FISHING

Reservoir fly-fishing for trout is the most popular form of game fishing today. When starting to fish any reservoir, the first consideration is the weather. If the wind has been blowing in a particular direction for several days previously, it is safe to assume that there will be fish around the windward bank. If the day is cloudy and overcast fish are more likely to be at the surface than if the day is bright. These clues will help you choose the method and place to fish.

When boat fishing, you can use a rudder or drift-controller if the reservoir rules allow. The method then would be to set the rudder so that the boat drifts along the bank, and to cast at right-angles to the boat. Allow the line to sink, and when it has gone through an arc and is straight behind the boat, retrieve your fly. Takes very often occur just as the fly is passing through the bend of the arc, because at this point it suddenly speeds up, and any

fish following will often be fooled into taking it rather than let it escape.

Floating line tactics

If fish are seen to be rising or feeding just under the surface, it is obviously sound tactics to use a floating line and a team of nymphs or wet flies. These are fished very slowly, across the wind, with no movement whatsoever, except the movement given by the drift of the boat. Fish moving up wind are very susceptible to this method, and if none are caught quickly when you know you have covered them, change the fly, or grease or degrease the leader in case you are not fishing at their depth.

If the boat is drifting fast, it is advisable to anchor in an area where fish are, and fish across the wind, again not retrieving.

Bank fishing or anchoring while boat fishing produces the best results as the water temperature begins to drop at this time of year. In general, the mood of everything beneath the surface begins

to slow down, so you need to fish your lines accordingly.

The best way to fish in such conditions is to use a static floating lure, which works very well if fish are seen to be attacking the fry. When trout use these bulldozing tactics they charge into a thick shoal of perch or roach fry, catching one and swallowing it down and stunning perhaps four or five more, leaving the stunned fry feebly flapping on or near the surface.

If the water is deep from the bank, use a sinking line which will enable you to retrieve slowly without snagging, or a floating line with a long leader. That is, of course, if you need to fish deep. Use the same flies as you would when boat fishing.

One spot from the bank might be fished very thoroughly, so if nothing is contacted, it often pays to move along. When the wind is blowing onto the bank, the wave action varies according to the depth of the water. In shallow water, more of the bottom is stirred up, which might attract feeding fish. This is something always worth considering, so try all depths of water possible from the bank until you start catching.

INDEX

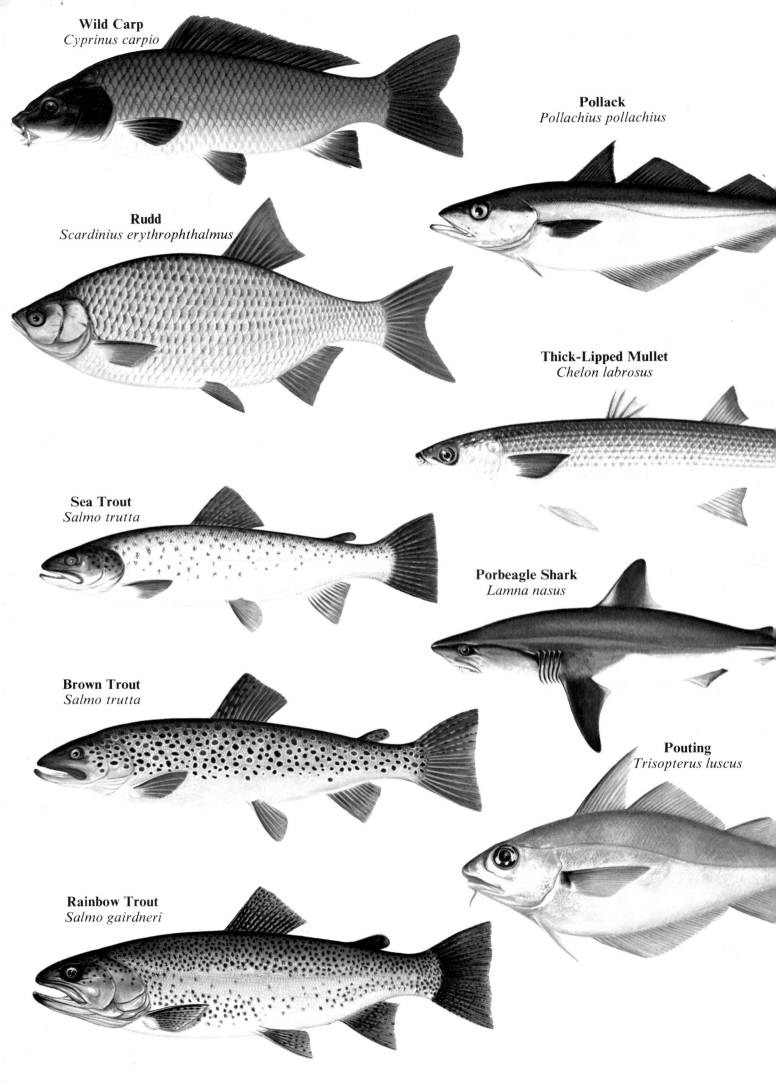

Wild Carp
Cyprinus carpio

Pollack
Pollachius pollachius

Rudd
Scardinius erythrophthalmus

Thick-Lipped Mullet
Chelon labrosus

Sea Trout
Salmo trutta

Porbeagle Shark
Lamna nasus

Brown Trout
Salmo trutta

Pouting
Trisopterus luscus

Rainbow Trout
Salmo gairdneri